Tolerance &
Education

W. Paul Vogt

Tolerance &

Education

Learning to Live With Diversity and Difference

SAGE Publications
International Educational and Professional Publisher
Thousand Oaks   London   New Delhi

For information:

SAGE Publications, Inc.
2455 Teller Road
Thousand Oaks, California 91320
E-mail: order@sagepub.com

SAGE Publications Ltd.
6 Bonhill Street
London EC2A 4PU
United Kingdom

SAGE Publications India Pvt. Ltd.
M-32 Market
Greater Kailash I
New Delhi 110 048 India

Printed in the United States of America

Library of Congress Cataloging-in-Publication Data

Vogt, W. Paul.
    Tolerance and education: learning to live with diversity and
difference / author, W. Paul Vogt.
        p. cm.
    Includes bibliographical references and index.
    ISBN 0-7619-0216-3 (cloth: acid-free paper). — ISBN
0-7619-0217-1 (pbk.: acid-free paper)
        1. Multicultural education—United States. 2. Toleration—Study
and teaching—United States. 3. Pluralism (Social sciences)—Study
and teaching—United States. I. Title.
LC1099.3.V64 1997
370.117—dc21   97-4675

This book is printed on acid-free paper.

98   99   00   01   02   03   10   9   8   7   6   5   4   3   2

Acquiring Editor: C. Deborah Laughton
Editorial Assistant: Eileen Carr
Production Editor: Diana E. Axelsen
Production Assistant: Karen Wiley
Typesetter/Designer: Danielle Dillahunt
Indexer: Mary Mortensen
Cover Designer: Lesa Valdez

Brief Table
of Contents

Detailed Table
of Contents

List of Tables

List of Figures

Preface

OTH THEORETICAL AND PRACTICAL GOALS
motivated me to write this book. My main theoreti-
cal aim was to determine whether education fosters
tolerance, as much research suggests, and more
profoundly, how tolerance is learned in schools and
colleges. It was my hope that understanding how tolerance is learned would
point toward some concrete guidelines about how to teach it—which was my
main practical aim. I believe I have attained, at least in part, both of those goals.
The following pages show that we can be very confident that the correlations so
often reported between education level (usually measured crudely as "time
served") and tolerance level indicate a true relationship, not merely a statistical
artifact. Further, because the research reviewed and synthesized in this book
identifies several ways in which the link between education and tolerance
occurs, practical suggestions for educators can be built on these research
findings. Many of the research conclusions about the relationship between

education and tolerance and many of the implications of those conclusions for practice are new. Some may be controversial, but I hope that they provide a basis upon which to build further investigations into the theoretical and practical links between education and individuals' attitudes and values.

My two purposes, theoretical and practical, have resulted in two conclusions. In Chapter 6, I discuss policy implications and list suggestions for practitioners, and in Chapter 7, I suggest what I believe to be among the more valuable directions for future research, including research on practice. Although I think these two chapters are two ways of looking at the same set of problems, I was not surprised when some colleagues who read early drafts were more interested in the suggestions for practitioners whereas others focused on the implications for researchers. Many readers of this book will also be more interested in one aspect of the relationship of education and tolerance. But I hope to have at least piqued their interest in the other side of the theory/practice divide.

Why tolerance? Of all the attitudes, beliefs, values, or virtues that one could study, what makes tolerance worth all this attention? Tolerance is not very exciting in comparison with, for example, resistance to persecution or altruistic self-sacrifice. Combating the evils of persecution can require heroic measures, and examples of altruism bring a lump to the throat. By contrast, tolerance involves the less dramatic virtues of self-restraint, deliberation, and forbearance. For most people most of the time, however, tolerance is much more important than fighting persecution or engaging in altruism. Most people have little ability or occasion to be altruistic saints like Mother Teresa or courageous resisters of evil such as Nelson Mandela. Most of us relate to other people and to our society in more prosaic ways.

Tolerance is minimal. It involves the lowest level of positive relation among individuals and among groups. It pales by comparison with altruism, universalism, caring, and understanding of others. But precisely because it is minimal, it is crucial. It is the first step that hostile groups can take to begin to establish peace, or, looking at it the other way around, the last line of defense against destructive conflict, even genocide. Tolerance is the first step toward civility— and the last bulwark against barbarism. When understanding, compassion, and altruism are in short supply, as they are from time to time, we can get by with tolerance. Tolerance is minimal, but it is foundational to a just society.

Tolerance is vitally important because of the inevitability of diversity and the apparent inevitability of stereotyping, bias, and prejudice. But discrimination and persecution are not inevitable. Tolerance keeps negative attitudes and beliefs from becoming negative actions. When tolerance is recognized as the final defense against discrimination and persecution, its importance is clear.

Tolerance is complicated. That is one of the reasons we have difficulty understanding how it is learned in schools and colleges. At the root of the complexity is the fact that tolerance always has limits. No one thinks that everything should be tolerated (consider, for example, the federal policy of "zero tolerance" for weapons in schools). Disagreement on what it is right and wrong to tolerate is inevitable in a democracy. Indeed, teaching tolerance effectively includes teaching how to think about both what *should* and what *should not* be tolerated.

No one strategy for teaching tolerance is always effective, but there are methods that, in circumstances we can identify, often work. This conclusion may be disappointing to true believers looking for a movement to join or a quick fix, but when the topic is as important as tolerance and education, it is better to build on complicated and limited truths than to try to put into practice inspiring oversimplifications.

Acknowledgments

ORE THAN MOST BOOKS, this one has hundreds of virtual coauthors. It is based heavily upon evidence gathered by other researchers. My methods have been "archival" as I sorted through the large collections of findings and theories in the five or six disciplines that have contributed importantly to my study of tolerance and education. Although I may have arranged the tiles in a different mosaic, a work of synthesis such as this one is possible only thanks to the labor of others. In addition to those mentioned in the references, several other scholars have helped more directly by reading and commenting on various drafts. Most important, Elaine Rosenthal Vogt has read and reread nearly every version of each chapter. I shudder to think of the number of errors, misinterpretations, logical lapses, and infelicities of style from which she has saved me.

Over the years, many colleagues and friends have read the manuscript in whole or in part. Fritz Ringer has been my intellectual mentor since graduate school. The several discussions he and I have had about education and culture and his critical readings of the manuscript have helped me better conceptualize the work as a whole. Daniel Levy gave the penultimate draft a particularly close and discerning read. Others who have helped by commenting on the manuscript, often extensively and penetratingly, include Mark Berger, Donald Biggs, John Bendix, Robert Hall, Brian McKenna, Maurice Richter, David Riesman, Mark Rodeghier, Douglas J. Simpson, and John Sullivan. Many other people made suggestions that I unavoidably incorporated without thanks.

Institutional support has also been important. Invitations to present preliminary findings at the University of Pittsburgh's History Department Seminar and the York University Tolerance Seminar were crucial in getting the work off the ground, as was a year's residence at the University of London's Institute of Education, which was made possible in part by a sabbatical leave granted by the State University of New York at Albany. Colleagues' comments on papers presented at meetings of the Eastern Sociological Society, the American Sociological Association, and the American Educational Research Association were very helpful, even (or especially) when I disagreed with those comments. Also, the opportunity to teach courses related to tolerance and education gave me the chance to learn from many students over the years.

Thanks to James T. Fleming, Dean of the School of Education at SUNY/ Albany, whose tolerance allowed me a very flexible work schedule during the final stages of writing and who always made it clear that my administrative duties need not be the end of my scholarly career. As always, C. Deborah Laughton, my editor at Sage Publications, helped with her enthusiasm for the project and her patience with late manuscripts. Diana Axelsen managed the book's final production with great insight and skill and continued improving the volume right up to the day it went to press.

Parts of early versions of the introduction and Chapters 1 and 5 were published in the *Review of Education, Pedagogy, and Cultural Studies,* volume 16 (1994, pp. 273-296 and 435-463; copyright 1994 Gordon and Breach Publishers). Thanks to Gordon and Breach Publishers (Lausanne, Switzerland) for permission to reprint portions of those pages.

I gratefully acknowledge the assistance of all the people and institutions mentioned above. I also acknowledge that with so much help and so many opportunities to "get it right," the book's shortcomings can only be my fault.

Introduction

Six Questions About Tolerance and Education

 ORE THAN 2,000 YEARS AGO, Plato asked in the *Meno,* What is virtue, and can we teach it? The questions asked in this book are parallel: What is tolerance? And can we teach it? The answer to the first question is crucial, for if we do not know what tolerance is, how can we possibly teach it? And as with virtue for Plato, we shall see that tolerance is much more difficult to define than it might seem. Even if we arrive at a clear definition of tolerance, however, it does not necessarily follow that we will be able to teach it. Plato, for example, after defining virtue, argued that it is innate, not learned, and therefore we cannot instruct others in how to be virtuous.

As with Plato's questions in the *Meno,* our two simple questions (What is it? Can we teach it?) imply subsidiary questions. If tolerance is learned, how and when is it learned? Is tolerance essentially a personality trait formed, if not in utero, at least in the course of early childhood socialization? If tolerance is that kind of trait, formal educational institutions will not be able to have much effect on it. On the other hand, if tolerance is learned in schools, *how* is it learned there? Is it taught as part of the curriculum or is it learned in more subtle ways? And, perhaps most important, if we can teach it, *should* we? It seems that we really have half a dozen questions. A quick review of these introduces what is to come in this book.

Question 1: What Is Tolerance?

Although there is some room for disagreement, and although the definition of tolerance is complex, there is a general consensus among researchers working on the issue. Most simply, tolerance is putting up with something one does not like. But that simple definition conceals a multitude of ambiguities. Here it is enough to say that tolerance often involves support for the rights and liberties of others, others whom one dislikes, disapproves of, disagrees with, finds threatening, or toward whom one has some other negative attitude. It follows from this definition that the opposite of tolerance is not prejudice, as is often assumed. Rather, the opposite of tolerance is *discrimination,* that is, taking action against people one dislikes or with whom one disagrees. Tolerance, by contrast, involves refraining from acting against people about whom one feels negatively. Tolerance generally requires self-control.

Defining tolerance is the main business of Chapter 1, where I delineate several forms of tolerance. When one calls an individual tolerant, one can be referring to a broad range of things, extending from personality traits through beliefs, attitudes, and behaviors. For reasons explained in Chapter 1, the focus in this book will be on attitudes and beliefs. Among beliefs of particular interest will be *values,* or beliefs about right and wrong. This concentration on attitudes and beliefs is a limitation, if a necessary one, because although attitudes and beliefs often influence behaviors, they do not completely determine behaviors. Yet self-control, which is a key component of tolerance, can arise only from an individual's attitudes and beliefs. Thus, studying attitudes and beliefs is a central part of studying tolerance.

In addition to tolerance being different things in the person described as tolerant, it can also vary according to the object of tolerance, the "toleratee," as it were. There are three overlapping but distinct categories of tolerance defined by its objects, the toleratees: political, social, and moral. These will be discussed throughout the book. Here I need only emphasize that many of the difficulties in the theory of tolerance and the empirical research on it stem from failure to distinguish among types of tolerance.

In addition to developing definitions—which draw from social psychology, sociology, political science, and philosophy—Chapter 1 also takes a brief look at the complex history of tolerance. Tolerance meant something rather different when it first emerged as a distinct idea in Europe in the 16th century from what it means today. Much of that difference is attributable to the ways tolerance has evolved in tandem with "rights." Understanding past and present struggles over either tolerance or rights requires that these concepts be studied together.

Question 2: Should We Teach Tolerance?

This is a different kind of question from most of the others addressed in this book; it is explicitly a values question. My answer and that of most educators is clear: Yes, we should teach tolerance. Many of the reasons we should teach tolerance stem quite directly from the definitions and historical account elaborated in Chapter 1. Hence, the positive answer to Chapter 2's question—Should we teach tolerance?—begins as an extension of the conclusions of Chapter 1. Social and individual reasons argue for promoting tolerance. First, if we want a society with both diversity and equality, some degree of tolerance is absolutely necessary. Diversity and equality cannot coexist without some tolerance. Second, if an individual is to be readied to cope in a pluralistic and egalitarian society, she or he will need, from time to time, some fairly well honed interpersonal skills, including skills of tolerance. The third, and most general, reason we should teach tolerance is that tolerance stands on the border between positive and negative relations among people. Tolerance guards against discrimination and internecine conflict; it is a rampart against injustice and belligerence. And tolerance opens the possibility of cooperation among antagonistic individuals and groups; it is a path to civility.

However, the answer to the question of whether we should teach tolerance is not always so clear—at least when we ask ourselves how much tolerance is wise and what in particular should be tolerated. Some tolerance of some things is probably inevitable, but saying that leaves most questions unanswered. For almost everyone, tolerance is an intermediate, partial value. In some instances tolerance seems inadequate; although it might be better than intolerance, it often falls far short of constituting what one might think of as values appropriate for a just community. In other cases, tolerating certain forms of behavior (hate crimes, for example) might be excessive; doing so could undermine a democratic society, and constitutional democracy is one of the main pillars of tolerance. The dividing lines between those circumstances in which tolerance does not go far enough, those in which it goes too far, and those in which it is about right are not easy to draw. They are inherently controversial, and they will always remain so in an open society. Thus, like the definition of tolerance, the issue of whether it is good to use educational institutions to promote tolerance is also more complex than it seems to most people when they first consider it.

These complexities and controversies lead us to our final task in Chapter 2, considering the main criticisms of tolerance as a social ideal. These are comparatively few in number, but they have been quite influential. An argument in favor of using educational practices to promote tolerance must examine these counterarguments to show their shortcomings.

Question 3: Is Tolerance Learned, Especially in Schools?

Tolerance is almost certainly learned, and learned in schools. Abundant evidence, reviewed in Chapter 3, shows that people who have had different post-infancy experiences express different amounts of tolerance. This has been found true in cross-national comparisons as well as in comparisons of different groups in the same society. Such evidence, although only correlational, is overwhelming: Different life experiences result in different kinds and levels of tolerance. Tolerance is learned. Education, age, and religious orientation are usually the most important predictors of tolerance. Certain personality characteristics and beliefs are also very strong predictors of tolerance, and these, in turn, appear to be influenced by education.

In most studies of adults' attitudes, education level is one of the strongest correlates of tolerance level, even after the effects of other demographic variables, such as age, income, religion, gender, and region of residence, are controlled for. This is persuasive, if not conclusive, evidence that years of schooling somehow foster tolerance. Controlling for certain beliefs, attitudes, and personality characteristics (e.g., commitment to democratic values, feelings of threat, and self-esteem) can importantly reduce the education-tolerance relationship, in part because those variables mediate the relationship (they are the causal links, so to speak) between education and tolerance.

Question 4: How Is Tolerance Learned in Schools?

We have stronger evidence *that* tolerance is associated with schooling than about *how* it is. In Chapters 4 and 5, four forms or processes of learning are identified as ways in which education may promote tolerance. Two arise from formal learning of the curriculum: (a) special instruction, such as in civic, moral, or multicultural education; and (b) students' general cognitive development as promoted by the curriculum. Two others involve more informal processes of socialization that take place in educational institutions: (c) intergroup contact in schools and (d) students' personality development as fostered by schooling. It is clear that these four processes are not mutually exclusive, but there have been few systematic investigations of how they might be related.

These four processes are addressed in Chapters 4 and 5, where a new theoretical approach to synthesizing currently available research on education and tolerance is developed. Chapter 4 considers what many students of attitudes and values consider most important: the indirect ways in which these are learned. By what subtle means are students' personality development and cognitive development influenced by schooling, and influenced in ways that encourage tolerance? Chapter 5, on the other hand, looks at direct attempts to teach tolerance, either by manipulating the social environment of students or by devising new curricula for them.

Question 5: Can We Teach Tolerance Directly?

Direct attempts to influence students' tolerance levels are easier to investigate than are indirect methods. Chapter 5 first examines the effects of contact among different social groups, a process partly tied to the history of school desegregation. The results of research in this area, while complicated, are generally encouraging for those who would wish to use schooling to increase tolerance. On the other hand, studies of the effects of direct instruction have often been discouraging. The fact that we have had little idea of how tolerance might be directly taught in schools has been disheartening for educators who want to use educational policy to foster tolerance. Until recently, there has been very little evidence that tolerance can be taught as part of the regular curriculum. But there is some evidence. Social psychologists have reported experimental results that suggest interesting paths for curriculum development. Several ethnographic case studies have yielded further evidence. And one quasi-experiment in particular that involved a tolerance curriculum for adolescents in Minnesota provides quite convincing evidence that the direct purposeful teaching of political tolerance can work. Chapter 5 examines the findings of these highly varied sources and draws conclusions that help us answer our final set of questions— about educational policies and research.

Question 6: What Are the Implications for Research, Policy, and Practice of the Answers to the Previous Questions?

While the causes and correlates of the association between tolerance and education are more complex than most researchers have imagined, enough is known to allow us to formulate persuasively strong guidelines for educational policy and practice. Knowing that different educational levels and processes affect different types of tolerance makes it possible for us to attack particular aspects of the complex of problems of tolerance and education one at a time— and to have reasonable prospects for success when doing so. Building on the discussion in the previous chapters, I argue in Chapter 6 that a careful disaggregation of tolerance and education into their distinct, if related, elements is a crucial first step toward finding the most effective approaches for educators to take. Given that there are three types of tolerance and four educational processes involved in teaching it, our investigations and applications need to be undertaken in at least 12 ways (4 processes times 3 types). Further, attention has to be directed to how these 12 ways can and do work in varying educational contexts and at different levels of schooling. Building on a discussion of these issues, I conclude Chapter 6 with specific recommendations for practitioners; these are designed to serve as guides to educators hoping to foster tolerance through schooling.

In Chapter 7, I draw some conclusions about how to organize further research so as to increase our understanding of the links between education and tolerance and, thereby, to help us design schooling to promote tolerance. Research can help us to form a realistic appraisal of the nature and limits of tolerance and how it can be influenced by educators. Research-based knowledge can go some way toward changing tolerance from a goal that is often voiced on ceremonial occasions and in official documents, but seldom realized, into a set of achievable educational objectives of considerable social consequence.

CHAPTER 1

What Is Tolerance?

The Basic Concepts

Tolerance is remarkably tricky to define. We must start with a definition, however, because if we cannot define tolerance, it will be hard at best to say anything coherent about how education might foster it or why we might want to teach it. We will not get very far by trying to stipulate one true definition of tolerance, appropriate for all circumstances. A better strategy is to begin with aspects of tolerance about which many people agree and then try to build theoretically on those. In the end we will discover a cluster of three overlapping types of tolerance, each of which can be expressed in several different ways.

Let us begin with a definition that can apply to simple interpersonal relations, but one that also has broader implications: *Tolerance is putting up with something you do not like—often in order to get along better with others.* A small example can illustrate. My wife likes to go to sleep early at night and to get up early in the morning; I prefer to stay up later and sleep in later in the morning. Many years ago we compromised and split the difference. We go to bed earlier than I'd like and later than she'd like. We both tolerate this vexation of our "natural" sleeping rhythms because doing so is good for our relationship. Of course, we had many other options besides compromise and tolerance, as people in similar situations usually do.

One alternative to compromise is persuasion and/or conversion. One of us could have convinced the other to come around to his or her way of thinking. But neither of us could persuade the other, so that alternative was eliminated. A second option, common in such cases, was also ruled out because we are equals: Neither of us could or would compel the other. Compulsion is, of course, a frequent alternative to compromise, especially when one party in a relationship has considerably more power. Other alternatives to tolerance my wife and I had were to fight about the issue all the time and to divorce. One of us could have decided that her or his sleeping habits were so important that inability to convert or compel the other meant that we had an intolerable, irreconcilable difference, and the marriage was doomed.

I have lingered over this small example because it illustrates several crucial points about tolerance. The first is that compromise entails tolerance. By definition, compromise involves settling for less than one wants so as to come to an agreement. Thus, any social or political system built on compromise will also be built on tolerance. If politics is the art of compromise, politics is also the art of tolerance—at least that is true for nonviolent, nonrepressive politics. Although a self-interested compromise is not tolerance, strictly speaking, tolerance is a precondition of such compromise.

A second key point is that tolerance is based on difference or diversity. If my wife and I had had identical sleeping habits, we would not have had to make a deal; we would have had nothing to tolerate. More generally, one precondition of tolerance is that there must be a difference, and the people involved must think that it is important. If people do not believe that the difference is important, if they do not care about it, it makes sense to say that they are *indifferent* to it, but not that they tolerate it. It makes even less sense to say that people tolerate diversity that they like. For example, many people like living in large cities because of the diverse languages, cultures, modes of dress, and so on that they encounter there. Such people do not tolerate diversity, they enjoy it. These basic distinctions among liking something, being indifferent toward it, and tolerating it are very important. Much unneeded debate about tolerance could be avoided were they kept in mind (Cranston, 1967; Crick, 1971; King, 1976).

The relationship of tolerance to other attitudes and behaviors is summarized in Figure 1.1. The figure shows two continua: one of positive and negative attitudes, the other of behaviors than might accompany those attitudes. The spectrum of attitudes extends from hate to love. The behaviors or actions, ranging from persecution to self-sacrifice, do not exhaust all possibilities; they are listed in the figure only as examples. The key point to note is that tolerance is not a logically coherent action for the middle and right-hand parts of the spectrum, for the range of attitudes extending from indifference or universalism through liking and love. Note also that the "distance" between discriminatory and tolerant behavior may be rather short. Tolerance is an option only when one dislikes something—or, in social psychology jargon, when one has negative affect toward an attitude object. This is the central idea that Sullivan and his colleagues have operationalized in their surveys of political tolerance when they have asked subjects if they dislike a group and only then asked them whether they would tolerate that group (Sullivan, Piereson, & Marcus, 1982; Sullivan, Avery, Thalhammer, Wood, & Bird, 1994).

A closely related point suggested by Figure 1.1 is that people could tolerate others whom they hate, but it is more likely for most people to tolerate others whom they dislike only a little. Sullivan et al., for example, have found that people tend not to be very tolerant of their "least-liked group." In short, although tolerance is possible at any point on the left-hand side of the spectrum, the further to the left one moves, the less likely it is. On the other hand, were a person actually to tolerate something he or she hated, this would count as more tolerance than if the person were to tolerate something about which he or she had less intense negative feelings.

Figure 1.1 also shows that tolerance generally means inaction, except to the extent that self-restraint can be called an action. To tolerate something is to have a negative attitude toward it, to be able to act against it, but to refrain from doing so. Of course, all inaction is not equal. The motive behind the inaction is crucial in determining whether it qualifies as tolerance. For example, most people surely would not count it as tolerance if someone refrained from acting against another because he or she was afraid to do so.

All this said, we can return to our (somewhat reformulated) definition of tolerance: *Tolerance is intentional self-restraint in the face of something one dislikes, objects to, finds threatening, or otherwise has a negative attitude toward—usually in order to maintain a social or political group or to promote harmony in a group.* The group can be small, such as a couple; it can be a large organization, such as a school; it can even be a society or a nation. The basic principle is the same. The harmony sought can be short-term or long-term. For example, tolerating disruptive political dissent, rather than repressing it, may not be conducive to order and harmony in the short run, but it may well promote the stability of a democratic society in the long run.

NEGATIVE   POSITIVE

ATTITUDES	hatred	strong dislike	mild dislike	indifference or universalism	mild liking	strong liking	love
EXAMPLES OF BEHAVIORS	persecute (tolerance)	discriminate against (tolerance)	no action (tolerance)	no action	no action	discriminate in favor of	self-sacrifice

Figure 1.1. Range of Attitudes and Examples of Behaviors Illustrating When Tolerance May Occur

In what sorts of social and political situations is tolerance likely? Certain conditions are conducive to tolerance; when they occur together, they make tolerance all but inevitable. The relationships may be summed up as follows:

> Diversity + Equality + Peace → Tolerance.

Figure 1.2. Conditions Conducive to Tolerance

That is, diversity and equality among people living in peace *necessarily* means that they have learned to tolerate one another. This does not mean that tolerance is inevitable in all circumstances, or even most. It is inevitable only when the conditions of diversity, equality, and peace pertain simultaneously.

An indirect substantiation of the relations among diversity, equality, peace, and tolerance is that people who argue against tolerance as a desirable or possible sociopolitical ideal usually do so by pointing out how one of the three preconditions to the left of the arrow in the above illustration (diversity, equality, or peace) is impossible or undesirable. Let us briefly examine each of these three kinds of counterarguments.

Arguments Against Tolerance

The Argument From Inequality

At least since the time of Plato's *Republic,* some political philosophers have argued that people are naturally, inevitably unequal. Hence, the best way to organize a society and run a government would be to give power to the most competent, to have an aristocracy in which the "best" would rule. This kind of argument, although common for most of the history of political thought, East and West, is pretty rare today. But it does follow that if equality is impossible (or a bad idea if possible), tolerance will have a very limited scope. The natural rulers will compel or convince the rest of the populace to do what they think is best. In such a society diversity will usually be quite limited as well.

The Argument About Diversity

Indeed, perhaps the most pervasive and persuasive type of argument against tolerance is based on concerns about "too much" diversity. The general idea behind this kind of argument is that we can best attain peace through unity. Tolerance, by contrast, is built on compromise among people with different interests and characteristics; tolerance is, in fact, an adversarial virtue. Some people think that, rather than tolerating diverse interests, we should reduce or tame diversity. Several types of arguments fit in this general category of peace through less diversity. First, those who wish to reduce diversity while retaining peace and equality usually support one form or another of left-wing communitarian social philosophy. Second, those who wish to reduce diversity to attain peace, but who do not care so much about equality, are more often found on the political Right, such as supporters of anti-immigration movements (compare Durkheim, 1961; Rahe, 1994). Finally, some wish to tame diversity by embracing it, liking it, loving it. They challenge the negativistic character of tolerance and say that we should respect and encourage, not merely tolerate, differences among our fellows.

The Argument From Conflict

The third form of argument against tolerance is in some ways the direct opposite of the second. Rather than advocating peace through less diversity, proponents of this view say that an equitable peace is not really possible. The general idea is that tolerance is of limited value because conflict, not peace, is the necessary condition of things. At least since Thomas Hobbes, social thinkers have argued that modern society exists in a state of relentless conflict among self-interested groups of unequal power. These groups struggle to impose social arrangements of benefit to themselves on all others that they can dominate. Theorists with this view of the world see tolerance, when it exists, as a sham or a trick; it is a means of social control imposed upon the weak by the powerful. At minimum, tolerance is more likely to serve the interests of society's dominant class than the interests of its subordinate classes (see Collins, 1975; Jackman & Muha, 1984; Marcuse, 1969; see also Chapter 2, this volume).

It is not possible here to attempt to refute these arguments or even to describe them adequately (for a good beginning, see Dahl, 1989). However, I may have elaborated my basic line of reasoning sufficiently for the reader to be convinced by the following conditional statement: *If* you value the coexistence of diversity, equality, and peace, *then* you must also make room in your catalog of virtues for tolerance. You cannot have all three (diversity, equality, peace) together without learning to put up with some things you do not like. Conversely, probably the best way to argue against tolerance is by attacking one of its three preconditions (diversity, equality, peace).

Such attacks on tolerance are certainly common enough, and there is at least a kernel of truth in each of the three kinds of antitolerance just discussed. Each points out limits on tolerance. And there are always limits to tolerance in all societies. Tolerance is generally assumed to be a virtue, but it is a qualified virtue and not an unalloyed good thing, such as honesty or kindness or wisdom might be.

Crime and Sin

Every society restricts diversity; each specifies a class or category of actions that are by definition not tolerated. That category is, of course, crime. Loosely speaking, crimes are things that societies do not like and that they officially act against. Crimes are punished. Societies differ in how they define crimes and in how severely they punish criminals, but all societies have the category. When we think of crimes, we usually think of acts; but traits, beliefs, and states of being (Jewish, homosexual, communist) have been declared illegal in some societies and officially prosecuted—that is, not tolerated (see the discussion below on objects of tolerance). Definitions of crime are usually closely linked to beliefs about morality—that is, to definitions of right and wrong conduct—which, in turn, are often, if not inevitably, supported by religious beliefs. Finally, to close the circle, when people have strong religious or moral beliefs, they usually think that "there ought to be a law" supporting those beliefs. What we might call the "theocratic urge" leads to huge controversies when a substantial number of people are outraged that their moral beliefs are not imposed on others by law. The identity of moral and legal rules is what is at stake, for example, in debates about the decriminalization and recriminalization of homosexuality and abortion.

When we speak of crime and punishment we speak of governmental action, which is why political tolerance is so important even if what is being tolerated is in no sense a political act. There is a separate category of governmental action that we might best call *toleration*. This occurs when a government establishes legal supports to protect individuals from others who would not tolerate them. An even more crucial type of toleration occurs when government sets limits on its own repressive powers. In the following pages I refer to these limitations as *toleration*—as distinct from *tolerance*, which is reserved for the interpersonal realm of individuals' attitudes and actions.

Both tolerance and toleration fall into a kind of gap between the unpleasant and the prohibited, between the immoral and the illegal, between sin and crime.

People who oppose any gap between legal and moral "oughts" have little patience with pleas for tolerance. Most people, however, tolerate at least a few behaviors that they believe are wrong but that they also believe ought not to be punished, ought not to be illegal. Survey research about racial attitudes provides an interesting example. In recent decades, most White Americans (approximately two-thirds) have disapproved of interracial marriages, but only about one-third thought they ought to be illegal (Davis, 1982; National Opinion Research Center, 1986).[1] Most people who fall within the gap (who do not approve but who do not think intermarriage should be illegal) would probably say that other people have a right to marry whomever they want. This illustrates another key component of our definition of tolerance: other people's rights. The things that people do not like but think ought to be tolerated are often rights and liberties, usually civil liberties and civil rights. We can thus give a more positive definition of tolerance: *Tolerance is support for the equal rights and liberties of others* (Corbett, 1982).

Which others? Answering that question points to different kinds of tolerance based on different kinds of diversity. The list of possible kinds of tolerance can be as long as a list of the kinds of human diversity: religious, ethnic, racial, political, moral, cultural, linguistic, and so on. But we can say a few things about the list that make it more manageable. Pride of place has to be given to religious differences and tolerance. The word *tolerance* was first used as we use it today to describe relations among religious groups. Gradually, it was applied also to political beliefs and actions, and from there its use spread to still other aspects of life. A brief look into the history of the concept of tolerance, and its sister concept toleration, will help us to understand more fully its contemporary meaning and will facilitate our further categorization of types of tolerance.

A Short History of Tolerance

Probably the earliest major work that discusses tolerance and toleration by name is Thomas Aquinas's *Summa Theologiae* (II, II, Questions 10 and 11). Aquinas held that true Christians need not be fanatics in all circumstances. His argument is ultimately pragmatic: If tolerance is good for the true faith, it can be employed as a temporary expedient; if persecution better promotes the ends of the true faith, then that is the preferred policy. In other words, one might calculate the consequences of one's actions and conclude that it is wisest to tolerate an evil, but one does so ultimately only to eliminate the thing one is tolerating. For Aquinas, tolerance is at best a strategy, not a virtue.

Tolerance began to become a virtue rather than a tactic only in the 16th century. The debates of that time between Christians who wanted to persecute heretics and those who favored tolerating them are the root of all modern Western conceptions of toleration. The question of whether heresy is wrong was hardly ever raised. The controversies were still mostly about means, not ends (see Bainton's introduction in Castellio, 1554/1931). Was a particular sort of persecution, such as roasting a person alive, an appropriate or just means to deal with the problem? Was it an effective means of extirpating heresy? Would banishment be a more "Christian" way to deal with the crime? Could preaching and teaching save more lost souls than torture and exemplary execution? These were the burning questions, so to speak. Although a few 16th-century theorists had moved beyond Aquinas's pragmatism to more general questions of justice and compassion, their early steps in this direction were tentative. But from that time on, controversies concerning tolerance have had the same basic form.

Social and political theorists have argued about what sorts of acts and beliefs should and should not be tolerated and have searched for principles that would make the decisions about boundaries less arbitrary, more rational, more persuasive, more just, or at least more workable. But there has always been a threshold, a point beyond which theorists argue that it is no longer wise or just to be tolerant. Among the better-known examples is Locke's *A Letter on Toleration* (1689/ 1968), in which he argues that Catholics (because they serve a foreign prince) and atheists (because they cannot be trusted to adhere to oaths) should be excluded from the full benefits of religious toleration—as they were in Britain for more than a century after the Act of Toleration of 1689. On the other hand, Locke also says that persons who would not tolerate others in matters of religion should not themselves be tolerated—surely the least influential idea in his famous tract. Locke's ideas anticipated the debates of a few decades ago about whether communists and other subversives should have the right to speak publicly, as well as current controversies over whether neo-Nazis and other racists should have the rights of freedom of speech and assembly.

Until well into the 17th century, it was fully possible to be proud of being intolerant, for tolerance was thought of as "lax complacency towards evil" (Labrousse, 1973). Whereas "toleration" had become a "reforming slogan" in the language of many 18th-century *philosophes,* the 1776 edition of the dictionary of the Académie française still defined it as acquiescence—as "sufferance, indulgence for that which cannot be prevented" (Merrick, 1990, chap. 6). Yet by the end of the 17th century, in the era of Locke and Bayle, it was becoming increasingly possible to claim that, although religious uniformity was to be preferred, some forms of religious dissent ought to be permitted and, more important, some means of achieving uniformity ought to be banned. Sweeping, general prohibitions of persecution and arguments for toleration appeared and sometimes replaced mere niggling over the details concerning what should constitute a "just" persecution. No one, Locke (1689/1968) says in his famous *Letter,* "neither individuals, nor churches, nor even commonwealths, have any just title to invade civil rights and rob each other of worldly goods on the plea of religion" (p. 85).

Such bold and high-sounding phrases should not, however, lead us to forget Locke's exclusion of Catholics and atheists from the protection of tolerance. Nor should we overlook the fact that it long remained dangerous to advocate toleration. That is why so many of what we now regard as classics in the literature of toleration were published anonymously (e.g., by Locke), under pseudonyms (e.g., by Voltaire), or only posthumously (e.g., by Bodin).

Just as it was becoming fairly routine in the 18th century for most advanced thinkers to advocate toleration, other politically advanced thinkers, especially those associated with the American and French Revolutions, came to see toleration as inadequate, as not a virtue at all. As Mirabeau put it, "The word tolerance . . . seems to me, in some respects, tyrannical in itself, since the authority who tolerates could [also] not tolerate" (quoted in King, 1976, p. 8). Thomas Paine was sharper still in making this point: "Toleration is not the opposite of intolerance, but is the counterfeit of it. Both are despotisms. The one assumes to itself the right of withholding Liberty of Conscience and the other of granting it. The one is the pope armed with fire and faggot, the other is the pope selling or granting indulgences" (quoted in Crick, 1971, p. 149).

The point has several times been made, and not only by revolutionaries. To tolerate, as Mirabeau and Paine understood it, implies that the tolerator has the authority or the power to *not* tolerate. Mirabeau and Paine considered certain liberties too fundamental to be thus restricted or provisional. As one historian of liberalism has argued, religious liberty was not achieved "without a long and arduous historical transition through successive stages of *that partial or defective liberty which is generally known as religious toleration.* Toleration . . . in contrast to liberty connotes that whatever immunity is enjoyed is regarded merely as a revocable concession rather than as a defensible right" (Ruggiero, 1942, p. 240; emphasis added).

This contrast between toleration and rights is a potentially important one. The status of, say, liberty of conscience certainly seems to change as it moves from something granted by an act of toleration to something protected by a bill of rights. Yet rights did not simply replace toleration; they were linked to it and remain so today. Toleration retains much of its value among contemporary social and political theorists because of its continuing connection to rights. But there is also a sense in which toleration can be thought of as a virtue or an ideal of conduct apart from its association with rights or its function as a stage on the way to rights. The evolution of toleration from the 16th through the 19th century illustrates how. From the time that toleration arose as a coherent concept in the 16th century, the fundamental question for governments and those who advised them was, How much deviance should be put up with before repressive measures must be taken? The most common answer in the 16th century was, *As little as possible.* By the mid-19th century, a different answer had gained currency: *As much as possible.* This idea is the essence of Mill's argument in *On Liberty* (1859/1979).

Toleration and rights can be thought of as a spectrum of degrees of legal protection for beliefs, practices, and characteristics. Some things are afforded hardly any protection; they are "barely tolerated." Others are guarded by impressive legal guarantees; they are "inalienable rights." Things that are tolerated are simply not prohibited; things that are rights are protected. If something is tolerated, one is *permitted* to do it. If something is a right, one is *entitled* to do it. Although there is thus clearly a distinction between toleration and rights, it is more one of degree than of kind. The boundary between the two concepts is often unclear—and, in the final analysis, neither makes much sense in the absence of the other.

Many of the differences between toleration and rights are rhetorical. The rhetoric of rights is much stronger than that of toleration, although that of toleration may more accurately describe how liberties have in fact been protected. Rights are thought of in the possessive, in terms of ownership: "I have a right to X." One usually acquires a right merely by being something: "I have a right to X because I am Y" [a French citizen, a human being, one of God's creatures]. Expanding the scope of a right is usually done through the argument that there is an *identity of being* between the candidate group and groups already protected. This pattern has not altered much since the 17th century. Think of the arguments of the animal rights movement or antiabortion groups: "Animals are Ys too"; "A fetus is Y, after all." Conversely, opponents of extending a right tend to argue, as they have historically, that there is some important difference between those already protected by the right and the candidate group (e.g., Blacks, Jews, women, animals, embryos). Rights are thought of as "natural," as part of the essence of being human; to deny them to the members of a particular group is to deny that those members are fully human. At minimum, rights have almost always been thought of as ideals with intrinsic merit. A "bad right" is a contradiction in terms.

The rhetoric of toleration is generally more modest. Toleration is usually seen as a sacrifice made for a higher end, or as part of some other valuable thing, very often a right. To use Berlin's (1969) famous distinction, toleration is a matter of negative liberty, of freedom *from*; rights are usually instances of positive liberty, of freedom *to*. The U.S. Bill of Rights, for example, is a clear case of the establishment of negative liberties, or toleration, through promulgation of rights against the state. The Bill of Rights limits the sphere of governmental action; "Congress shall make no law" is its most important phrase. The contemporaneous French Declaration of the Rights of Man and the Citizen, on the other hand, enumerates positive rights, such as the right to participate in government. The differences between the two lists of rights are not very substantial, however. The negative freedoms of the one imply the positive freedoms of the other, and vice versa. Only with freedom of speech and association, for instance, which are negative freedoms in that they bar government interference, is the positive liberty of meaningful participation in government possible.

The shift from toleration to rights involved three related changes. The first was a change in emphasis, both in theory and in policy, from *permitting* to *protecting* certain freedoms. The freedoms of speech and press provide the clearest examples. The idea that these liberties are good in themselves and should be encouraged, not merely allowed, had gained some currency by the 17th century, as is illustrated by some of the forceful expressions in Milton's "Areopagitica," but a fully libertarian theory of freedom of the press was not developed until very late in the 18th century (Levy, 1985, pp. 93-97).

The second change signaling the de-emphasis of toleration and the rise of rights came when the *burden of proof* shifted from those arguing for tolerance to those arguing for repression. Movements in this direction are easily discernible in Western Europe and North America by the 18th century. Freedoms of speech and press, to continue with that example, ceased being only tolerated liberties and became protected rights when the burden of proof in slander and libel cases shifted from the defendant to the accuser—whether that was an individual who had purportedly been wronged or a government claiming that an utterance or publication was treasonable, an incitement to riot, a violation of an official secrets act, or a case of seditious libel. Yet, no matter how well established their status as rights, freedoms of speech and press have never been boundless. The crimes of libel, slander, obscenity, blasphemy, and sedition still exist. They define the official limits of the right of free expression, or, for it is the same thing, the official limits of toleration of expression.

From the 17th century on in the British Empire, it is more useful to think of the narrowness or broadness of free speech and press than of their presence or absence. When the crimes of libel, slander, and so on are loosely defined, so that convicting a defendant comes easily (the prosecution's burden of proof is light), freedom of speech and press are narrow. Conversely, when those crimes are strictly defined and the burden of proof is so heavy that conviction is rare, the freedoms are broad (Schauer, 1982). For most of the 18th century in the North American colonies, a mixed situation existed. Prosecution for seditious libel was fairly common, and such prosecutions effectively restricted freedom to criticize the government, but convictions were quite rare. The law caught up with practice in the United States with the adoption of the Bill of Rights in 1791.

The third aspect of the shift from toleration to rights came as sovereign powers began to impose general, formal, and prior self-limiting restrictions upon their own powers of repression. Tolerance by a government requires that it exercise self-restraint, but this may be done merely on a case-by-case basis. Rights, on the other hand, cannot exist unless it is generally known in advance what will and will not be tolerated. In the case of freedom of the press, when it is established as a right, the government announces (by statutes, court rulings, or constitutional provisions), *prior* to knowing the content of any particular publication, that there will be no punishment for anything printed—unless, of course, certain limits, which are also made fairly explicit in advance, are transgressed. To the extent that the limits are loosely defined and not made explicit in advance, the government exercises, at best, a narrow tolerance rather than protects a broad right. Rights have always been limited, but to the degree they have been limited arbitrarily, they are no longer rights and are, at most, the weakest form of toleration.

A regime of rights can be said to have been established when all three transitions have been made: from permission to protection, from burden of proof on the would-be tolerated to the would-be repressor, and from ad hoc indulgences by governments to acts by which governments rigorously define liberties and their limits. Each change is more a matter of degree than of kind, but it is safe to say that in a dozen or so nations (Britain, Canada, France, Holland, and the United States, among others) by the 20th century the weight had shifted from the mere tolerance side of the balance to the full rights side.

Even when a regime of rights exists, however, tolerance and toleration do not disappear; they play a crucial role in maintaining such a regime. Persons in a society where citizens have rights automatically incur obligations to respect those rights. An individual's freedom of speech, for example, depends not only on the government, but on other individuals' willingness to tolerate speeches they dislike. If they do not do so, the government may compel them, and thus protect the right. But there is a limit to how much governments can, in the face of concerted opposition, protect the rights of an unpopular minority. Unless something like a culture of tolerance exists in a population—or at least in its most influential groups—rights are insecure.

Toleration is also crucial in a regime of rights because rights come into conflict—more accurately, the rights of some persons can come into conflict with the rights of others. When the state intervenes to settle rights disputes—as it must often do in complex societies with multiple claimants voicing conflicting rights—it has to rank some rights (or claimants) as more important than others. For a regime of rights to exist, the state must do this in a nonarbitrary way.

The theorizing involved in ranking rights claims has usually taken the form of debates about how to avoid the more harmful mistake. Schauer (1982) illustrates this kind of reasoning by pointing to the rules of due process of law. These rules make it difficult to convict innocent persons, but they also make it difficult to convict guilty persons. Strong due process rules are justified as long as we believe that punishing an innocent person is less "tolerable" (more harmful, the worse mistake) than freeing a guilty person. We must tolerate some (how many?) criminals' going free as the price of making it unlikely that innocent persons will be unjustly punished. Applying the same kind of reasoning to free speech produces a similar balance sheet. When free speech is a strongly established right, the mistake of overregulation of possibly "good" speech is considered worse than the mistake of underregulation of "bad" or harmful speech (Schauer, 1982, pp. 137-138, 186-187).

In sum, tolerance and toleration are broad concepts. They range from ad hoc permissions and pardons by private individuals to prior guarantees and protections by the state. Rights can be thought of as strong, assertive versions of toleration, and tolerance as the weakest kind of recognition of a right. Most civil rights are forms of toleration and/or began as such. Both toleration and rights are limited, usually by legal definitions; they end where illegality begins. Both toleration and rights are closely tied to the principle of equality before the law. Most edicts, patents, and acts of toleration have promulgated equality before the law for individuals who had been denied it; civil rights legislation has largely done the same. Toleration and rights have been historically linked and have gained strength from their association.

One of the most thorough and enlightening controversies concerned with tolerance and the legislation of morality occurred in Britain about three decades ago. It provides a revealing case with which to conclude this historical survey and this phase of our effort to define tolerance. The debate over whether private homosexual acts of adult males should be illegal began in earnest in the mid-1950s and largely ended in 1967, when the British Parliament passed the Sexual Offences Act. This law decriminalized homosexual activity between consenting adult males (female homosexuality had never been against the law).

In 1957, a parliamentary committee issued a document, known as the Wolfenden Report, that recommended that private homosexual acts no longer be subject to legal prosecution. The Wolfenden Report, like most serious debates about what private conduct should and should not be illegal, is largely a footnote to Mill's *On Liberty* (1859/1979). Mill's solution to the "demarcation problem" (between the legal and illegal) is persuasive in part because it is disarmingly simple: If an individual's conduct is "self-regarding," if it has no influence on or causes no harm to others, it should be tolerated; that is, it should be subject to no penal sanctions. Mill introduces many qualifications to his maxim that an individual's "purely self-regarding conduct cannot properly be meddled with" (p. 96), but he never wavers in his conviction that unless an act harms another, it is not even eligible for legal restriction. The Wolfenden Report's conclusion that there are some things that are simply not the government's business, and that "it is not . . . the function of the law to intervene in the private lives of citizens, or to seek to enforce any particular pattern of behaviour" is clearly inspired by Mill's arguments. Ironically, so was the main line of attack on the report, which claimed that homosexuality causes real social harm and should thus be a candidate for suppression.

The British jurist Lord Devlin headed the opposition to the Wolfenden Report. Over a period of about 8 years, he and H. L. A. Hart, an Oxford legal philosopher, led a debate that reached deep into British society. In *The Enforcement of Morals* (1965), Devlin argues that society "has a prima facie right to legislate against immorality as such" (p. 11). Because immorality, whether public or private, harms society, "it is not possible to set theoretical limits to the power of the state to legislate against [it]" (p. 12). There are limits, but they are relative and practical rather than absolute and theoretical. Those limits are set by the standards of morality prevalent in a given society at a given time. "Legal sanctions," Devlin contends, "are inappropriate for the enforcement of moral standards that are in dispute" (p. 90), but when "opinion is solid" (p. 69), when "every right-minded person" (p. 15) reacts with feelings of "intolerance, indignation, and disgust" (p. 17), the law should almost always back those sentiments with legal sanctions. How does one determine who "right-minded persons" are and what their sentiments are? According to Devlin, this is so obvious as not to require discussion in many instances. For more difficult cases, he would use the standard of what the "reasonable man" thinks—what he thinks in the jury box, after a process of deliberation, and with the kind of certainty required for 12 members of a jury to come to a unanimous decision. Practices that are condemned after that rigorous test and with that degree of certainty should be prohibited by law, for their mere existence undermines the integrity of society by eroding its moral standards—regardless of whether the acts are committed in public or in private. Thus, Devlin accepts Mill's "harm principle," but argues against the notion that acts committed in private can cause no harm.

In his reply to Devlin, Hart (1963/1982) claims that there can be a difference between a moral evil and a genuine threat to society. He notes that Devlin has produced no evidence that "deviation from accepted sexual morality, even by adults in private, is something which, like treason, threatens the existence of society" (p. 50). Right-thinking individuals may be distressed, their feelings may be hurt, by "the bare knowledge that others are acting in ways . . . [they] think wrong" (p. 46). But legal action cannot properly be taken against a practice unless it can be shown to do injury according to "some criterion of 'harm' . . . independent of the (alleged) immorality of the conduct" (p. ix). This is the interpretation of the harm principle that won out in British jurisprudence.

But even if we wish to base our decisions about tolerance on the harm principle, it is not sufficient. For an act to be eligible for prohibition, it must be shown to cause harm. But some acts that cause harm must be tolerated. If you write a book, for example, a reviewer can cause you serious harm (to your feelings, to your bank account, to your reputation) by writing a highly critical review of that book—much more harm, in all likelihood, than he or she could do to you with a punch in the nose. The lesser harm need not be tolerated, but the greater harm has to be endured. Why? Because the lesser harm (the nose punch) violates your right to security of person. All persons have, in Mill's terms, a "distinct and assignable obligation" to respect your rights. No such obligation protects you from the greater harm (the nasty book review). The review violates no right. It is a harm, but it must be tolerated, because you have no right to be a famous author or to get rich from royalties. The inseparability of rights and tolerance is nicely illustrated by this example. Although the harm may be considerable, most of us would likely conclude that society should neither prevent nor punish it. One of the prices that authors must pay for living in a society where they have the right to freedom of expression is having to tolerate the same freedom in others, even when it leads to harmful book reviews.

▒ The Concept Analyzed

The preceding analysis of the concepts of tolerance and governmental toleration and my review of the history of the application of tolerance and toleration suggest broad categories of tolerance. In this section, I think it is best first to define tolerance by reference to the objects of tolerance, by what or whom is being tolerated. I will then classify tolerance according to the traits and states of individuals who are tolerant.

Tolerance Defined by Its Objects (Toleratees)

By *political tolerance,* I mean tolerance of acts in the public sphere, such as giving a speech, demonstrating, distributing leaflets, organizing meetings, and so on. Political tolerance in the United States often is referred to as *civil liberties.* Political tolerance is fundamental because it is important for winning and maintaining tolerance of other kinds.

By *moral tolerance,* I refer to tolerance of acts in the private sphere. Most typically and controversially in recent decades this has concerned sexual conduct, such as "living in sin," pornography, homosexuality, and abortion. The issue in matters of moral tolerance is usually whether private acts should be subject to public control. A related issue is just what acts should be considered "private," that is, which acts are matters over which governments should have no control.

By *social tolerance,* I mean tolerance of people's states of being—that is, of characteristics people have at birth (such as skin color) or as the result of early socialization (such as language). Such "ascriptive" characteristics are sometimes not in themselves objects of tolerance or intolerance. Rather, what is at issue are acts, whether public or private, held to be "inappropriate" for people with such characteristics. For example, in the United States before the 1960s and in South Africa before the 1990s, the use by Blacks of the same public facilities (such as water fountains or beaches) as Whites was often not tolerated. In more extreme situations, merely having a characteristic or belief, regardless of whether it leads to an action, has been grounds for persecution or discrimination—and to opportunities for their opposite, tolerance. In such situations, not persecuting or not discriminating counts as tolerance. One can go further in one's opposition to persecution than mere tolerance. A hero such as Schindler comes to mind, but his example, although related to our subject, carries us to areas of investigation beyond those we can pursue in this book.

The categories of tolerance are not rigid. For example, one characteristic of democratic intolerance is that it tends to focus on individuals' acts, not on their traits. In the British example discussed above, it was not illegal to *be* a homosexual, it was illegal only to engage in homosexual *acts*. In this terminology, then, homosexuality was on the borderline between moral (private act) and social (state of being) tolerance. Something similar was true of communism in the United States in the 1950s. It was not, strictly speaking, illegal to be a communist, or to believe that communism is a good social system, but it was illegal to do things that communists were thought to do, such as plan to overthrow the government.

Although the three forms of tolerance are distinct, they overlap. Political tolerance is the easiest to define. It is also probably the form of tolerance that is easiest to defend, at least in the courts, in the United States, because it is clearly a constituent part of democracy and is written into the U.S. Constitution. One can oppose political tolerance only by opposing democracy, because a "democracy" without civil liberties would be a sham. Democracy entails the freedom to oppose the government, to disagree publicly with government policies. This freedom is clearly linked to the other two sorts of tolerance, because governments regulate the social and moral spheres. Political tolerance allows individuals to oppose (or demonstrate in favor of) such regulations, and political freedom is often key to the attainment of social and moral rights and liberties. For example, the entering wedge of the civil rights movement for racial equality in the United States was the political right of the people peaceably to assemble and petition the government. This is why political tolerance is the most fundamental type: Other kinds of tolerance often have to be established by battles in the public sphere.

Activities in the private, or moral, sphere are perhaps the most interesting and most contested today in the political arena, and the same primacy of political tolerance is true here. The gay rights movement is a good example. The viability of that movement ultimately depends on political rights or political tolerance. Homosexuality is a private act. It may also be a social category (a state of being)—depending on how the debate about the genetic determination of homosexuality turns out. But ultimately the battle for sexual privacy for homosexuals will be won or lost in the public, political arena.

Religion is the paradigm case of the links between political rights and private conscience. Religion was once largely a public (political) matter. Religious dissent was regarded as something like treasonous in Elizabethan England. The whole idea that there could be a private sphere in important matters such as religion was rejected by many who felt that, by definition, deviance in key values harms the society and the polity. With the separation of church and state, religious acts and beliefs became private (moral) matters. Tolerance frequently involves this kind of shifting of activities out of the public realm and into the private sphere. When that shift occurs, the main governmental regulation of private acts becomes a form of toleration, usually, the prohibition of discrimination or intolerance.

Interestingly and significantly, when this stage is reached, tolerance can become offensively inadequate, especially to the people who are the objects of social tolerance. People can and do understandably resent being tolerated (disliked but put up with) because of the color of their skin, their religion, their native language, or their sexual orientation. This has led some commentators to conclude (mistakenly, in my view) that tolerance is an antiquated value, appropriate only to an unequal era when White folks might have condescended to tolerate Black folks on "their" beach. Such an attitude would indeed be offensive, but that should not be allowed to obscure the fact that it was through political tolerance (the rights of free speech, press, and assembly) that the *right* of all to equal access to public facilities was won. And if groups now subject to discrimination because of their states of being ultimately gain rights, it will be as a result of the combination of two forces: legal guarantees of political toleration and cultural values that support tolerance.

Because *social tolerance* refers mostly to tolerance of "race" and "ethnicity," I want to devote a few lines to these concepts, both of which are hotly contested and, to a large extent, meaningless. In one sense, races do not exist. The idea of color-coded biological groups (yellow, red, black, brown, white, or whatever) is, scientifically speaking, a joke, in poor taste. Although there are certainly inherited physical traits in human populations (height, nostril width, amount of melanin, and so on), physical anthropologists are largely agreed that there is as much trait variation within "races" as between them. This is doubly true of ethnic groups. Trying to find objective criteria by which to place people into categories such as "Hispanic" or "Asian and Pacific Islander" is an honest classifier's nightmare, attempts by the U.S. Bureau of the Census to reify these categories notwithstanding (Hodgkinson, 1995).

On the other hand, although races do not exist, *racists* do. Although ethnic groups are worthless as scientific categories, ethnocentrism pervades social life. In short, the categories exist in people's minds even if, upon close examination, they are useless as objective sorting concepts. As categories, both race and ethnicity lack the most fundamental characteristic of coherent categories: They are not mutually exclusive. However, most people routinely use categories of race and ethnicity as though they were meaningful—and, in a sense, they are.

Their meaning is social; they are socially learned constructs, hallucinations really, but constructs that are as real as can be in their consequences. People use the categories of race and ethnicity to stereotype, to discriminate in favor of or against—and to tolerate. Therein lies their importance for this study. Racial and ethnic categories, arbitrary as they may be, are socially ascribed labels that have very real consequences for individuals and groups. As long as that is so, researchers will have to find ways to investigate these phantoms. My great worry in so doing is that by studying these social illusions, I will contribute to further reifying them.[2]

Tolerance Defined by the Tolerators

One final way to categorize kinds of tolerance is to ask what kind of cognitive/emotional state tolerance represents in the individuals who are doing the tolerating. What does it mean to say that an individual is tolerant or is engaged in tolerating? There are five general types of answers to that question. Tolerance can be a *personality trait,* roughly the opposite of the "authoritarian personality" (Adorno, Frenkel-Brunswick, Levinson, & Sanford, 1950; see also Young-Bruehl, 1996). Most sociologists and political scientists treat tolerance as an *attitude,* a disposition to act favorably or unfavorably toward someone or something. Tolerance can also be a *belief* or *commitment.* One might have a very negative attitude toward flag burners, for example, but believe that they have the right to thus express themselves; one could even be committed to defending that right. Finally, to tolerate can be to engage in *action,* such as refraining from discriminating against; or it can even involve action to bar the discrimination of some persons against others (working for a civil rights organization or participating in a counterdemonstration, for example).

If we put together these five affective/effective states of individuals who tolerate (trait, attitude, belief, commitment, action) with the three kinds of tolerance defined by the objects of tolerance, we get 15 possibilities, as illustrated in Figure 1.3.

One of the reasons discussions of tolerance can generate more heat than light is that these distinctions are not always clear to the discussants. When we ask, Does education foster tolerance? we are really asking 15 questions; we are asking about 15 categories of phenomena, ranging from moral traits through political actions. Add to this the fact that education is far from unidimensional— because there are many types, levels, and kinds of educational experiences—and the possibility for misunderstanding grows rapidly. These issues will be pursued

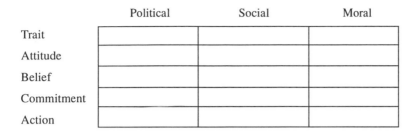

Figure 1.3. Tolerance Categorized by Objects of Tolerance and the Affective/Effective States of Tolerating Individuals

at greater length later in this book. Here it suffices to make one general and one specific remark. First, progress in understanding the connections between tolerance and education depends in part on our paying careful attention to the nuances among the different subcategories of tolerance. Second, in this book I will discuss all three broad types (political, social, and moral) but only two of the individual states in detail—specifically, I will focus on attitudes and beliefs (including values). This is not only helpful, because it reduces the number of subcategories from 15 to 6, but it is also necessitated by the comparative paucity of evidence about tolerant traits, commitments, and actions. Furthermore, tolerance cannot be studied without an examination of attitudes and beliefs. An action, or an inaction, that might qualify as tolerant does so only if the tolerator has a prior negative attitude or belief about the toleratee and only if the action or inaction or self-restraint is motivated by particular attitudes or beliefs—for example, that the toleratee has rights. In all cases, attitudes and beliefs are an integral part of tolerance—more so than traits, commitments, and actions, which, accordingly, will be discussed less thoroughly.

The terms used to describe attitudes and beliefs vary widely. *Attitude,* for example, is often broadly defined to include traits and beliefs, which are then sometimes referred to as different kinds of attitudes. Many researchers make no distinction between beliefs and commitments, but would rather talk of differences in strength of attitudes or strength of beliefs. Further relevant concepts that add to the confusion are *values* and *norms.* Values can be thought of as broad or general attitudes, such as honesty or compassion for the unfortunate, or they can be defined as beliefs about right and wrong. A norm is a socially enforced value; it is a rule (or belief) about how to behave, about good conduct. By these definitions, tolerance can be thought of as a norm or a value as well as an attitude or belief. Of course, one could say that a value is a belief that one ought to have a particular attitude and that a norm is such a belief when it is socially enforced. At this point the confusion that ensues becomes overwhelming.

These differences in terms in the research literature are mostly nominal, despite strenuous debate among scholars about "correct" meanings. The basic concepts and the ways they will be used in the pages that follow are clear enough. We will be dealing with various kinds of feelings (attitudes) and thoughts (beliefs) having to do with tolerance. We will examine attitudes and beliefs about putting up with something one has negative thoughts or feelings about. Usually, if one advocates or engages in such self-restraint, it is in the name of making social life possible.

Conclusion

My efforts to define tolerance in this chapter have involved looking at it in four ways. First, I have located tolerance in the context of related attitudes, beliefs, and behaviors (such as universalism, indifference, prejudice, and discrimination). Second, I have addressed tolerance in conjunction with the related concept of governmental toleration. Third, I have demonstrated that the definition of tolerance may vary depending upon the "object" toward whom it is directed, which results in three main subtypes of tolerance: political, social, and moral. Fourth, I have reviewed the kinds of personal cognitions, affects, or behaviors involved in tolerance and have specified five: personality trait, attitude, belief, commitment, and action.

All this said, it is clear that a full definition of tolerance is complex. Any attempt to teach tolerance will be similarly complex. Subsequent chapters in this volume address those complexities. However, before turning to the issue of how to teach tolerance, we need to address the question of whether we ought to do so. This is the subject of Chapter 2.

2

Should We Teach Tolerance?

HOULD WE TEACH TOLERANCE? If so, why? Answers to these questions are fairly simple, as they are more or less straightforward extensions of the concepts discussed in Chapter 1. On the other hand, as with most discussions of oughts and shoulds, with prescriptive controversies, the arguments are fairly theoretical or philosophical, more so at any rate than in subsequent chapters. In general, my positive answers to the questions of whether and why we should teach tolerance are comparatively short. In fact, a large part of this chapter is devoted to answering counterarguments, including attacks on structural-functionalism and critiques of "bourgeois" democracy offered from the perspective of one form or another of "conflict theory." I begin with the general case for teaching tolerance, and then proceed to a detailed consideration of counterarguments. Finally, I conclude with a reprise of the argument that in a complex and diverse society tolerance is crucial and must be fostered, this time folding in arguments drawn from social and cognitive psychology's study of stereotyping and prejudice.

The Case in General

Tolerance involves skills and understanding necessary for individuals to function in modern diverse societies. By extension, the viability of modern diverse societies requires that the individuals who live in them know how to cope with diversity and the conflicts that inevitably accompany diversity. To conclude that tolerance is a fundamental value in our society, we need not agree with Mill that differences among individuals, even differences that we might find objectionable, are "experiments in living" that enrich us all (if they do not violate the "harm principle"). Nor do we have to agree (although I do) with one modern philosopher who argues that conflicts over values are "welcome signs that we are on the right track" (Kekes, 1993, p. 31).

The importance of tolerance rests on the more modest claims that (a) diversity and conflict are inevitable and (b) tolerance provides procedural minima for dealing with diversity and conflict that do not violate other fundamental values, such as justice, liberty, and equality. Whether one welcomes diversity and conflict or is resigned to them or hates them, they are facts of life. Like it or not, there is always a range of opinion on any issue. (Indeed, the presence of a range of opinion about something is largely what we mean when we call something an *issue*.) And, like it or not, there will always be some issues on which the range of opinion is broad. Abortion is a good example of such an issue in the contemporary United States. Tolerance is mostly a procedural value for dealing with such issues; it is not in the first instance a substantive value. It is a preliminary condition for dealing peacefully with issues where opinions and values are as divisive as those about abortion. Tolerance, then, mere tolerance, is insufficient for most conceptions of what a good society would be. But mere tolerance is one of the functional minima for life in the modern world. Tolerance allows a society's values to evolve peacefully. Where tolerance is not present, well-known horrors are found (pogroms, lynchings, terrorism, assassinations, ethnic cleansing, and the like). If opponents cannot agree to tolerate one another long enough to begin discussions aimed at finding some common ground, the main alternative is one form or another of war (or hostile "standoff"). Of course, sometimes opponents do go to war, and some wars are "just wars," causes worth fighting for. But in most circumstances, other means of conflict resolution are preferable.

Alternatives besides war and tolerance exist. Most of them involve moving society in the direction of less diversity. Anti-immigrant sentiment and the movement to make English the official language of the United States are examples of opposition, perhaps growing opposition, to diversity. But, barring an authoritarian revolution, U.S. society is likely to continue with its present high level of political, social, and moral diversity. If this is the case, the need for tolerance will persist. For the foreseeable future, a citizenry equipped with the procedural value of tolerance will be better able to deal with the inevitable substantive differences among individuals and groups in the population. Students who leave school without those skills and understandings will be ill prepared to live in U.S. society. And U.S. society, as a society built upon the values of equality, liberty, and justice, will be jeopardized if tolerance is maintained only by constitutional law and is not also supported by a broad band of citizens who are committed to it as a value.

In contrast, the so-called elitist theory of democracy holds that the opinions of the mass public are largely irrelevant, because the masses do not participate to any significant degree in the political system (see, for example, Lipset, 1981). In response to this theory that the shared values (culture) of the citizenry do not matter, Gibson (1992b) has demonstrated through ingenious analyses that an intolerant climate of opinion is important because it contributes to "a culture of political conformity" (p. 339) in which citizens do not feel free to express themselves on controversial issues because they believe "that there are significant personal costs to be paid for expressing one's views" (p. 342). In brief, one of the contributions a culture of tolerance makes to a democratic society is that it nurtures individuals' sense of freedom to participate in the political system.

Tolerance may be a rather negative-sounding, limited, even mean-spirited sort of virtue. One might ask, Can we not have higher goals than putting up with one another? Yes we can, and we ought. But if we have pluralism, and if the differences among people are important, we need tolerance. Tolerance is the fundamental value that makes possible managed conflict, in which there are limits on what is allowed in the competition of values that characterizes a diverse society. Tolerance sets limits on what the powerful can do to the weak, on what majorities can do to (political, social, or moral) minorities. And in a society as diverse as the United States, everyone is a member of some minority group, usually more than one.

John Rawls takes a similar position in his widely discussed *Political Liberalism* (1993). Rawls maintains that a society must be built upon principles of political toleration if it is to be a fair system of cooperation among free and equal citizens. This is because the natural outcome of reasonable human activity in a free society is more diversity, not less. Even under idyllic conditions—a society with no prejudice, ignorance, or self-interested bias—reasonable people will still often disagree over basic values, philosophies of life, and political doctrines. The nature and limits of knowledge, what Rawls calls the "burdens of judgment" (pp. 54-58), make disagreement among reasonable people (to say nothing of unreasonable people) normal and inevitable. There can be no one true, comprehensive doctrine in a free society. In such a society, reasonable people must learn to live with diversity, and the political rules of the society must include a central place for toleration. Toleration may have begun as a modus vivendi—a way to end religious wars, for example—but, Rawls asserts, it can eventually, in the course of social and political evolution, become a value in its own right.

Charles Lindbloom, in a pragmatic account of the policy-making process, comes to roughly the same conclusions as does Rawls about the inevitability and desirability of diversity (Lindbloom & Woodhouse, 1993). Because of human cognitive limits, there can be no single best solution to any social problem (see also Simon, 1983). Diversity of interests is inevitable and is, moreover, a good thing, because it permits more intelligent policy making. Competing groups, each arguing its own case, reduce the likelihood that something important will be omitted from consideration: "As the diversity of those participating influentially in policy making increases, the number of important considerations neglected will decrease" (p. 31).

This general argument has been made in many ways and constitutes an identifiable theme in Western thought, from Locke and Mill through Rawls and Lindbloom. My citing more instances of this line of argument is unlikely to convince anyone as yet unconvinced. In sum, my view (and my main reason for writing this book) is that citizens in a socially diverse democracy need to understand something like the following "facts of life," as summarized in the rationale for a university course on tolerance that I teach from time to time:

> A person cannot like everything, and everything a person dislikes will not be illegal. Thus, everyone will need to tolerate at least some things. The need for tolerance is a fact of life in societies that afford persons considerable individual liberty and that also contain high levels of social and political diversity. The only way to reduce the need for tolerance is to reduce liberty or diversity or both.
>
>   On the other hand, since tolerance is not indifference or permissiveness, being tolerant does not require that we do nothing about what we see as wrong. Because we are compelled by law and morality occasionally to tolerate practices we find abhorrent, or at least to limit the actions we will take against them, it

does not follow that we can do nothing. We may campaign, lobby, preach, advertise, organize, and demonstrate. By being tolerant we do not lose our freedoms of expression and assembly. In short, others have to tolerate us. That is part of the deal (and the beauty of the deal) that makes a democratic polity and society possible.

Students who leave school not having learned some version of the "lessons" included in the above statement, and who cannot see the practical implications of those lessons, are lacking fundamental knowledge crucial for themselves and for their society. Schools should provide that knowledge if they can. The rest of this volume is devoted to the questions of whether and how they do so. But before we turn to those issues, we need to consider carefully some influential counterarguments. Thus far, the implicit counterarguments I have addressed have come mostly from the political Right, but there is also a left-wing critique of tolerance that has ancient lineage (see the quotations in Chapter 1 from Mirabeau and Thomas Paine). In the next section, I briefly address modern versions of this critique of tolerance.

Left-Wing Critiques of Tolerance

Functionalism Versus Conflict Theory

Almost any general discussion of the aims and consequences of education influenced by sociological work is interpreted by first placing the discussion into the battle of the "paradigms": functionalism and conflict theory. The locus classicus for this approach is the work of Karabel and Halsey (1977; see also Hurn, 1993). Readers accustomed to using these categories will suspect that my argument for why we should strive to use educational institutions to promote tolerance is a variant of the now largely discredited functionalist approach. This makes it worthwhile to put the argument for the centrality of tolerance into the context of that debate.

Functionalists focus on social systems and on how their parts operate to maintain the society as a whole. Conflict theorists, in contrast, stress the distinctness of social groups and how their interests divide the society. In its simplest form (believed by no scholar I have ever met, but often "refuted" by critics), functionalism leads to the conservative and naively optimistic belief that, as in Voltaire's parody, "all is for the best in the best of all possible worlds." Conflict theorists, on the other hand—by asking of any social policy or value,

Who benefits?—take a much more cynical view of society and stress domination of the many by the few. As Hurn (1993) and Karabel and Halsey (1977) have pointed out, however, the dichotomy between functionalism and conflict theory conceals some strong similarities. Adherents of both paradigms agree that the education system tends to promote values that perpetuate the existing society. The question is whether this is a good thing (as functionalists usually claim) or a bad thing (as conflict theorists most often say). Thus, the argument between conflict theorists and functionalists basically boils down to an evaluation of the society and/or the standard of comparison that should be used. For example, functionalists tend to compare the current social situation with the past (the bad old days), whereas conflict theorists more often compare it to an ideal future.

A second difference between functionalists and conflict theorists is that functionalists tend to talk about the good of society as a whole, whereas conflict theorists stress differences among self-interested groups, particularly how dominant groups arrange social institutions for their own benefit. Again, these two approaches are not mutually incompatible. Although it is useful for pedagogical purposes to dichotomize them in introductory sociology courses, the two paradigms are not of much use in investigations of particular questions in educational or social research. The nub of my view about tolerance is that it is crucial for social peace, which I consider a good thing, and one that benefits society as a whole. This is the functionalist "side" of this book's thesis. But something that benefits society as a whole will usually also benefit disproportionately those who are dominant in that society (the conflict theory "side"). It is not the case that the two kinds of benefits always work in concert; they can often have opposite effects for the society and for certain of its members. For example, the growing inequities in income and wealth in the United States since the 1980s are probably not good for the society as a whole, but they certainly appear to be good for the society's economic elites.

Suppose that we can agree that tolerance is good for society as a whole and therefore that it is a value that can be embraced as a general one. This seems to be a functionalist conclusion. But even if a society is agreed on the universal benefits of tolerance, this will not end conflict about how much and what kinds of tolerance are to be promoted by the society. Different kinds of tolerance will be more immediately beneficial to some groups. Obvious examples include the advantages of freedom of the press, which tend to be most keenly appreciated by journalists; likewise, the procedural guarantees of the Fourth, Fifth, and Sixth Amendments can be cherished by defense lawyers and those accused of crimes, while the same rights can seem annoying technicalities to law enforcement officials. Further examples include the benefits of freedom of religion for religious minorities and the value of the right to privacy for gays and lesbians. Most generally, and in the long run, I believe that tolerance is good for the stability of society, and therefore it is good for those who benefit most from the status quo. But tolerance is also good for those groups that would be oppressed without it.

Another similarity between most variants of functionalism and conflict theory is that they both see education systems as exerting very powerful influences on individuals. Functionalists see the consequences as being for the benefit of society as a whole, whereas conflict theorists see that influence as reinforcing society's elites. Thus, neither functionalism nor conflict theory denies that schools can and do teach values; rather, they differ mostly over who benefits from those activities. But they may be alike in the extent to which they exaggerate schools' influence. In later chapters, I will show that although education is often the most powerful predictor of variance in tolerance, most of that variance is not explained by education—or any other variable that we know how to measure.

One influential variant of conflict theory developed by John Meyer (1977) is specifically agnostic about whether schooling does or does not teach values or anything else. Meyer considers the key fact to be that people believe that different amounts and kinds of schooling have different effects, therefore they believe that manipulation of amount of schooling is a fair way to allocate scarce resources in a society. An extension of Meyer's approach (and also a return to his sources) would be to use Weberian concepts and see tolerance as part of a U.S. "status culture." People at different educational levels have different status cultures. Although this may easily be true, it does not tell us how tolerance has become part of the status culture of the highly educated, or whether they have acquired that culture in educational institutions, or whether educators should try to teach it.

In sum, although in certain portions of this book I draw on the work of functionalist theorists (see especially my use of the works of Durkheim and Dreeben in the discussion of "personality development" in Chapter 4), this is irrelevant to any judgment of the book's validity. For those who prefer to judge a work mainly on the grounds of whether it is based in functionalist or conflict theory, I would say that many aspects of this book are compatible with each, and that the much-discussed paradigm clash is not very revealing for our topic. When it comes to assessing the value of tolerance in a modern society, I would agree with Simmel (1955) and Coser (1956), who long ago pointed out that, within bounds, conflict can be functional. Indeed, as we shall see in the following subsections, that is precisely the problem as far as other critics are concerned.

A Critique of Pure Tolerance

A set of arguments similar to the critique of functionalism informs the work of Robert Paul Wolff, Barrington Moore, Jr., and Herbert Marcuse, in their volume *A Critique of Pure Tolerance* (1969). There is probably no work better known for its apparent opposition to the main line of argument in this book. And given that it is hard to think of three more widely respected social theorists, their critique deserves careful consideration. *A Critique of Pure Tolerance* is really three separate essays with a few common themes. The first theme is that tolerance can be a sort of trick. As the authors put it in their preface, "For each of us the prevailing theory and practice of tolerance turned out on examination to be in varying degrees hypocritical masks to cover appalling political realities" (p. vi).

A second theme is the perils of indifference. All three authors are on guard against indifference. Tolerance taken too far, they say, can become an excuse for doing nothing, for going along with whatever or whoever is in power. A close relative of indifference is relativism, which is the issue most central in Barrington Moore's essay, "Tolerance and the Scientific Outlook." Moore is especially worried about "watery toleration of every doctrine," which can add up to a refusal to judge, a form of "intellectual cowardice" (p. 54). After warning the reader against flaccidity and relativism, Moore turns to an advocacy of political tolerance and democracy and an analysis of the "prospects for tolerant rational discussion" (p. 73).

It is easy to agree with Moore on all these points. First, pure relativism is an intellectually incoherent doctrine, because it affirms that one can affirm nothing. Pure relativism has nothing to do with tolerance as discussed here. In my view, the capacity for tolerance has a lot to do with probabilistic ways of thinking, which are often confused with relativism (see Chapter 4). Second, I have tried in Chapter 1 to distinguish tolerance sharply from indifference, which is what the three authors of the *Critique* sometimes mean by "pure" tolerance. It makes no sense to say that one tolerates something about which one is indifferent. Indeed, at no point in this book will the reader encounter a plea for pure tolerance, with no limits and unchallenged by no other competing values. It would be absurd to make such a plea. Tolerance is always limited by and alloyed with other values (social order, for example). The most important questions pertaining to tolerance are not whether we should favor or oppose it as the sole organizing principle of society. Rather, serious discussion has to focus on where tolerance fits in the mix of other values and where the boundaries separating what is to be tolerated and what is not should be drawn.

The best-known essay in *A Critique of Pure Tolerance* is probably Marcuse's "Repressive Tolerance." Marcuse's basic point is that in an Orwellian world, where meaning is controlled by the media, which are controlled by oppressors, freedom of speech has little import. In a debate between unequal opponents in front of an audience that has been brainwashed to believe the stronger opponent, mere formal equality may simply legitimate the system by making unequal contests look fair. Thus, in "a repressive society, even progressive movements threaten to turn into their opposite to the degree to which they accept the rules of the game" (p. 83). Nonpartisan tolerance or "pure" tolerance, because "it refrains from taking sides . . . , actually protects the already established machinery of discrimination" (p. 85). Marcuse's solution is that we ought have no tolerance for "false words and wrong deeds"; rather, we should focus on a "liberating tolerance" (p. 88). This adds up to "intolerance against movements from the Right and toleration of movements from the Left" (p. 109). Marcuse admits that "to be sure, this is censorship" (p. 111). Who will be the censors, deciding what is worthy of being tolerated? The answer for Marcuse boils down to this: people who agree with Marcuse (*la gauche, c'est moi*). Even were one to agree with Marcuse about the effects of tolerance, his solution would be an ill-advised policy. Without the maligned "rules of the game," issues would be decided through pure power struggles, and, in the United States, people who agree with Marcuse would almost always lose.

The most important essay for our purposes in *A Critique of Pure Tolerance* is Robert Paul Wolff's "Beyond Tolerance."[1] Wolff's main point is that tolerance is central to the theory and practice of pluralistic liberal democracy. His critique of that form of democracy is then extended to a critique of tolerance. Although it is true that pluralistic democracy is inconceivable without tolerance, the converse is not necessarily true. Wolff cannot be faulted for his summary of the arguments for tolerance (pp. 20-23). But his main quarrel is not with tolerance; it is with pluralism. Wolff's complaint is that pluralism "always favors the groups in existence against those in process of formation" (p. 41). It is hard for a new group to get a hearing. Many groups go unrecognized because they do not have the resources to make their case and be admitted into "the circle of the acceptable" (p. 44). A pluralistic system, in short, is not completely fair. Bigger, stronger, richer groups almost always win, and they often have narrow, selfish interests that make them "fatally blind to the evils which afflict the entire body politic" (p. 52). Tolerance is guilty by association with pluralism. To the extent that tolerance can make an unfair fight look fair, it can be said to legitimate an unfair system. But what is the alternative? Eliminate tolerance and make the system even more unfair? It is hard not to agree with much of what Wolff says.

Who could deny that in a competitive system, big strong groups win more often than small weak ones? But the solution is not to reduce the limited protections that tolerance provides for small weak groups—even if big strong groups might disingenuously claim that those protections amount to equality.

Jackman's "Velvet Glove"

More than any other scholar, Mary Jackman is known for research results and interpretations of those results that are at odds with the conclusions and arguments of this book. Jackman has claimed that there are only very small links between education and tolerance, and her interpretations of those links are different from mine. We will return to measurement issues (how we size up education's association with tolerance) in Chapter 3. Because this chapter deals with values, or normative questions, I focus here more on Jackman's interpretations of her results, which have been very influential. Jackman's work on the subject of education and tolerance stretches over two decades. We are fortunate that she has recently published *The Velvet Glove* (1994), in which she pulls together the implications of her wide-ranging arguments. The nub of her position in that book is captured by its title, which refers to an emperor who said that he ruled with an iron fist—clothed in a velvet glove. In Jackman's view, tolerance forms part of the fabric of the velvet glove that disguises brutal power relationships.

Jackman designed her work on tolerance in essentially the same way tolerance is conceptualized in this book. She took the notion of tolerance often used in political studies (support for the liberties of others about whom one has negative beliefs or attitudes) and applied it to the social realm, especially interethnic studies (Jackman, 1977). Unlike in the study of politics, *tolerance* in the study of ethnic relations has usually meant any positive thought or feeling, anything that is not prejudice; *prejudice* has also been loosely defined as any negative attitude or belief. Jackman's approach was a big advance over such loose operationalizations. She put her ideas about the definition of tolerance into practice in a 1978 article titled "General and Applied Tolerance: Does Education Increase Commitment to Racial Integration?" That article stimulated considerable controversy, not so much about Jackman's findings (which were drawn from publicly available surveys) but about her explanations of them.[2]

Jackman introduced an analytic distinction common in studies of political tolerance (e.g., Prothro & Grigg, 1960) between support for a general principle and support for a specific application of the principle. She did this by comparing two measures: Support for Integration (SI) and Government Action (GA), each composed of answers to two questions. We need to look at the measures in some detail here, for the debate over the interpretation hangs on an understanding of the details. The first "abstract principle" question asked of respondents was, "Are you in favor of desegregation, strict segregation, or something in between?" The second question was not as abstract or general, although it was part of the general tolerance measure. Respondents were asked which statement they agreed with: (a) "Whites have a right to keep Negroes out of their neighborhoods if they want to" or (b) "Negroes have a right to live wherever they can afford to, just like anybody else." Responses to the two questions were coded to yield an 8-point scale.

For the application (GA) scale, Jackman asked the following:

Should the government in Washington—
  (a) see to it that Negroes get fair treatment in jobs or
  (b) leave these matters to the States and local communities?

Also asked was this question:

Should the government in Washington—
  (a) see to it that white and Negro children go to the same schools or
  (b) stay out of this area as it is none of its business?

It is important to note that this second set of questions asks about "the government in Washington" as much if not more than about integration. Jackman was certainly right to label this her Government Action scale. The problems arose when she claimed that if a person did not get a high score on the GA scale, his or her score on the SI scale was pretty meaningless. That is, if an individual did not support federal intervention, he or she did not "really" support integration. What good is it, Jackman asked, to be in favor of something "in principle" if you will not support policies to back up your principles?

How did people at different education levels score on these two scales? The association with education was very clear and direct for the SI scale (integration in general and support for open housing). For example, in 1972, on the 8-point Support for Integration scale, the scores for whites with 0-8 years of education, some high school, high school degrees, some college, and college degrees were, respectively, 4.5, 5.0, 5.7, 6.3, and 6.8 (Jackman, 1978, p. 319). This is precisely the kind of clear, direct, linear relationship that has led most researchers to posit a causal link between education and "tolerance" (variously defined). But the scores for Government Action were not so clearly linked to education level. Only college graduates had scores noticeably higher than those of the rest of the population.

It is also interesting to see the change over time in the scores. Surveys were conducted in 1964, 1968, and 1972. The scores for all education groups went up on SI (general tolerance), and the scores for the more-educated groups tended to go up faster (about a point on the 8-point scale), although the pattern was not perfect. On GA (applied tolerance) only the scores of college graduates clearly increased (half one point on the 8-point scale). Each of these results represents quite a lot of change over a relatively short period. However, the change in attitudes cannot be attributed to rising education levels, because education levels did not increase much in the 8 years in which the surveys were conducted. But people with higher levels of education seemed to be more open to influences originating in the broader society. This was especially notable on the GA/applied scale.

A second way to look at this issue of change over time is to examine the percentage of variance explained by education as estimated by the R^2 statistic, which Jackman provides for both scales. Again the pattern is the same: more modest levels and levels of growth for GA than for SI. Again, the coefficients are largest and most frequently attain levels of statistical significance for college graduates—more than for any other group (see Jackman, 1978, p. 311, Table 2). For our purposes, however, the main point is that the percentage of variance explained by education increased on both scales over this 8-year period, as can be seen in Table 2.1.

Jackman carried her analyses further, but we will not follow those analyses here for two reasons: First, enough has been said for us to be able to examine the construction she puts on the data, which is our main task in this chapter; second, most of the rest of her analyses were done with the education variable measured in three categories, not five. By eliminating the highest category of education (college graduation, the best predictor), Jackman squeezed too much of the variance out of the variable to make her analyses with the collapsed categories interesting. This problem was rectified in a later article (Jackman & Muha, 1984), which we shall examine shortly.

So why, according to Jackman, do Whites, including highly educated Whites, get higher scores on Support for Integration than on Government Action? One possibility, suggested by several of Jackman's critics, is that they do not like "the government in Washington" (Kuklinski & Parent, 1981a, 1981b; Margolis & Haque, 1981). At minimum, it is impossible to tell whether people answering the questions were responding to school integration or to the federal government, because the questions include both. Jackman's (1981b) answer is otherwise: "The most credible interpretation of lack of support for government

TABLE 2.1 Percentage of Variance Explained by Education, R^2

	1964	1968	1972
Support for Integration (general principle)	7	9	11
Government Action (specific application)	0	1	2

action in a specific policy area remains lack of support for the policy goal involved" (p. 169). If you do not support the means, Jackman seems to be asking, can you really claim to support the end? And if people do not truly support the end via the means, how do we interpret the increasing scores, especially among the highly educated, for Support for Integration? Basically, her answer is that more-educated people better know what the "socially correct" answers are (see the discussion of "social desirability bias" in Chapter 3). Giving "socially correct" answers to the general questions is relatively painless, because simply answering does not commit one to take the applied steps that would really make a difference. When it comes to really making a difference, well-educated Whites, just like less-educated Whites, retreat. But those with more education know how to cover themselves in a cloak of moral enlightenment.

There are several responses one might make to Jackman. Most important, the basic logic of her argument is flawed. Although it is true that a person who is opposed to any and all means to bring about an end might be said to have a questionable level of support for that end, this is an extremely limiting case. Looking at it the other way around, merely because a person does not favor every means by which an end could possibly be achieved, it does not follow that he or she is opposed to the end. Say that a couple claims to be very upset by the policies of a new Republican majority in Congress, but they don't take out a second mortgage on their home and send the proceeds to the Democratic National Committee. They don't put their money where their mouth is. Does this mean they "really" like Republicans? Not necessarily; they just don't dislike Republicans enough to jeopardize their own financial future. Jackman might reply that this example is just the limiting case at the other extreme. If federal intervention is the only effective means to bring about integration, saying you are in favor of integration but opposed to federal intervention is contradictory. Her argument here is similar to the "symbolic racism" argument (Sears & Allen, 1984). As Jesse Jackson put it in response to those who claimed to favor desegregation but opposed busing to bring it about, "It's not the bus; it's us."

But why do Whites who are opposed to federal government action to bring about applied tolerance bother to support integration as a general principle?

Jackman's explanation has grown increasingly cynical about "dominant group" motives over the years. In 1978, she argued that their commitment was "superficial." By 1984 she had switched to an "ideological refinement" explanation. Education helps people "become state-of-the-art apologists for their group's social position." People with advanced educations "are the most sophisticated practitioners of their group's ideology" (Jackman & Muha, 1984, pp. 751-752). Jackman explained away as an ideological sham the comparatively small ties she found between education and attitudes. Her quantitative results were based on one survey in one year (1975). The statistical associations of education and attitudes in that survey, although smaller than those found in many other studies, are not radically different in kind. But although the data need not detain us, Jackman's interpretation of them is very important—if for no reason other than that the article "Education and Intergroup Attitudes" is one of the most widely cited on the subject.[3]

Most scholars who have disagreed with Jackman have assumed that her data and her reporting of them were fine (see Chapter 3 for a discussion of the data); they have quarreled more with her interpretations. Jackman admits that her explanations "go well beyond the data presented in this paper" (Jackman & Muha, 1984, p. 759). Because those interpretations are most fully elaborated in *The Velvet Glove,* we can get the best view of them by examining that work. Tolerance, Jackman claims, is a conflict reducer. By reducing conflict, tolerance "places more weight on societal stability than on the substantive resolution of group differences." Like Wolff, Jackman (1994) notes that tolerance "lends itself more easily to the pluralist view of a society unmarked by deep rifts between have's and have-not's" (p. 46). According to Jackman, because contemporary U.S. society is deeply riven, tolerance is misleading at best, because it promotes the idea of pluralist unity. Perhaps Jackman is right that the idea of tolerance can lead people to be overly optimistic about equality in U.S. society, but what are the practical implications of that argument? Should we reduce tolerance? Can there be any sense in which less tolerance would improve things for members of disadvantaged groups in modern society?

Jackman's main complaint against tolerance is indirect. Tolerance is complicit in maintaining a regime of individual rights and is thus linked to one of the biggest barriers to social justice in U.S. society. The problem is that dominant groups use "varying forms of ideological persuasion" (p. 1), such as tolerance, and this "obscures the bare bones of expropriation" (p. 9). The central form of ideological obfuscation is individualism. What is wrong with individualism? Two things, says Jackman: It makes the "rights of groups" seem "illegitimate and unreasonable" (p. 89), and it deflects attention from equality of outcomes (for groups) to equality of opportunity (for individuals). Jackman frequently writes as though the idea of individual equality of opportunity were something recently dreamed up by clever apologists for the status quo. She often refers to "this shift in the meaning of equality to connote equality of opportunity" (p. 224) and to how "equality is quietly transmogrified into equality of opportunity" (p. 365). Historically, of course, this is quite backward. Equality of outcomes for groups is by far the newer idea in the United States. It is more accurate to say that subordinate groups have raised the stakes by asking for equality of outcomes than to claim that dominant groups have changed the idea of equality by making it more individualistic.

Basically, Jackman is convinced that dominant groups in society want to maintain their advantaged position. It is hard to argue with that. The problem is that she then explains all facts with one nonfalsifiable theory. Is the dominant group less rigid than it once was? This is merely another way for it to extend its "insidious reach" (p. 70). Do some Whites make crude racist stereotypes? This shows that they are racists. But most do not do this. Do many more Whites draw more modest distinctions "with care" and avoid treating Blacks as members of an undifferentiated category? This is merely a much more clever way of keeping Blacks down. And most clever and subtly racist of all, Jackman concludes, "some whites disclaim racial differences altogether" (p. 337). There is probably no way to convince Jackman that any change in attitudes or beliefs on the part of members of the dominant group (that is, White males) could ever amount to social progress. What some might view as progress Jackman would claim is simply dominant groups' rendering institutions "morally palatable to those whose compliance sustains them" (p. 68).

I simply am not persuaded by this argument. It obscures under one overarching conspiracy theory too many real differences. Some of Jackman's contentions are persuasive, particularly those that parallel ideas outlined in the section above on functionalism and conflict theory. As I have noted, it has been suggested that the maintenance of a peaceful, stable society will often disproportionately benefit a society's privileged groups. But Jackman talks only of benefits to privileged groups and never of the advantages of tolerance for unpopular minorities or society as a whole. Thus, according to the old formula, she is right in what she affirms, but wrong in what she denies. In any case, it is hard to see how society's less fortunate members could ever benefit from having fewer individual liberties and less tolerance. Readers who are persuaded otherwise by arguments such as those of Jackman and Marcuse probably will not care much about the origins of tolerance and whether it can be taught in schools. They might even believe that it should not be taught in schools, because in their view, tolerance is an ideological ploy that serves to legitimate an unfair social system.

Whenever one discusses values questions, one eventually arrives at a point where further argument seems futile. It is always tempting, however, to try to go a bit further—so here goes. It is hard to conceive how a society can progress by denigrating its most progressive values, such as tolerance and individual liberty. More important, how can the cause of egalitarianism be served by disarming the main weapons that small, weak, unpopular groups have in a democratic society—freedom of speech, the right of assembly, and equal protection under the law? Critics are correct to point out that tolerance is importantly related to notions of individual rights, liberties, and opportunities. Hence, tolerance gets swept up in the debate over "group rights." In my view—and I think of myself as an egalitarian on this point—the problem with the principle of group rights is that it is hard to confine it to the rights of disadvantaged or oppressed groups. If group rights become an accepted norm, what is to prevent dominant groups from demanding their group rights, too? Indeed, historically, societies in which group rights have been a strong social and political value have been rigidly inegalitarian. The two most obvious examples are the caste system in India and the various "estate" systems that prevailed in Europe before the democratic revolutions of the 18th and 19th centuries.

Much of the argument for the importance of tolerance in social, political, and moral life (and therefore the case for teaching it in schools) is a version of the case for democracy. Ultimately, most of the arguments critical of tolerance (especially those made by Marcuse, Wolff, and Jackman) are arguments against particular forms of democracy. Saying this does not settle much, because arguments for democracy and by its critics are hardly simple (Dahl, 1989). Tolerance can and surely does exist in nondemocratic societies. But democracy cannot long endure without some types of tolerance. Putting up with losing an election is the most obvious example of political tolerance. And when your side wins an election, putting up with criticism of your policies from those you just defeated is a kind of tolerance even more important for the survival of democracy. Hence, if one supports democracy, one must logically support political tolerance. A democratic society entails political tolerance, and, if not quite as obviously, it usually implies social and moral tolerance as well.

In addition to the argument that in bourgeois societies, tolerance is a trick to keep the oppressed from turning revolutionary, there is a somewhat parallel argument that tolerance and democracy may be fine for prosperous societies, but they are luxuries that poor societies, and especially the poorest people in them, can ill afford. What good is freedom of speech, it can be asked, when one does not have enough to eat? Often such questions are versions of the "repressive tolerance" argument: Tolerance, civil liberties, and the like deflect attention from the main issue, which is the construction of a society where the most important right of all is ensured—the right to eat. In poor societies, the argument goes, the only beneficiaries of civil liberties are rich elites.

Against this argument, several scholars have made an overwhelming case for exactly the opposite view. Most persuasive to me is the work of Amartya Sen (1995) and Partha Dasgupta (1993, 1995), at least in part because these scholars are far from "Eurocentric." Their conclusions are fairly simple, although based on uncommonly rigorous scholarship. Famine and disease are found less frequently in poor societies that have democracy, open government, and civil liberties than in poor societies without these advantages. As Dasgupta (1995) concludes, "Even in poor countries political and civil liberties go together with improvements in other aspects of life, such as income per person, life expectancy at birth and infant survival rate" (p. 45). To summarize my argument: Democracy, rights, liberties, and tolerance are good for societies as a whole and for the people in them, including poor people and those subject to discrimination. That is why we should promote them in schools if we can.

Prejudice, Bias, and Stereotypes

Social psychologists have long warned that it is naive to expect stereotyping, prejudice, and overgeneralizing to disappear (Allport, 1954; Simon, 1993; Tajfel, 1978). In specific situations, we can reduce the overwhelming drive of humans to overgeneralize, but we can never eliminate it. The alternative is James's "bloomin' buzzin' confusion." We need to generalize in order to think, and in one sense all generalizations are overgeneralizations, because all generalizations are, at best, only generally true. Stereotypes are merely our generalizations about groups of people. Stereotypes are judgments about the personal traits of categories of people; they may be positive as well as negative. Although no particular stereotype is inevitable, the process of generalizing about groups of people probably is. According to the authors of the most fully elaborated view of the inevitability of stereotyping, "People can't afford . . . to do without stereotypes" (Leyens, Yzerbyt, & Shadron, 1994, p. 1). Indeed, "people use stereotypes as explanations like scientists use theories" (p. 14).

This idea of the universal tendency to prejudge, and the related phenomenon of maintaining distance from those we judge to be different, has been recognized about as long as social psychologists have worked on these issues. For example,

Hartley (1946) found that people unwilling to accept members of various ethnic groups into their midst also rejected association with "Wallonians," "Danireans," and "Pireneans"—three fictitious groups. This was perhaps not quite as silly as it seems. Some people may just not like foreigners, including those from places they have never heard of. The tendency to be very quick to have negative reactions toward out-groups, even fictitious out-groups, has been linked with modern trends in cognitive psychology.

People seem to be willing and able to discriminate against out-groups, or at least to be biased against them, almost without exception (for one area of exception, high-status out-groups, see Sidanius & Pratto, 1993). There is little disagreement among social psychologists doing laboratory research that people tend to view members of their own groups more positively than they do members of other groups. People usually find it easier to remember bad things about out-groups and harder to remember good things about them. Experimental subjects have revealed such biases and have done such discriminating even when the groups in question were created through wholly artificial divisions invented only for the experimental situation (Tajfel, 1978). But as Messick and Mackie conclude after an extensive review, "Nearly 20 years after the discovery that mere categorization produced intergroup bias, an adequate theory of the phenomenon has yet to be developed" (quoted in Leyens et al., 1994, p. 68). In the short term, for this discussion, the lack of an adequate explanatory theory is not crucial. The fact is more important than its explanation; the inevitability of stereotyping and bias is why tolerance is vitally important.

Groups with visible markers of their status are particularly susceptible to bias and discrimination, which is why, when there are no outward signs, people often create them. From the Blues and Greens of the Byzantine Empire, through the yellow star, to the colored kerchiefs of the Crips and Bloods, visible markers have always been helpful to the discriminator. (They are also used as positive emblems or totems of in-groups, of course.) Ethnic conflict can be fierce, but even when there are no obvious ethnic differences, clashes between groups can reach suicidal proportions with surprising speed. For example, Somalia, a nation more united in ethnicity, language, and religion than virtually any other African nation, has been the site of an intensely bloody civil war. The slaughter in Cambodia is another instance of conflict seemingly out of all proportion to the differences among the groups involved (Staub, 1989). What these examples show is that it is very difficult to predict intergroup conflict using only information about the degree of "real" diversity in a society.

Former havens of tolerance can change quite rapidly. Spain before the 16th century was one of the few places Muslims, Christians, and Jews coexisted, although they lived mostly in separate enclaves. Under Muslim rule, Christians and Jews were tolerated, although they did not really have rights (compare Netanyahu, 1995). But Spain rather quickly became a synonym for, the paradigm case of, religious repression. For a few decades the former Yugoslavia (especially Bosnia) was looked upon as a model of interethnic and multireligious cooperation and harmony. The same was true for Lebanon, and especially Beirut. This is not the place to develop a macrosociological theory of how "models" of tolerance may be particularly susceptible to vicious repression and suicidal civil war (see my discussion of the "paradox of diversity" in Chapter 5). It is enough here to point out that the urge to discriminate and dominate persists even in social circumstances that seem also to provide the strongest grounds for optimism about intergroup harmony.

Whatever the ultimate reason, as Rothbart and John (1993) conclude, "intergroup bias . . . appears to be ubiquitous" (p. 34). Although there is much debate among researchers, there is broad agreement that "we tend to perceive groups other than our own as too homogeneous" (p. 40), and those perceptions are almost invariably negative. Over the past couple of decades, psychologists have done extensive work on human cognition as it pertains to the possibility of changing stereotypes. Most studies have found that, given our understanding of how the mind works, changes in biases or stereotypes are quite unlikely. There are, for example, a wide variety of cognitive "mechanisms that serve to protect beliefs from disconfirming information" (Rothbart & John, 1985, p. 88). But, although cognitive psychologists have well explained why attitudes do not change and have documented "the self-perpetuating nature of prior beliefs" (p. 99), we know from other evidence that attitudes and beliefs do change. If they did not, we would all still be as foolishly racist as our grandparents. Some of us still are, of course, and many people two generations ago were quite enlightened. But there is very strong evidence of dramatic changes in Americans' attitudes over the past 50 years (Schuman, Steeh, & Bobo, 1985). In any case, "the conditions favouring flexibility or perseverance [in beliefs] are still a matter of intense investigation" (Leyens et al., 1994, p. 202).

I think it is fairly easy to resolve an apparent contradiction about attitude change. We know from social surveys that there has been much attitudinal change, but we also know from psychological research that strong forces discourage people from changing their attitudes. First, the two research traditions work with very different time frames: Social psychologists often look for attitude change in short experiments lasting perhaps an hour or two, whereas survey researchers make attitude comparisons over several years, sometimes decades. Second, we need to distinguish among types of attitudes. Psychologists have mostly studied stereotypes, biases, and prejudices. But the absence of changes in these is not the same thing as the absence of any change. Even if we are largely stuck with our stereotypes, at least as first impressions (Devine, 1989), we do not have to act on them, and they do not necessarily determine our attitudes and beliefs about the rights and liberties of others—including others about whom we hold stereotypes. Biased perceptions, prejudices, and stereotypes are not incompatible with tolerance. In fact, it is precisely because we seem to be "hardwired" stereotypers that we need tolerance. And some evidence indicates that, for example, Whites' stereotypical attitudes about Blacks are changing more slowly than Whites' support for Blacks' rights and liberties—to buy a house, to join a club, to intermarry (Dowden & Robinson, 1993). In short, Whites may not stereotype much less than they did a decade or two ago, but they are more tolerant; they are more supportive of the rights and liberties and legal and institutional equality of people they continue to stereotype. That is progress. In subsequent chapters, we will see that this progress is partly attributable to schooling. In this chapter, I argue that it ought to be furthered by schooling when possible.

A diverse society contains not only real differences among people, but also the absurd ones we make up. And evidence about what leads us to hold on to or to persist in our beliefs is not well understood. To summarize: Although particular stereotypes may be subject to change, stereotyping is inevitable. Humans are categorizing animals. Because of our limited cognitive capacities, we need to oversimplify greatly in order to act (Simon, 1983). The huge research literature on the issue of why stereotyping is ubiquitous (see Leyens et al., 1994, for a review) contains quite a bit of controversy about the details. However, there is widespread agreement that stereotyping is part of human cognitive and social nature. This is what is most important for our purposes. Our nature as stereotypers is one of the reasons social diversity will always pervade society. And diversity, it will be recalled, is one of the conditions conducive to and necessitating tolerance (see Figure 1.2). Should we ever come up a little short on real diversity, we seem bound to make up the deficit by stereotyping.

In sum, people process information in a broad range of ways. These extend from quick and easy stereotyping to "effortful consideration of individuating information." People are more likely to stereotype when they are highly aroused (angry or happy) and when they are tired (Leyens et al., 1994, pp. 117-118). One interpretation of tolerance, parallel to the "sober second thoughts" definition from political science, is that tolerance involves "effortful consideration" in matters where the modal response is quick and easy stereotyping. But whatever the source of the disliked differences, there will always be many of them, which, in turn, will always provide ample opportunities to tolerate.

Conclusion

How important is it to teach tolerance, in comparison, say, to appreciation for diversity or reducing prejudice? I would say tolerance should be our first aim. Other ends may be higher, but we have just reviewed considerable psychological evidence that reducing prejudice, to say nothing of increasing positive beliefs about out-groups, can be extremely difficult (and perhaps, in some senses, impossible). Tolerance is a more attainable virtue, and for that reason may be more important than feelings of brotherhood or appreciation of diversity. Tolerance is minimally necessary for civil society. Although I could easily be persuaded that we should aim higher than mere tolerance, tolerance should be our first step; it is the lowest acceptable level of intergroup harmony. After we have attained it, we can perhaps move to higher ground.

We do not have to eradicate prejudice or eliminate stereotyping to attain tolerance. Tolerance is more of a behavioral disposition, whereas prejudice is more of a feeling. People do not always simply act on their feelings. Indeed, people can be tolerant of a group, in the strict definition of the term, only when they have negative feelings toward it. In other words, prejudice does not necessarily lead to intolerance. There is a difference between having a negative feeling about a group and denying that group's members basic rights. We do not have to change people's feelings to promote their being more civil toward one another.

A well-known line of research suggests that eliminating stereotypes and eradicating prejudice are not necessary preconditions for civil social interaction (Devine, 1989; compare Fazio, Jackson, Dunton, & Williams, 1995). People with high and low levels of prejudice do not differ much in their initial reactions to members of an out-group. Most Whites, for example, initially react on the basis of broadly shared cultural stereotypes when encountering Blacks. (Other stereotyping interactions, especially Blacks' perceptions of Whites, have been studied much less extensively.) But nonprejudiced Whites do not stop at this knee-jerk level of appraisal. They use their reflective, conscious, controlled attitudes and beliefs to direct their behavior. One's gut reaction is not the only "true" measure of what one is.[4]

Negative affect toward outsiders is "normal"—that is, it is statistically common and takes little thought or effort. But that does not mean that it is admirable, nor is "normal" the only alternative. Much that is admirable in human life is not "normal" (i.e., easy and common)—for example, playing the violin, writing computer programs, or tolerating those who frighten us because they are different. The lesson of tolerance is that some portion of our negative affect toward outsiders must not result in negative action against them if we are to live in social conditions of decency and civility. The lesson is particularly difficult precisely because tolerance is always limited in its application. Knowing how to live in a civilized society means knowing how to think about where and on what principles to draw the boundary between what is to be tolerated and what is not. It is a lesson so crucial to democratic society that an education system in a democratic society should try to teach it.

The next chapter reviews evidence that tolerance is learned and taught, perhaps sometimes unintentionally, in the education system. Subsequent chapters are devoted to discussion aimed at determining *how* that happens and whether we can use our knowledge of how it happens to make recommendations for educational and social policy.

CHAPTER 3

Does Education Really Foster Tolerance?

NE OF THE MOST CONSISTENT FINDINGS in modern survey research is the strong link between education level and social and political tolerance (Davis, 1975, 1982; Hyman & Wright, 1979; Lawrence, 1976; Nunn, Crockett, & Williams, 1978; Stouffer, 1955). Researchers have devoted considerable attention to establishing that a correlation exists between education and tolerance, to measuring its size, and to determining education's rank in a list of other variables that correlate with tolerance level. That research is reviewed in this chapter, and in the remainder of this book I will make an effort to explain the causes of the connections between education and tolerance. Most attempts to explain how education promotes tolerance have been rather casual post hoc speculations resting only lightly upon empirical data. Most typically, researchers have tried to account for a statistical association by borrowing an idea or two from some convenient theory of learning, personality, or attitude development.

Causal conclusions are notoriously problematic in the social sciences, of course, but by taking stock of the available explanations for the persistent associations between education and tolerance, and by building upon those explanations in Chapters 4 and 5, we can arrive at persuasive conclusions about the ways in which education promotes tolerance. These conclusions will allow me to recommend some strategies for educational policy and practice in Chapter 6 and to suggest some guidelines for further research in Chapter 7.

▓ Arguments That Education
May Not Promote Tolerance

I must begin by noting that some researchers have denied the existence of strong and meaningful correlations between education and tolerance. Below, I take a close look at their arguments and attempt to answer them as a prolepsis to the positive findings presented later in the chapter.

Skepticism About Survey Research

The key method used in gathering most of the findings discussed in this book is one form or another of survey research. Doubts about that method must be addressed, because many of the conclusions presented here are based on evidence gathered by researchers who asked people about their beliefs. Although most people would probably agree that survey research has proven a useful tool in some fields (predicting how people will vote or what they will buy, for example), many critics question the validity of surveys for addressing sensitive topics such as social, political, and moral attitudes. There is a huge literature on the validity of survey research, and I can do no more than touch on it here. In general, my position is that although a healthy skepticism is always a good idea, with this or any other research method, nihilism about the results of survey research is not justified. When we want to know about people's attitudes and beliefs, we have few alternatives but to ask them. Attitudes and beliefs are subjective; they cannot be observed. Whereas asking someone, "Did you vote in the last election?" requests objective information that could in principle be checked, asking a person, "Which candidate do you like?" is, in principle, subjective; there is no objective way to verify what someone likes (Turner &

Martin, 1984). Answers to questions about attitudes and beliefs have to be accepted on trust. People who think other people are all congenital liars should not bother reading the results of survey research—or those of other methods that depend on people to tell the truth, such as interviews and psychological experiments. That position—trust no one—can be honestly held, and is a coherent position, but it is one that is too skeptical, in my view. Taken seriously, it would make social life impossible.

What is not honest, however, is to be a "skeptic when convenient" (SWC). SWCs believe the results of survey research when those results support their interpretations (often claiming, however, that they "already knew" that). But when survey answers do not conform to their prior beliefs, they become skeptical. Believing survey research when it advances one's argument and doubting it when it does not shows at best little critical self-awareness and at worst a lack of intellectual probity. Be that as it may, despite the limits on our knowledge of how to ask good questions or how much we can trust the answers, if we want to study crucial social issues such as tolerance and its causes, we have little choice but to ask people questions and put some degree of confidence in what they tell us.

The main criticisms of survey research I will deal with here can be categorized as versions of the following four beliefs: (a) People do not always tell researchers what they really think. (b) Sometimes people do not actually know what they really believe about questions on surveys, but they offer top-of-the-head answers anyway. (c) Even assuming that people know what they think and are willing to share it, the survey situation and the kinds of questions used in surveys are usually so flawed that it is nearly impossible to interpret respondents' answers. (d) Finally, and most damning of all according to many critics, what people say and what people do are not necessarily the same. A large literature exists on each of these topics. I will review the main points relevant for our purposes.

People Do Not Tell the Truth

There are many reasons for assuming that people do not tell researchers what they really think or feel or believe, or what they would do or have done. The particular kind of skepticism about survey research most important for those who claim that highly educated people do not really tend to be more tolerant is one version or another of the *social desirability hypothesis*. The argument goes as follows: Well-educated people are good at taking tests, at giving the "right," or socially desirable (in this case, tolerant) answers; but this does not mean that educated individuals are in fact more genuinely committed to tolerant norms. The educated are merely better at deception. Hence, according to this argument, most research probably overestimates the "true" tolerance levels of the highly educated and thus exaggerates the tolerance gap between people with more and less education.

Although the social desirability hypothesis has considerable intuitive appeal for many people, there is very little evidence to support it, in part because much of the research on social desirability bias has been badly flawed (DeMaio, 1984). Despite the fact that social desirability bias is an "implicit, but untested, assumption of most researchers" (DeMaio, 1984, p. 272), it does not pose a serious threat to the main findings of this book; one reason for this is that "people who have a high tendency to respond desirably do not necessarily agree on what is desirable" (p. 278). Of course, one could ask subjects what they think are desirable answers and use their responses to challenge their responses to other questions, but the circularity of such a procedure renders it pointless and absurd.

Furthermore, it is actually easier to make the opposite case—for what might be called the social self-confidence hypothesis: Highly educated people tend to be more self-assured and are, therefore, less likely to be intimidated by the interview/survey situation and more likely to answer accurately. Also, because people with extensive educations are more likely to be aware of the purposes and methods of survey research and to understand that their responses will be anonymous, they are more, not less, likely to give responses that reflect their "true" attitudes, even if those attitudes do not conform to standard notions of what is desirable. If the social self-confidence hypothesis is correct, most reports of the gap in tolerance levels between the more and less educated probably underestimate the actual differences (compare Schuman, Bobo, & Krysan, 1992, on the F scale).

Perhaps the best, although indirect, evidence we have for social desirability bias comes from survey respondents' reports of their behaviors that can be verified. This is not the same thing as being able to check on the reporting of attitudes and beliefs, but results of this kind of research are suggestive of the magnitude of the problem (see the subsection below on attitudes and behavior, what people say as a guide to what they do). Well-known among such studies are those pointing to the fact that a higher percentage of people answering surveys claim to have voted in the last election than did in fact vote. The differences are not huge, but they are serious—2% in one study, 8% in another (Hyman & Wright, 1979, p. 14; see also Inkeles & Smith, 1974, pp. 252-253).

More interesting are longitudinal studies of reports of educational attainment and achievement, which provide much better, more direct, evidence—and evidence about one of the key variables in this book. The National Longitudinal Study of the Class of 1972 (NLS 72) followed some 20,000 high school graduates for a period of 14 years (1972-1986) and studied their occupational and educational histories, among other things. Adelman (1994), who has made a special study of the issue, is "skeptical about using survey data to determine educational attainment" (pp. 10-11). Upon checking the college transcripts of the NLS respondents, he found, for example, that some 6% of those who claimed to have earned a doctoral or first professional degree had not even earned a baccalaureate, and nearly 12% of those who said they had earned a bachelor's degree had not done so. Although falsehood rates of 6% and 12% are shocking and disheartening for those who rely on surveys, it must be remembered that these dismaying results did not pertain, respectively, to 94% and 88% of the respondents. We do not know the exact extent of the misreporting, because Adelman provides only some dramatic illustrations rather than a systematic account, but a reasonable guess would be that 10-20% of respondents exaggerate their educational attainments and 80-90% do not.

Further interesting evidence comes from a study of reports, by students and their parents, of elementary students' grades. Alexander, Entwisle, and Bedinger (1994) found that parents and students routinely expected grades higher than those that were earned. More to the point, students and parents in the fall semester often recalled or reported the previous spring's grades (in third-grade math and reading) as being higher than they were. Although all socioeconomic and ethnic groups tended to overreport, this tendency varied by group. Parents were generally more accurate than their children, and the least accurate (most exaggerated) parental reports came from those with the lowest levels of education. Children of parents with lower levels of education were also more likely to inflate their past performance. The relation was not linear; whereas the lowest education group was the least accurate in predicting or reporting, there were no differences among the middle and high education groups.

What does this mean for our subject? Because we cannot check attitudes in this way—only self-reports of behaviors and events—it is not easy to tell. I would guess that social desirability bias might well increase reported tolerance levels and that it is probably even more likely to increase reported education levels. Will the bias produce results skewed in the same way for the same people? Again, there is no way to tell, no direct evidence, although we might suppose that people who exaggerate the one would be likely to inflate the other. We can be sure, however, that there must be a ceiling effect; that is, people with the highest true levels of either education or tolerance will be less able to inflate their responses. This means that social desirability bias probably tends to reduce overall variance in both variables (education and tolerance), and therefore reduces the size of the measured associations between them. In short, when we mismeasure, we are likely to underestimate, not overestimate. This is all quite speculative, of course, but I see no reason to believe that this sort of bias would dramatically alter the measured associations between tolerance and education, except to reduce them under certain conditions.

The main conclusion that education level is positively related to tolerance level is jeopardized only if we assume that people with truly high education levels would be especially likely to lie about how tolerant their attitudes and beliefs are. It is more likely, I think, that people who exaggerate in one area would also do so in the other. I have laid out the possibilities (assuming that no one underreports education and tolerance levels) in Figure 3.1. Cell 1 in the figure represents those respondents who report true tolerance and education levels. My working assumption is that most people fit into this group. The second biggest group is probably in Cell 4—those who exaggerate both levels. If everyone exaggerates by a like amount, there is no problem from the standpoint of the researcher. The biggest problems arise if many people fit into either Cell 2 or Cell 3. People in Cell 3 are those who inflate their education levels but give true reports of their tolerance levels. They might do this if they care more about what the interviewers think of their education levels than of their tolerance levels. On the other hand, if people care deeply about what the interviewers think of their tolerance levels, but not their education levels, they might exaggerate their tolerance only, not their education. These people would fall into Cell 2.

It is very hard to estimate what is more socially desirable, being tolerant or being highly educated. Given that it is hard to tell what is more likely to lead to social desirability bias, there are no grounds for assuming that people exaggerate only their tolerance levels. In my experience, this is the assumption most widely shared among researchers, but no evidence supports the idea that people try to put themselves in a good light only in terms of their tolerance levels, and not their education levels. In fact, we *know* only about people misreporting their education levels.

People's inclination to overreport educational achievement and attainment would, *if anything,* tend to suppress evidence of the effects of education on tolerance. This is true for two reasons: First, the ceiling effect makes it difficult for the highly tolerant and highly educated to inflate their levels even if they wanted to do so; second, there is substantial if indirect evidence that all forms of misreporting (such as acquiescence bias—see below) are more common among the least-educated respondents. Given this, it is fair to conclude that if we could somehow always measure "true" levels of education and tolerance, the

Tolerance Level

		True	Inflated
Education Level	True	1	2
	Inflated	3	4

Figure 3.1. Types of Possible Misreporting by Subjects

relationship between the two would be *stronger* than the already robust associations now reported in the research literature. But, for the purposes of this book, I will take a more cautious approach and assume that misreporting does not lead to underestimates of the associations between tolerance and education, although it probably does.

In sum, neither the social desirability nor the social self-confidence hypothesis is supported by enough evidence to justify worrying about skewed results in the research on education and tolerance levels. In the absence of such evidence, it is most reasonable to assume that highly educated adults are neither more nor less likely to respond dishonestly to attitude surveys about their education and tolerance levels and, therefore, that the correlations found in the huge literature on the subject, in all probability, reflect something real about the influence of education on attitudes and beliefs.

People Do Not Know What They Believe

A more serious limitation to survey research than the possibility that people lie on surveys is that they may not know how they feel or what they believe about particular issues, but they will answer questions about them anyway. I hesitate to conclude that people do not know what they believe or that they do not really have attitudes—the "nonattitude" theory (Converse, 1964). Rather, I think it is more accurate to say that people often do not have attitudes that they have thought through completely enough to be able to give quick but definitive one-word answers to potentially difficult questions. One of the reasons survey answers can be biased by small changes in wording (see the following subsection) is that people believe that they *ought* to have opinions or attitudes; this sometimes leads them to respond to survey questions with the first thing that comes to mind (Chong, 1993). Such quick answers given in the "pop quiz" context of a survey may or may not reflect the conclusions respondents would come to upon greater deliberation. People's first reactions are not always their "true" reactions (Devine, 1989), or the ones that will determine their actions. However, quick, thoughtless reactions are what may be obtained by many surveys. As one survey respondent put it: "A lot of these questions you're asking me . . . I really haven't thought about. . . . Maybe, if I thought about them a little bit more, I'd come up with a different answer" (quoted in Chong, 1993, p. 871).

The question of whether people have attitudes and actually know what they believe is quite a bit more complex than is usually realized, and has been studied extensively (for a sophisticated and thorough review, see Smith, 1984a). The line of research was begun by Converse (1964), who labeled as "nonattitudes" answers to interviewers' questions that reflected respondents' lack of any real opinion or knowledge. Important evidence came from longitudinal surveys on which Converse found low correlations between individuals' answers to the same questions 2 years apart. Converse divided people into two sharply distinct groups: those who had attitudes and were consistent in their responses and those who had no attitudes about the issues studied and whose responses were random. Subsequent research on the varieties of nonattitudes has revealed "a continuum of attitudes/nonattitudes" that Converse's "black-and-white model tends to obscure" (Smith, 1984a, p. 220). For example, some people who answer "don't know" to survey questions are quite well-informed but undecided, whereas others simply do not know or care much about the issues.[1]

Another indication of nonattitudes is that perhaps one-fourth to one-third of respondents to attitude surveys or similar measures will give opinions about fictional issues—the "Bishop-Schuman amendment to the 1980 labor relations bill," to make one up—rather than admit to having no knowledge or opinions. The best-known example of this is the experiment mentioned in Chapter 2 in which many subjects were willing to express their attitudes toward "Wallonians" and other groups of "foreigners" made up by Hartley (1946). Of course, a positive or negative expression about Wallonians is probably not just a random response, but rather a general expression of attitudes toward unknown foreigners. In any case, opinions on such fictional topics are less commonly given when subjects have the option to reply that they "don't know."

How often do such behaviors differ by education level? Not as often as many researchers have supposed, but when differences have been found they have been in the predicted direction: Measurement error of this kind is less common among more highly educated respondents. Generally, more educated subjects are more likely to have substantive opinions. When they answer "don't know" it is more likely that they are undecided rather than uninformed (Smith, 1984a).

We cannot ignore these sources of measurement error, but, for reasons laid out above in the section on social desirability bias, if anything, what we know about these measurement problems leads us to predict that the relations between education and tolerance are stronger than most statistical associations reveal. To repeat: I am not assuming that they are stronger (even though there is some evidence that they are stronger), I am only denying that they are weaker (because there is no evidence they are weaker).

Probably the most widespread version of this kind of argument against taking survey results at face value is the "symbolic racism" literature. The basic assumption is that any declines in measures of White racism cannot be real. Despite dramatic declines in Whites' expressed racial prejudice (Davis, 1992; Schuman, Steeh, & Bobo, 1985), it is too early to take heart. Rather, the argument goes, White racism must have taken some new, more subtle form. The feelings are the same, but the manner of expressing them is new and indirect (Huddy & Sears, 1995). Whites now offer explanations and rationalizations for their prejudices that are not race based. For example, Whites might claim to favor increased opportunities for Blacks, but oppose affirmative action; or they might say they support school integration, but oppose busing to achieve it. Consciously or not, they are using symbols, such as quotas and forced busing, to express their racism. Proponents of the notion of symbolic racism often claim that Whites' unconscious feelings are more racist than their conscious beliefs. Ultimately, of course, there can be no answer to those who think they know your unconscious feelings better than you do. But enough evidence (reviewed briefly in Chapter 4) has accumulated against symbolic racism theory that its supporters have greatly moderated their claims in recent years.

The Questions Do Not Reveal What People Think

Questions can be inadequate to the task of inquiring into what people think in many ways. One of the earliest tendencies that researchers discovered was *acquiescence bias,* or the inclination of some respondents to say yes to all questions so as to appear agreeable. Although this problem has been reduced by asking some questions negatively—Do you favor X? Do you oppose X?—it can be argued that even this easily remedied problem remains potentially serious (Jackman, 1973; Ray, 1983; Schuman & Presser, 1981, pp. 229-230). Mueller (1994) has persuasively shown that differences in question wording during the "mother of all opinion polling frenzies" made it very difficult to gauge something as apparently clear-cut as the strength of Americans' support for the Gulf War. Depending on how the questions were worded, Mueller found, estimates differed dramatically. Survey researchers have long been concerned with the problem of how apparently slight differences in question wording can influence results.

A striking example is the "forbid-allow" problem, which is surely one of the largest wording effects ever documented (Schuman & Presser, 1981, p. 280). Questions were asked as follows: "Do you think the United States *should forbid* public speeches against democracy?" and "Do you think the United States *should allow* public speeches against democracy?" (emphasis added). Clearly, a no answer to one question is logically equivalent to a yes answer to the other. But logical equivalence does not necessarily yield attitude equivalence. In 1976, for example, the results were approximately as shown in Table 3.1. Logically, the figures on the diagonals (i.e., yes, forbid; no, not allow) should be the same if question wording has no effect, but there is a 25% gap between the two versions of the "same" answer.

What do results like these mean for the findings presented in this book? First, although a difference of this magnitude is substantial, it is not overwhelming. We can still say that a majority would support free speech, but we would be unclear about the size of that majority (55% or 80%). Second, because this is as large a difference as one is likely to get, one has to exercise caution, but reasonable interpretations are not impossible. We can also say quite a bit about the education levels of people for whom the forbid-allow wording difference is likely to matter (see also Hippler & Schwarz, 1986). Forbid-allow differences are less great for college-educated respondents. In general, when there are biases due to wording, response set, and question order, they are smaller among the more educated, especially the college educated. Basically, responses of college-educated subjects are more consistent across differences of question wording and order (Sniderman & Piazza, 1993). In the specific case at hand, using either question (not forbid or allow), "education is positively related to support for free speech" (Schuman & Presser, 1981, p. 278). And what is most important, the positive association of education and tolerance persists almost regardless of how the tolerance questions are worded, although different wordings can change the size of the relationship (see the discussion of political tolerance later in this chapter).

What People Say Is a Poor
Guide to What They Will Do

Even if people tell the truth and actually know what they believe, and what they believe is accurately captured by survey questions, it still might not be the

TABLE 3.1 The Forbid-Allow Problem (Free Speech)

	Forbid (%)	Allow (%)
Yes	20	55
No	80	45

case that people do what they say. In other words, attitudes do not predict actions, beliefs do not cause behaviors, talk is cheap. So, *do* attitudes and beliefs influence behaviors? The answer is very clear: sometimes.

Attitudes are imperfect but useful predictors of actions. A large research literature has developed based on attempts to assess when internal states (attitudes and beliefs) are more and less likely to lead to action (Ajzen & Fishbein, 1977; Fazio, 1986; Fishbein & Ajzen, 1975; Jackman, 1976; Kelman, 1974; Schuman & Johnson, 1976). Most researchers are agreed that the more specific the attitude, the more likely it is to influence an action. It is not hard to see why. Voting behavior provides a clear example. Figure 3.2 lists hypothetical survey questions meant to uncover voters' attitudes. As predictors of behavior, they are arranged from the specific to the general, from strong predictors to weak predictors of whether someone will vote for Candidate X.

Much of the literature concluding that attitudes do not predict behavior takes very general attitudes (for example, Do you like politicians?) and shows how they are "contradicted" by people's "actions" (such as voting for Candidate X). But there is no necessary contradiction. One could dislike politicians but vote for Candidate X because one believes she is the best of a bad lot, far preferable to her opponent. The same kind of reasoning is true when we look at normative beliefs. Here researchers have pointed out contradictions and inconsistencies in Americans' beliefs large enough that many scholars have been led to doubt that the beliefs matter (see, e.g., McClosky, 1964; Prothro & Grigg, 1960). The kind of difference is captured in the following extreme example: "Do you think democracy should be defended?" followed by "Should the KKK be allowed to march?" When it is discovered that substantial numbers say that they defend democracy but oppose the KKK's march, the rhetorical question researchers ask becomes: How could one purport to defend democracy and then say the KKK should not be allowed to march? The answer, of course, is that it is quite easy. One could make a good argument on either side—that tolerating or repressing the KKK (or communists, or hate speech) defends democracy. I think that the case is almost always stronger for tolerance than for repression, but that does not mean that the opposite case reveals some fatal contradiction.

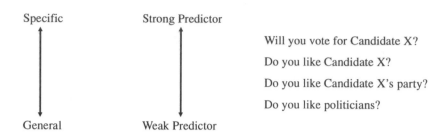

Figure 3.2. Attitude Specificity as a Predictor of Behavior

Finally, although this kind of result is often reported, it is not, of course, strictly speaking, an attitude-behavior contradiction. It is, rather, a "contradiction" between general and specific attitudes (Ajzen & Fishbein, 1977).

Do actions speak louder than words? Perhaps, but they do not always speak more clearly than words. Most important, words do not always give a more flattering portrayal than deeds. The locus classicus for research on this question is an article by LaPiere (1934) in which he describes his extensive U.S. travels in the early 1930s in the company of a young Chinese couple. "In something like ten thousand miles of motor travel, twice across the United States, up and down the Pacific Coast, we met definite rejection from those asked to serve us just once" (p. 232). Then, some months later, LaPiere wrote to 250 establishments that had served them, asking whether they would serve Chinese customers. More than 100 wrote back to say that they would not or do not serve Chinese customers. The moral of the story? It may be easier to claim to be "good" than to act that way, but not in this case. Owners of motels and restaurants who claimed to be "bad" had "graciously" served LaPiere and his companions.

The conclusion most researchers have drawn from this research is that actions are somehow "real," whereas verbal attitudes are just so many words (see Deutscher, 1966, 1969; LaPiere, 1934, 1969). I believe it is more accurate to say that words and deeds can be independent; they are strikingly so in LaPiere's classic study, but not in the expected way. Social desirability bias would have owners claiming enlightened beliefs but acting in a bigoted way, when the reverse was true. Most generally, it is just as easy to lie with actions as with words (think, for instance, of bringing flowers to a social event you dread attending and giving them, with a smile, to the hostess you detest). As Schuman and Johnson (1976) succinctly put it, "Behavior rather than attitude may be insincere" (p. 195).

Most reviews of studies on the question have found that on the whole there is a substantial relationship between attitudes, variously defined, and actions.

Of course, any connection with nonattitudes would be small; because the predictor is random, it can predict nothing. But among people with clearly thought-out attitudes and beliefs, the correlations can fall in the .40 to .50 range (Schuman & Johnson, 1976, p. 181). How big is that? Schuman and Johnson summarize it well: "The typical associations reported [between attitudes and behaviors] are small or moderate only in terms of expectations that they be very large; they are not particularly small in comparison with magnitudes reported in social research generally" (p. 166).

Attitudes, in the most general sense of the term, are crucial to an understanding of actions. It is hard to see how someone could act in any way, positively or negatively, toward persons or groups without some sort of mental disposition toward them. One might think of "attitude as an integral part of action" (Kelman, 1974, p. 321), or as a type of transmitter from beliefs to intentions, which are then the proximate cause of behaviors (Fishbein & Ajzen, 1975). Another way to express the relationship is to say that when intentions are well formed (but only when they are well formed), they "mediate the effects of attitudes on behavior" (Bagozzi & Yi, 1989, p. 277). Fazio's (1986; Fazio, Jackson, Dunton, & Williams, 1995) claim is different: Attitudes influence perceptions, which influence beliefs, which influence actions. Most of these claims have reasonably strong empirical backing even though the basic concepts are still not well defined—for example, some researchers treat intentions and beliefs as components of attitudes, whereas others treat them as separate entities. But it requires more skepticism than I can muster to deny that various kinds of internal states—beliefs, values, attitudes, perceptions, intentions—have consequences for external actions or behaviors. How do we, as researchers, learn about these internal states? Often, the best we can do "is to ask and then to listen as well as we can" (Schuman & Johnson, 1976, p. 202).

Actions and behaviors do not matter as much for the study of tolerance as they might for research on other topics. Tolerant attitudes and beliefs most often restrain action, or cause people to inhibit what might otherwise be their behaviors. The typical pattern is as follows: I dislike Group X; I could act against it, but I am not going to do so, at least in certain ways. There are tolerant behaviors, of course, such as writing a letter to a newspaper supporting the rights of an unpopular group. Interesting evidence on this question of tolerant actions comes from survey experiments conducted by Marcus, Sullivan, Theiss-Morse, and Wood (1995), who conclude that tolerant attitudes and normative tolerant beliefs (support for democratic norms) have strong and independent effects on respondents' intentions to act in tolerant ways. But, in general, tolerance involves inaction. And "the tolerant, who may tend to be more politically involved overall, are generally unwilling to indicate an intention to do what is necessary to protect a noxious group's civil liberties." Intolerant persons, on the other hand, usually indicate a stronger willingness to act. The McCarthy era is merely the best known of the many "unsettling examples of intolerant activity and tolerant passivity" (Marcus et al., 1995, pp. 206-207). More generally, a tendency for "the conservative position [to be] held with more passion by its supporters than is the liberal position by its supporters" has been noted by more than one researcher (Schuman & Presser, 1981, p. 250).

To repeat, most often in this book we are not examining the attitude-behavior link at all. Rather, our focus is on education, attitudes, and beliefs and the various ways in which these three are related. I have reviewed the connections with action only because many believe that unless a link with action can be established, research on beliefs and attitudes is useless. The association of attitudes and actions is neither simple nor automatic. One very important reason is that people usually have more than one attitude about particular issues or social problems, and those attitudes can conflict. A person might strongly believe in free speech and also hate a particular group that is demanding free speech rights. One of these attitudes will probably be stronger than and override the other, but this does not mean that the weaker attitude is unreal or that it has no influence on behavior.

Conclusions About the
Limits of Survey Research

The caveats with which we must approach conclusions drawn from survey research do not, in my view, detract from the general finding of a statistical association between amount of education and level of tolerance. That relationship occurs virtually however tolerance is measured. On the other hand, although there is widespread agreement that the survey research discussed in this book is *reliable,* considerable concern persists about whether it is valid, about whether researchers are measuring what they think they are measuring. And there is no simple statistical test for determining that. If the result popped up on some surveys but not others, we might attribute the relationship between tolerance and education to random effects or measurement error or some sort of bias. But given the very large number of studies over several decades (later sections of this chapter provide a review) pointing almost unfailingly to the same result, using not only survey methods but also interviews (Chong, 1993), we are safe in concluding that an association exists. But how big is it? Is it big enough to be practically significant?

Questions About the Size of the Relationships

Even though most researchers have found statistical associations between tolerance and education, considerable debate remains about the magnitude of the correlations and whether they are big enough to matter. The majority of researchers have found that, even after controlling for other variables that might account for them, the correlations remain robust and, indeed, that education is often the most powerful of all variables explaining differences in individuals' tolerance levels. Examples from two well-known studies in the field can illustrate. Nunn et al., in a 1973 replication of Stouffer's 1954 survey, found that respondents who were college graduates were more than four times (84% versus 19%) as likely to score high on a tolerance scale as were respondents with only a grade school education—almost exactly the same ratio Stouffer found in 1954. Even among older respondents (60 and older), who as a group had lower tolerance scores, the same four-to-one ratio existed—65% versus 14% (Nunn et al., 1978, pp. 59, 81). In an extensive review of surveys on the effects of education on social and political attitudes, Hyman and Wright (1979) found gammas (i.e., coefficients of association between ordinal variables) showing robust relationships between education levels and tolerant attitudes. Examples include education level and frequent churchgoers' willingness to allow a speech against religion (.42) and education level and younger respondents' (aged 25-36) favoring the freedom of Blacks and Whites to intermarry (.57); on the intermarriage issue for older respondents (aged 61-72), the gamma remained significant at .40 (pp. 103, 109).

How important are the statistical associations of the size typically found between tolerance and education? How big are they really? There is no one answer, because education and especially tolerance have been operationalized in several different ways, and the associations between them have been variously measured. I think it is safe to say, however, that they are substantial by the standards of most social science research as well as by the standards of research in other disciplines predicting human outcomes. The relation between tolerance and education is quite a bit bigger than, for example, the correlation between consumption of eggs and heart attacks or that between regular exercise and longevity. Associations between education and tolerance levels are more similar in size, for instance, to those between the occupational status of parents and that of their children. In multiple-regression studies the proportion of total variance in tolerance explained by all the variables taken together often ranges around 20-30%. This is substantial, but is far less, for instance, than the percentage of variance in faculty salary explainable by most multiple-regression models; that is about twice as big, usually in the range of 40-60% (e.g., Bellas, 1994; Fairweather, 1995; Lillydahl & Singell, 1993).

But the importance of a statistical association is only partly determined by the size (absolute or comparative) of the relation between the predictor and outcome variables. For example, the relation between exercise and longevity, although very modest, is also very important, for two reasons: First, it is literally a matter of life and death; and second, it is possible to control the predictor—one can exercise more or less. A person's genetic inheritance is probably a much bigger determinant of his or her longevity. Yet genes are "unimportant" in one sense: There is nothing one can do about them. On the other hand, exercise, although having only a small effect on how long a person will live, is "important," largely because it is subject to the individual's control.

Hence, the size of an association between two variables is only a first step toward assessing its significance. However, even if we accept the larger estimates of the size of the association between education and tolerance, the amount of the variance in tolerance explainable or predictable by differences in education is not overwhelmingly determinative. Even bivariate correlations of $r = .50$, pretty much the upper limit, mean that education would successfully predict only 25% of the variance in tolerance. As a rule of thumb, it would be unrealistic to expect to predict more than one-fourth of individuals' tolerance based on their education levels. Even 15% is rare. On the other hand, one-fourth or even one-tenth can be thought of as a large fraction—if tolerance is important and if we have substantial influence over the educational processes that foster it. It is my argument that both of these are true. Tolerance is very important, and we can significantly influence it by education (more, for example, than we can influence longevity by exercise).

Some researchers—Mary Jackman and John Sullivan the most important among them—have argued vigorously for revising downward our estimates of the size of the correlations between various measures of tolerance and education levels. Considerable controversy surrounds their methods and conclusions, and I have discussed their important works elsewhere in this volume. For our purposes at this point, it is enough to note that no one has ever persuasively argued that education in general systematically decreases tolerance as a whole; nor has anyone ever demonstrated that education in the United States usually has no effect on tolerance. Even Jackman has found statistically significant associations and has speculated about their causes. And Sullivan's findings, although showing quite modest direct associations between education and tolerance, have led to very successful attempts to design and implement a tolerance curriculum (see Chapter 5).

Qualifications Due to Varying Effects
and Measures of Education and Tolerance

In some respects, one could consider it surprising that there is *any* relation (much less a strong one) between education, crudely measured as years of schooling, and answers to highly specific questions about social, moral, and political attitudes. Viewed from that perspective, it is hardly remarkable that every form of schooling is not always and equally associated with all forms of tolerance in all circumstances. Discussing some situations in which increased education may not lead to increased tolerance is perhaps as revealing as analyzing those situations in which it does. There are five specific contexts in which the association between tolerance and amount of education is smaller than has usually been found. These are discussed in turn below.

Definitions and Measurements

One situation in which the relation between tolerance and education is smaller than usual is partly an artifact of measurement and definition. Defining tolerance more stringently and requiring that respondents meet more demanding criteria before they are called "tolerant," even when justifiable on theoretical grounds, may sometimes have the artifactual effect of reducing tolerance levels. For instance, to be considered tolerant, Sullivan, Piereson, and Marcus (1982) require subjects to tolerate not just any group they dislike, but the group they most dislike (their "least-liked group").

Levels and Kinds of Education

Another qualification concerning the association between years of schooling and tolerance is that not all years contribute equally. For example, the average difference between survey respondents with 10 versus 12 years of schooling is usually not nearly as large as that between respondents with 12 versus 14 years. That is, 2 years of college often have a bigger influence than 2 years of high school (see Bird, Sullivan, Avery, Thalhammer, & Wood, 1994).

Types of Tolerance

It is also quite clear that different types of tolerance (i.e., political, moral, and social) can be affected differently by education. Even within a general category, specific differences can be very large. For example, in the realm of social tolerance, education is likely to have a more positive effect on Whites' support for interracial marriage than on their support for affirmative action. And in the case of political tolerance, as Hall and Rodeghier (1994) point out, education has varying effects. Although education has a general tendency to promote tolerance by increasing commitment to civil liberties, it also promotes commitment to orderly, nondisruptive political procedures and to the values of white-collar, educated people. Hence, education may reduce tolerance for some actions, such as disruption, violence, and blue-collar protest. More broadly, as Davis (1985) has noted, the varying effects of education can counteract or suppress one another: For example, more education is associated with more liberal attitudes, but it is also associated with higher income, which in turn is associated with less liberal attitudes.

Different Nations

The association between tolerance and education varies across countries. In New Zealand, Israel (Sullivan, Shamir, Walsh, & Roberts, 1985), and some European countries (Weil, 1985), for example, the link between education and tolerance is less strong (when it exists at all) than it is in the United States. Although other studies suggest that the connection between tolerance and education is quite widespread (Inglehart, 1990; Inkeles & Smith, 1974; Miller, Slomczynski, & Kohn, 1985), Sullivan and his colleagues, who have made the most extensive comparisons, have found the association between education and tolerance to be most pronounced in the United States. However, in one particularly interesting study of Bulgaria and Romania after the fall of their Communist regimes in 1989, the connections between ethnic tolerance and education were found to be substantial (McIntosh, MacIver, Abele, & Nolle, 1995). This is especially impressive because the two countries constitute a stringent test. In each, the ruling majority ethnic group is confronted with a previously dominant minority ethnic group (Turks in Bulgaria and Hungarians in Romania) demanding rights such as instruction in their own language. It would not be unreasonable to expect education to have reduced tolerance in these two countries. The schools under Communism promoted harshly assimilationist ideologies. Nonetheless, surveys in 1991 and 1992 showed that education had a direct positive association with tolerance in Romania and an indirect positive association (through its effect on political ideology) with tolerance in Bulgaria.

It remains wisest at this point, despite a growing body of international evidence to which I will refer from time to time, to limit our generalizations about links between tolerance and education mainly to the United States. First, however, I need to digress briefly to mention the relations between tolerance and education in one more country, because that country appears to constitute an overwhelming counterexample to the general line of argument in this volume: Germany under the Nazis.

A frequent and understandable question is: If education promotes tolerance, how could a highly educated people like the Germans, in a nation that probably had the best education system in the world, have supported the Nazis—surely the incarnation of the most evil intolerance? Although I think a good case could be made that nations with highly educated populations are more likely to have constitutions based on toleration and governments that do not systematically attack the civil liberties of their citizens, that is not the case I am trying to make in this book. Here I am concerned with the attitudes and actions of *individuals*. But nations are made up of individuals, one might reply, so the question remains: How could a nation with so many highly educated individuals have become so intolerant? This is an extremely important question, and one that deserves more careful scrutiny than I can give it here. Yet I must address it briefly. Four points may help explain why this horrifying counterexample does not invalidate the general line of argument that differences in individuals' education levels can partly explain differences in their tolerance levels. These points also serve to clarify the nature of this book's central theses.

First, the education level of the German population in the generation or two before the National Socialists came to power was not particularly high by European standards. And although the German higher-education system was indeed very good, the vast majority of the German people, whose educations ended by age 14, had no contact with it.[2] The schools that most Germans attended were politically reactionary, often preaching a rabid nationalism, and were sharply divided along class lines.

Second, when the Nazis came to power, they immediately set about crippling the higher-education system (which is only now fully recovering). The Nazis believed that an independent university was a potential threat to their regime. Their repression of the universities is indirect evidence, from a despicable source, of the validity of the view that higher education "threatens" to have a liberalizing effect.

Third, the appropriate comparison, parallel to those that are being made in this volume, is between the education levels of individuals who supported the Nazis and the education levels of those who opposed them. The parallel argument would be that opponents of the Nazis likely had higher education levels than did Nazi supporters—a plausible generalization as I read the historical research on the subject, but a generalization that would be very difficult to

demonstrate conclusively. The historical evidence is too incomplete for us ever
to move beyond endless rounds of example and counterexample on this topic,
important though it is.[3]

Fourth, and most important, education is neither a necessary nor a sufficient
condition for tolerance. To return to an earlier example, education promotes
tolerance, perhaps, much as exercise promotes longevity—it helps, but it is no
guarantee. A nation with a high proportion of regular exercisers among its
citizens could be expected to have a higher average life expectancy than a nation
with fewer exercisers—but only if the effects of exercise are not offset by other
events and conditions such as poverty, war, and air pollution. But, ultimately,
this is not our comparison. We are, to continue the analogy, looking at the average
longevity of individuals within a single nation based on whether or not they
exercise regularly. It is a fundamental mistake in reasoning to take facts about
national differences and use these to draw conclusions about individual differences. For example, Kenya probably has more champion long-distance runners
per capita than any other nation in the world. However, the average life
expectancy of Kenyans is very poor. One would surely not want to argue on the
basis of the Kenyan life expectancy that jogging is bad for your health. The
argument about Nazi Germany is flawed in the same way. Just because Germany
had a good system of research universities and the Nazis came to power there,
we would not be justified in concluding that education promoted fascism or
inhibited democratic values such as toleration.

Education systems may be and have been used (with varying effectiveness)
to promote widely different ideologies, some hospitable to tolerance, some not.
Ultimately, my claim is that when one controls for the specific cultural and
political contexts in which education occurs, there remains a tolerance-generating
residual effect.

Generation or Era Effects

The final qualification about the relation between years of schooling and
tolerance level is the possibility of a time or era effect. Our knowledge of the
association between education and tolerance is strongest for the past three
decades, since 1960 or so. Allport (1954) did not believe that more-educated
people were more likely to be racially tolerant. On the other hand, Myrdal (1944)
believed that tolerant racial views were the direct result of higher levels of
education. And Stouffer (1955) found a strong association between education
and political tolerance in the early 1950s, but it is possible that the link was
weaker for racial tolerance at the time.

Turning to today, there is a fairly widespread belief that people—especially young, well-educated people—have been moving toward a kind of conservatism that includes less tolerance. The media are fond of reporting racial tensions on campuses and interpreting them as a sign of changing times. Maybe schooling did promote liberalism in earlier generations, the argument goes, but after a generation of conservative administrations in Washington, perhaps things have changed. What evidence do we have for this? Unlike before the 1950s, today we have extensive trend data about social and political attitudes (Davis, 1992; Inglehart, 1990; Steeh & Schuman, 1992), and a huge majority of the evidence points in the same direction: There is no indication of a general conservative trend in attitudes about racial issues. Young, highly educated people are not less likely than they were a generation ago to voice support for tolerance in attitude surveys. Skeptics may feel that talk is cheap, and that interracial actions matter more than attitudes. In reply, we might point to one classic measure of race relations: intermarriage. Black-White intermarriage, although still uncommon, has increased dramatically since 1960. The number of Black-White married couples more than quadrupled in the years between 1960 and 1991—from around 52,000 to more than 230,000 (U.S. Department of Commerce, 1992).

Perhaps the best-known version of the "conservative era" argument is Alexander Astin's (1993). Although Astin does not directly discuss tolerance, he does address the related issue of whether and how education brings about changes in students' attitudes. I shall discuss two of his conclusions: (a) that entering college freshmen today are less liberal than they were a couple of decades ago; and (b) that today college does not do much to influence students' attitudes in a liberal direction. Part of the reason for the second finding is the first—that is, college does not liberalize students because there are fewer liberal students and therefore there is less liberal peer influence.

It is important first to remember that the dependent variable for each of the claims (students are less liberal than they used to be; college does not make them more liberal) is students' self-identification. What Astin has correctly measured is the popularity of a label. It seems clear that it is less fashionable for students to label themselves liberal than it once was. But as Astin points out, albeit too briefly perhaps, general labels matter less than attitudes about particular issues. Here the picture is more complicated. Let us take Astin's two conclusions one at a time.

First, Astin concludes that entering college students have steadily become less liberal. Table 3.2 briefly reports freshmen's attitudes on select issues, particularly issues related to tolerance, and compares these with the liberal self-label. The table shows clearly that although use of the self-label of liberal

TABLE 3.2 Trends in Freshmen's Attitudes (in percentages)

	1966	1970	1978	1986	1990
Liberal self-identification		33.5	23.6	22.0	22.6
Support free speech on campus	60.5	66.8	79.4	74.4	
Support legal abortion		56.7	58.6	64.9	
Say school busing is okay			41.5	56.1	56.7
Favor a national health plan			60.7	62.1	73.7

SOURCE: Dey, Astin, and Korn (1991, pp. 122-125).

has declined, answers to other questions show a broadly liberal trend (see also Shea, 1995, 1996). Furthermore, students appear substantially more liberal than the general population. Perhaps Astin's findings have been somewhat misreported or have been examined only superficially.

Astin's (1993) second conclusion is more germane to our concerns in this volume: "Our analyses fail to support the traditional notion that attending college has a liberalizing effect on students' political identification" (p. 89). Again, this conclusion refers to students' self-labeling. But Astin also provides extensive data on specific attitudes for a large longitudinal study of entering freshmen in 1985 and 4 years later, in 1989 (the apex of the Reagan-Bush era, one might note). Not surprisingly, the best predictor of political attitudes upon graduating from college in 1989 was attitudes upon entering in 1985 (see the similar finding for ninth graders in Bird et al., 1994). Astin was not dealing directly with tolerance, but one of his questions, concerning free speech, is typical of the sort found in tolerance scales. A second example, showing the largest change among Astin's items, concerned abortion (see Table 3.3).

The net change is important, but even more interesting from our perspective is that these relatively "small net changes conceal a great deal of switching around during the college years" (p. 107) in both directions. For instance, about 16% of students increased their support for free speech, but 11% reduced theirs. Likewise for abortion: Around 23% changed their views in favor of legalization, but another 5% moved in the opposite direction (Astin, 1993, pp. 144-145). This "switching around" provides important clues about how education influences political and social attitudes.

Students entering college in 1985 (and probably in other years) usually graduated with the same attitudes they began with. However, for those who changed, the most likely sources of influence (in order of importance) were peers, faculty, and major field of study. For example, students who went to a

TABLE 3.3 Attitude Change During College Years

Issue	1985	1989	Net Change
"College officials have the right to ban persons with extreme views from speaking on campus." Percentage disagreeing	78.7	82.9	+4.2
"Abortion should be legalized." Percentage agreeing	55.1	72.7	+17.6

religious fundamentalist college and majored in business or mathematics were less likely to move in a liberal direction than were students who went to a nonsectarian college and majored in sociology or English—and this conclusion remains firm even after many background variables are controlled for. The general lesson to draw from Astin's work, and one that is stressed as one of the most essential points in this book, is that we can best assess education's effects on tolerance when we examine various aspects of the educational experience in greater detail than has been done in most previous studies. The mere number of years of schooling alone, although it tends to be moderately associated with individuals' tolerance, is a poor measure at best of the effects of education on attitudes.

We have seen, in sum, that five broad categories of qualifications can limit or complicate the simple model of education → tolerance: definitions and methods of measurement, kinds and levels of education, kinds or objects of tolerance, different places, and different eras. Yet the statistical associations between education and tolerance variously measured in many studies are generally robust, despite these qualifications. We turn now to a detailed review of these positive statistical associations between education and tolerance.

Review of Evidence That Education Promotes Tolerance

It will be helpful to begin our review of the evidence by recalling what we mean when we say that education fosters tolerance and how this fits in with other information about what influences people to believe what they do. The words in bold in Figure 3.3 highlight our focus on the link between education and tolerance, whereas the rest of the figure reminds us that there are prior influences

Background → **Education** → **Tolerance** → Intentions → Actions

Figure 3.3. Prior Influences on and Subsequent Effects of the Education-Tolerance Link

on this link. Also, attitudes and beliefs can subsequently affect intentions and actions.

A large range of background variables—such as gender, religion, ethnicity, personality type, intelligence, and parents' income—surely influence the amounts and kinds of education people receive and thus indirectly influence tolerance through education. Such background characteristics sometimes also influence tolerance directly, a claim most frequently made about personality types (Adorno, Frenkel-Brunswick, Levinson, & Sanford, 1950; Young-Bruehl, 1996). But in most studies, the indirect effects of background, through education, are much stronger than the direct effects of background.

At the other end of the causal chain, there is the question of whether tolerant attitudes and beliefs influence intentions and actions or behaviors. Intentions are inserted here because they are often seen as a crucial link between attitudes and behaviors, and because they have frequently been used as a proxy measure for actions, because actions are notoriously difficult to study directly. Although there is strong evidence that tolerant attitudes and beliefs influence "behavioral intentions" and individuals' responses to questions about how they would act in hypothetical situations (Marcus et al., 1995), intentions are not our focus. Nonetheless, it is important to note that tolerant attitudes and beliefs are not without influence on intentions. We also need to remember that tolerance most often means inaction or behavioral self-restraint, which is another reason the link with actions is problematic for the particular attitudes we are studying.

A typology loosely borrowed from Merton (1976) is also useful for reminding us of our target. In this typology, tolerant individuals are those whose attitudes and beliefs fit in Cell 1 in Figure 3.4, that is, those who are prejudiced against a group and who nonetheless support its rights. Cells 2 and 3 are examples of more typical patterns, that is, lack of prejudice leading to support for a group's rights and presence of prejudice leading to lack of support. Cell 4 is probably least common of all and might even seem like a logical contradiction. But it is conceivable that one could be not prejudiced against a group and still not support its rights, perhaps because one has a realistic, nonprejudiced view of the particular group. Our target is Cell 1. Such individuals are not as rare as one might think, depending on how one defines "support a group's rights." But,

Prejudiced Against a Group

		Yes	No
Support a Group's Rights	Yes	1	2
	No	3	4

Figure 3.4. Relations Among Prejudice and Rights

because of the focus of much extant research, we will often have to make do with Cells 2 and 3, and take prejudice (and its lack) and support for a group's rights (and its lack) as approximations of our real object of study.

Given the very large number of studies relevant to our topic, this review of them will necessarily be selective. The focus will be on the studies in which we can have most confidence because they use large, well-designed samples, because they extend over substantial periods of time, and/or because they build cumulatively on important research traditions. Our objective is not an exhaustive survey, but rather one that is sufficient to make the point that education is almost always one of the most important variables associated with tolerance. The review is divided into sections reflecting different kinds of tolerance— social, moral, and political—as defined by objects of tolerance. First, we will survey non-Jews' attitudes toward Jews. Second, we will examine Whites' attitudes and beliefs about Blacks, including their support for policies to promote racial equality. Third, we will investigate moral tolerance by studying attitudes toward atheists, homosexuals, and abortion. Finally, we will conclude with our paradigm case and the one with the longest research tradition: political tolerance and civil liberties for political nonconformists.

Anti-Semitism

Persuasive evidence about the links between education and tolerance comes from a series of studies of anti-Semitism and unprejudiced attitudes about Jewish people. As I have noted several times, being unprejudiced is not the same as being tolerant, but the two are closely enough related to make it worthwhile for us to survey some of this evidence. Many of the results closely parallel those we will find when we look at other aspects of intergroup attitudes. The work of Martire and Clark (1982), which builds on the earlier work of Selznick and Steinberg (1969), can be taken as broadly representative of the literature on

TABLE 3.4 Anti-Semitism Among Non-Jews, by Education Level, 1981
              (in percentages)

	Prejudice Level		
Education Level	*High*	*Mid*	*Low*
Less than high school	28	38	34
High school graduate	26	35	39
Some college	16	23	61
College graduate or more	15	19	66

SOURCE: Adapted from Martire and Clark (1982, p. 36).

anti-Semitism (see also Quinley & Glock, 1979). The relation of level of prejudice against Jews and education is very clear, as shown in Table 3.4. Martire and Clark found that respondents with a college degree were about twice as likely to be low in prejudice as those with less than a high school education.

Of the wide range of demographic variables Martire and Clark studied, only three had an independent ability to explain differences in anti-Semitism—education level, age, and race: "After controlling for these three, we find that other demographic variables add little or nothing to our ability to explain the variation in anti-Semitic beliefs" (p. 37; see also p. 116). Of these three variables, education was the strongest. As Table 3.4 shows, "some college" was the key breaking point, a finding that parallels many other studies of attitudes. The gap in anti-Semitism between those who did not graduate from high school and those who ended their educations with high school ranged from 2% to 5%. Similarly, those with some college and college graduates differed from 1% to 5%. But the gap between the high school and college groups is from 10% to 22%.

However, the relationship between education level and prejudice against Jews has varied over time. This is not a simple, stable relationship. Between 1964 and 1981, anti-Semitism declined, but so did the relation between education and unprejudiced attitudes toward Jews. The prejudice gap associated with education narrowed. This was mostly because people with lower levels of education became less anti-Semitic, but it was also because those with higher levels of education became somewhat more anti-Semitic. Attitudes about specific groups clearly fluctuate with conditions. For example, much of the change in educated persons' overall anti-Semitism scores in the early 1980s was attributable to foreign policy issues and criticism of Jewish loyalty to Israel (Martire & Clark, 1982, p. 38). Nonetheless, in both the 1960s and the 1980s, the relation between advanced education and low anti-Semitism was very strong. It was not mostly due to or explainable by other variables, such as the low income, low occupational status, or downward mobility of the less educated (Martire & Clark, 1982, pp. 61-62; Selznick & Steinberg, 1969, pp. 138, 179).

Perhaps the most interesting relationship between education and attitudes (because it went against the main pattern) concerned the right of members of a private club to exclude individuals from membership solely because they are Jewish. In 1964, education and income were both good predictors of support for this kind of discrimination. College graduates who made more than $15,000 annually (about 5% of the population at the time) were the most discriminatory. More than half of them (52%) defended this "right" to maintain social distance. It was also true, however, that college graduates were the group that contained the largest number of people most strongly opposed to this form of discrimination. In the 1960s, social club discrimination was an issue that divided the highly educated, and the key factor that made a difference among them was their income level: Those with higher educations but lower incomes opposed the discrimination; those with higher educations and higher incomes favored it. Many commentators have interpreted anti-Semitism as a distinctly middle-class form of prejudice, but this example seems to indicate that it is a bias more common in the upper class (Selznick & Steinberg, 1969, pp. 86-88). This example is interesting for our purposes because it is one of the few suggesting that education, especially interacting with income, may strengthen a discriminatory belief. This unusual example complicates but does not fundamentally alter the basic pattern.

There was another important area, although not a counterexample, in which education made no difference in attitudes. In the 1964 sample, there was no variance by education level among non-Jews who would disapprove if their children married Jews—the proportion was about 40% for all education groups. Since that time, however, actual intermarriage rates have increased. This is easiest to see by looking at the proportion of Jews who have "outmarried." Before 1965, about 11% of Jews had outmarried. In the period 1965-1974, this figure rose to 31%, and by 1985-1990 it had climbed to 57% (Dinnerstein, 1994, p. 241). In general, surveys in the 1990s have found that the connection of low prejudice scores with education is still strong and, even more striking, that anti-Semitism is, by any measure, at a historic low point (Smith, 1991).[4] The main exception to this trend of declining prejudice is in the attitudes of African Americans toward Jews.

Differences in trends in anti-Semitism between Blacks and Whites are summarized in Table 3.5. The gap between Blacks and Whites in anti-Semitism grew from around 8 points in 1964 to around 20 in 1981. Declining White scores

TABLE 3.5 Mean Anti-Semitism Levels, by Race, 1964-1981

	1964	*1981*
Whites	40.4	32.7
Blacks	48.5	52.6

did more to create the gap than did rising Black scores, but both occurred. One of the reasons for these differences is that although education levels have gone up for both groups, education is less associated with the reduction of anti-Semitic attitudes among Blacks than among Whites. The overall raw difference cannot easily be explained by education. Rather, it probably has more to do with the nature of contacts between Jewish and Black people; these contacts have often been less intimate than those between Jewish and non-Jewish White people (see the discussion of intergroup contact in Chapter 5).

A 1992 survey by the Anti-Defamation League of B'nai B'rith found that 37% of Blacks versus 17% of Whites held strong anti-Semitic beliefs. Although college-educated Blacks were considerably less likely to accept strong anti-Semitic stereotypes (27%) than were Blacks without a college education (46%), the college-educated Black rate was higher than the overall White rate (Dinnerstein, 1994, p. 318). Thus, even among the major demographic group with the most significant levels of anti-Semitism in the United States, there is evidence that higher levels of education work to reduce prejudice. Finally, a study by Sigelman, Shockey, and Sigelman (1993) allows us to compare Black and White levels of stereotyping of Hispanics as well as Jews. Even though Blacks tend to stereotype Jews negatively more than do Hispanics, as far as the effects of education are concerned, we find the same basic pattern for all groups: Education tends to lessen negative stereotyping by both Blacks and non-Jewish Whites about both Hispanics and Jews.

Black anti-Semitism did not pop up out of nowhere in the 1960s and 1970s, as some journalists have claimed. Blacks were already complaining about "exploitive" Jewish shopkeepers in the 1930s and 1940s, and Jewish-owned businesses were sometimes targets of Blacks in the riots in Harlem and Detroit in 1943. Poorly educated Christian (and Islamic) fundamentalists of any racial background in the United States have always been more susceptible to anti-Semitism, and a disproportionate number of African Americans fit that demographic profile. But there is probably more involved here than differences in education levels and religious fundamentalism—I suspect a version of symbolic racism. Jews were long the main White group that Blacks could safely criticize; Blacks could unite with their actual oppressors (mostly Protestants) in a common dislike of Jews. Yet Blacks and Jews were also fairly natural allies; both worked hard, and often together, for the passage of the Civil Rights Act of 1964. After that date, the interests of the two groups more frequently diverged (for a fuller account, see Dinnerstein, 1994). In sum, since the mid-1960s many incidents widely reported in the press seem to indicate discouraging prospects for improvement of relations between Jewish and African American people. It must delight neo-Nazis and other racists to see the targets of their hate engaged in internecine conflict (Ezekiel, 1995).

We can conclude this discussion with an examination of the results of an excellent study presumably showing that education's effects on reducing anti-Semitism are not as strong as I have been claiming. Weil's (1985) general position is one of "skepticism regarding the usual claim that education has a universally liberalizing effect on values" (p. 459); he says that "education's effect on liberal values is *by no means* universal" (p. 469). I have never actually seen any research publications in which "universal" effects have been claimed. "Universal" would mean that education *always* makes *any* value of *every* person more liberal. That is an absurd claim, of course; it is a straw man—easy, if pointless, to defeat. Weil's findings are important, even though the "spin" he puts on them is somewhat misleading. Weil has studied anti-Semitism in four nations: France, Germany, Austria, and the United States. He has found that education's effects on anti-Semitism often vary; they are stronger in some countries than in others. The pattern of results fits Weil's hypothesis that in countries with long-established democratic traditions and substantial religious diversity, the education system will be more effective at teaching tolerance. This may be true for two reasons: First, the education system is likely to teach values that are already well rooted in the society; second, the values that the schools teach are more likely to be retained by students if they conform to, and are thus reinforced by, broad societal values. Although education is related to intergroup tolerance in some nations with very limited democratic experience (see McIntosh et al., 1995, on Romania and Bulgaria), Weil is surely right to claim that when the "official culture" is tolerant, schools will do a better job of teaching tolerance. This qualification that education's effects may vary by country is certainly true. But that in no way weakens the actual point (not Weil's straw man) that scholars have made: Among the variables used to try to explain differences in tolerance levels within the United States, amount of education is almost always the most significant variable, the one that explains the most variance. As Selznick and

TABLE 3.6 Percentage of Whites Scoring High on Anti-Negro Scale, by
Education Level, 1964

Education Level	North	South	Total
Less than high school	58	86	68
High school graduate	41	77	49
Some college	25	50	32
College graduate or more	16	43	23

SOURCE: Selznick and Steinberg (1969, p. 176).

Steinberg (1969) put it, "Education does not tell the whole story. . . . But no other factor has an impact approaching that of education" (p. 186).

Whites' Prejudices and
Support for Blacks' Civil Rights

Whites who are prejudiced against Jews are also very likely to be prejudiced against Blacks. Indeed, those with low levels of education have been found to be prejudiced against just about everyone—including, in 1964, men who wore beards. Table 3.6 summarizes the education levels of Whites who scored high on an anti-Negro scale used by Selznick and Steinberg (1969). It is instructive to compare the pattern in this table with the column in Table 3.4 on high levels of anti-Semitism by education. The relationship is stronger for Whites' attitudes toward Blacks than for non-Jews' attitudes toward Jews. Also worthy of note is that the level of anti-Negro sentiment was much higher in 1964 than the level of anti-Semitism.

Another difference in patterns in the two types of bigotry, and one that brings up an important theme that has directed much scholarship, is the difference between stereotyping and general attitudes on the one hand and support for specific policies on the other (Sniderman & Piazza, 1993). These two hardly ever match exactly *for* any group *about* any group. The contrast is especially interesting when it comes to Blacks and Jews. As Selznick and Steinberg (1969) note: "Support of discrimination against Jews is generally less prevalent than acceptance of anti-Semitic beliefs. The opposite appears true of anti-Negro prejudice: support of discrimination far exceeds acceptance of traditional stereotypes" (p. 172). What this shows is that we need to examine not only attitudes and beliefs about different groups but also different kinds of attitudes and beliefs. Again, we see that the association between education and tolerance is multifari-

TABLE 3.7 Percentage of Whites Who Approved of School Integration, by Education Level, 1956 and 1963

Education Level	North		South	
	1956	*1963*	*1956*	*1963*
Grade school	50	60	5	20
High school	63	75	15	32
Some college	75	86	28	48

SOURCES: Hyman and Sheatsley (1956, 1964).

ous, because the concept of tolerance contains many components. Chapters 4 and 5 will examine how the concept of education is also multifaceted (see Williams, 1988).

One of the earliest and best-known sources for data on Whites' attitudes about Blacks is a series of four articles published in *Scientific American* by Hyman and Sheatsley (1956, 1964), Greeley and Sheatsley (1971), and Taylor, Sheatsley, and Greeley (1978). These articles summarize the results of surveys conducted by the National Opinion Research Center (NORC) dating back to 1942. The authors focus mostly on trends over time, but also report differences in attitudes by education level over time and for different regions of the country. The educational results are very clear, especially for some issues. For example, Whites who approved of school integration were distributed by education as is shown in Table 3.7. Here we see that the relation between education and support for school integration was strong and remained strong as overall support of integration grew quickly (by the 1980s, approval of integrated schools would reach above 90% in both the North and the South; NORC, 1986, 1994).

Although the gap between the South (the old Confederacy) and the North (the rest of the country) narrowed rapidly between 1956 and 1963, and has now all but disappeared, the relation of education to approval of integration was strong in both years and both regions. On other issues, the pattern varied. On the question of Blacks living in White neighborhoods, for example, residents of the North were much more liberal, but there were almost no differences among northerners by education level. This was probably because the association of education with support for integration was suppressed by education's association with higher income, which tends to reduce commitment to residential integration.

The large changes in Whites' attitudes toward Blacks between 1956 and 1963 that are the focus of the *Scientific American* articles cannot be attributed directly to education. The attitude changes were much too fast (10-20% in 7 years) to be accounted for mainly by increasing education levels. Rather, in the 1950s and 1960s, adult segregationists were changing their views. People with higher levels of education may have changed their opinions faster. However, in the long run, all groups changed their attitudes. Still, the association of attitudes with education level persisted.

One of the big questions dividing scholars is how to explain the broad trends in the liberalization of the population since World War II. Of the several types of explanations, none can be tested directly without massive longitudinal data of the sort we are unlikely ever to have. The authors of all four *Scientific American* articles insisted that members of all age and education groups, including people who had long ago left school, changed their minds. This is an example of an "era effect" explanation. The era since the end of the Second World War has been one of rapid change in matters of intergroup relations, and people changed their minds to go along with court decisions and legislation. This explanation is almost certainly partly correct.

Another main type of explanation for changes in racial attitudes involves "generational replacement": Older, more bigoted people die off to be replaced by younger, more enlightened ones. But this raises the question, Why are the younger cohorts more enlightened? One explanation, the "aging effect," is simply that they are younger, and younger people are always more open to new ideas. This would mean that any gains in liberalism, including tolerance, would be temporary, lasting only until the baby boom generation reaches its dotage. Thus, it could be that as the average age of the population increases there will be a conservative turn, but the evidence we have strongly suggests that aging alone will not bring about this result. Rather, in recent decades, members of all age groups, including the oldest, have dramatically increased their support for school integration and increased their opposition to laws against marriage between Blacks and Whites.

Leaving aside the "just because they're young" explanation, for which there is very little evidence (Davis, 1992, p. 281; see also Cutler & Kaufman, 1975), there are two prominent explanations as to why newer generations have become less open to racist stereotypes and more open to laws against discrimination. One is that the era in which members of these generations were raised (post-World War II) was relatively prosperous, and the security of growing up in a prosperous era made them more liberal. The other explanation is that members of the newer generations are better educated. In the long run, rising levels of education could account for much of the change in attitudes. The education level of the population has gone up sharply in recent decades. For example, in 1960 about 23% of the adult population had at least some college; by 1980, 38% did.

The decrease in the proportion not graduating from high school is also impressive: In the same 20-year period, it dropped from 47% to 25% (Abramson, 1983).

This does not resolve the matter, however. The interpretive problem is clearest in a recent debate over the causes of increasing "postmaterialist" values since the Second World War (Abramson & Inglehart, 1994; Duch & Taylor, 1993, 1994; Inglehart, 1990). The measure of postmaterialism is composed of several items; prominent among them is support for democratic values, including tolerance and free speech. According to Inglehart, the main cause of the change in attitudes is psychological. The socialization experiences of adolescents have changed dramatically in recent decades. Adolescents have become much more economically secure during their formative years and thus less interested in the materialistic values of earlier generations. Education is strongly correlated with postmaterialism, but that is because "education is a powerful indicator of the respondents' economic security during their formative years" (Abramson & Inglehart, 1994, p. 798). Duch and Taylor (1993, 1994) claim, on the other hand, that education is the best predictor of postmaterialist attitudes because education influences the attitudes; it is not a proxy for something else (see Chapters 4 and 5 for more discussion of this topic).

This dispute should not detract from the main point, however: National survey evidence shows that the relation of individuals' tolerance and education levels is quite strong, and it has been strong just about as far back as we have extensive and reliable survey data. For instance, in reviewing the results of 16 national surveys conducted between 1954 and 1977 on the attitudes of some 22,000 adults, Smith (1981b) found, as did the authors of the *Scientific American* studies examined above, that attitudes toward school desegregation were directly related to education. Briefly, the more educated the respondents, the more likely they were to favor integrated education. This was true at the end of the period as well as at the beginning, and it was true despite the fact that educational level was measured very crudely. As was common practice at the time (and since), education was measured solely by number of years of schooling completed. The population was divided into three groups: fewer than 12 years, 12 years, and more than 12 years. Despite the resulting suppression of the variance in education, the relation of education to attitudes remained strong. For example, in 1954 the three education groups (less than high school, high school graduate, and some college) were "tolerant of desegregation" in the following proportions: 46%, 66%, and 75%, respectively. By 1977, the figures were 75%, 90%, and 96%. Smith concludes, however, that the big change in tolerance of educational desegregation was not accomplished by educational means. The change occurred in all age groups, at all levels of education, and in all regions of the country. Smith attributes the attitude shift to an era effect in which everyone changed in roughly the same amount—but, because of ceiling effects, as support for integration became nearly universal, the gaps narrowed between regions and educational groups.

It is impossible to resolve completely the issue of the importance of aging effects, era effects, education effects, and cohort effects with the data we currently have or are likely ever to have. We can say that researchers using different databases and different statistical techniques differ on the "mix" of the most probable sources of attitude change: change because of a different climate of opinion that affects all age and education groups, change because newer generations replacing the old grew up in different psychosocial circumstances, change because newer generations are more highly educated (compare, for example, Firebaugh & Davis, 1988; Miller & Sears, 1986). My preference is for a mix of the three that differs somewhat depending upon the issues (race, free speech, gender equity, and so on).

One point is fairly clear, however: Most Whites surveyed who have expressed pro-integration beliefs were not just going along with the crowd and saying what they believed everyone else believed. When Whites were asked not only whether they were for or against strict segregation, but also how they thought other Whites would answer the question, they routinely overestimated the amount of prejudice in other Whites' responses. For example, 4% of respondents from the North with some college themselves favored strict segregation, but they estimated that 40% of other Whites did (corresponding figures for the South were 12% and 72%, respectively). In fact, Whites were more likely than Blacks to overestimate the proportion of Whites favoring strict segregation (O'Gorman, 1979; see also Sniderman & Piazza, 1993).

For whatever reasons, the long-term "climate" of opinion has continued moving in a "liberal" direction, despite some fluctuations in short-term "weather" conditions (Davis, 1992), and the effect of education remains clear over time, even when related variables are controlled for (Condran, 1979; Corbett, 1982; Steeh & Schuman, 1992). The relation holds when one examines attitudes not only about general principles, such as favoring integration, but also about policy implementation, such as favoring a law to enforce integration (Davis, 1992; Steeh & Schuman, 1992). Looking at pooled results from NORC surveys from the early 1970s to the late 1980s and 1994 (the most recent year for which data are available), we see continuing important changes in racial attitudes of Whites. There was no "conservative" turn in the early 1990s. Table 3.8 displays four examples. Given these continuing trends, we are left with the problem of explaining "the frequent news reports of decreasing liberalism among young

TABLE 3.8 Changes in Whites' Racial Attitudes, 1972-1994 (in percentages)

	1972-1974	1987-1989	1994
Favor school busing	14	28	31
Oppose laws against Black-White marriage	61	73	84
Favor open housing	34	53	62
Oppose Whites' right to keep Blacks out of neighborhoods	55	74	83

SOURCES: Davis (1992, Table A1) and National Opinion Research Center (1994).

people" (Steeh & Schuman, 1992, p. 360) and ultimately, therefore, in the general adult population.

Given that there was no decline in the liberalism and tolerance of young people entering adulthood from 1960 to 1990, why do so many people think there was such a decline? Answers are necessarily speculative, so here are my speculations, my three guesses. First, some of the misreporting may reflect wishful thinking. As I recall, the press has been heralding the conservative turn of American youth since 1971. I suspect wishful thinking because even journalists cannot be devoid of all memory and incapable of realizing that they have been routinely announcing the same "news" for a quarter century. Second, some assessments of how "conservative" youth are today may be a result of our expectations running ahead of reality: Our standards have gone up faster than our behavior has improved. Any relatively "minor" racist incident on a college campus today is likely to be widely reported in the press, including incidents on campuses that did not even accept Blacks as students 30 or 40 years ago. Instances of racism that once would have gone without notice are now shocking because our criteria for acceptable behavior have become more stringent. Third, there may simply be a need for news. The headline "Youth Same as Last Year, Survey Shows" is unlikely to sell many newspapers. In sum, regardless of the reasons for the misreporting, our evidence in the 1990s is the same as it was in the 1960s: On most issues, more education leads to more social, political, and moral tolerance, especially among young people.

A crucial measurement issue that influences how we see attitudes and their relation to education is whether we should look at related attitudes one at a time or add them (or average them) into scales and indices. Depending upon the topic one is investigating, either strategy can be appropriate. But there is one consequence that should be mentioned at this point, because it is especially noticeable in matters of race attitudes. The connection between education and tolerance, or between education and lack of prejudice, is usually stronger when indices and scales, rather than individual questions or items, are used. Scholars wishing to argue that the education-tolerance link is less important will naturally favor the item-by-item approach, so they can focus on exceptions to the rule. On the other hand, researchers wanting to emphasize the education-tolerance connection will tend to use indices in which embarrassing exceptions are averaged away. It seems to me that quite a few such value-laden measurement choices are made by researchers, but the selection is more important than that. Assuming it makes sense to sum the items in an index, the index will be better able to indicate differences (variance) in attitudes with which variance in education can be associated (Corbett, 1982).

The summing or indexing strategy was used to good effect in the later *Scientific American* articles discussed above. Attitudes were measured on a 7-point "pro-integration scale." Six education categories were used, ranging from elementary school through graduate school. The results were very clear. In 1963 and 1970 surveys, for example, a steady progression in the pro-integration score occurred—from about 2.5 to 3 for those with elementary educations to about 5.5 to 6 for those with graduate school educations (Greeley & Sheatsley, 1971). It is also interesting to note, given the discussion of Black anti-Semitism above, that Jews were consistently more likely to score high on this pro-integration scale than were members of any other religious/ethnic group. The average Protestant respondent scored about the same as did the high school dropouts, whereas the average Jewish respondent had roughly the same score as people with postbaccalaureate degrees.

Research in the 1980s and 1990s has gone considerably further than the *Scientific American* reports of the 1950s, 1960s, and 1970s in uncovering subtle relationships between education and beliefs and attitudes about race. This greater subtlety has been concentrated on the attitudes half (as opposed to the education half) of the equation, but gives us some important data we need to clarify our problem. In 1985, Schuman et al. systematically pulled together the results of just about every reliable survey of race attitudes that had been conducted through the early 1980s. They used the same crude, three-category measure of education (fewer than 12 years, 12 years, more than 12 years) common at the time and since. This is one further indication that researchers studying the education-attitude link have often been much more interested in examining the dependent variable (attitude) than the independent variable (education). Despite this shortcoming, which is often forced on researchers by the nature of the data with which they have to work, Schuman et al.'s findings remain very important. First, Whites' support for integration declined "when the degree of integration proposed would make whites into a minority," and it declined for "highly educated [more than 12 years of school] respondents" as well as others, to the point that they were "no longer in the vanguard" (p. 116). But they were not in the rear guard either. When the dependent variable was the willingness of Whites to be in a minority, Whites with higher levels of education responded in about the same way as those with lower levels of education (but see Chapter 5).

The association of attitudes with education also tended to be sharply reduced when Whites were asked about policy implementations rather than general principles, especially if the policies involved federal intervention. As I have already discussed, commentators often take this result, the principles-implementations gap, to mean that Whites are not really serious when they say they favor integration; the gap supposedly shows that Whites have learned to conceal, symbolically, their racism. Although plausible, this interpretation is called into question by the fact that the same gap exists for Blacks. For example, virtually all Blacks surveyed said that they favored school integration, but over the years studied by Schuman et al., only about half of them favored busing to bring it about. Unless about half the Black population is made up of anti-Black racists, opposition to busing cannot be taken as a measure of anti-Black racism.[5] It is true that the principle-implementation gap was bigger for Whites than for Blacks on most questions of racial equality,[6] but it is hard to imagine any group and any issue where there would not be some such gap between desired ends and approved means, especially when those means are mandatory. As Schuman et al. (1985) note, "There are some legitimate reasons for questioning almost any nonvoluntary change" (p. 158). And the federal nonvoluntary aspect is key to these particular survey responses: The support of Whites and Blacks for federal government action to desegregate schools has declined since the mid-1960s (p. 148; see also Sniderman, Tetlock, & Carmines, 1993a).

Schuman and Bobo (1988a, 1988b) conducted a series of survey experiments in 1985 and 1986 that further refine our understanding of Whites' attitudes and their associations with education. They found that sometimes changes in the kinds of questions asked made important differences. For example, on the question of whether Whites think that Black and White children should go to the same school or different schools, the association of education level with the tendency to say the "same school" was large and positive (gamma = .55). But when the phrase "or do you favor something in between?" was added as a choice, enough Whites (11%) picked this option to reduce the gamma to statistical nonsignificance (1988a). On the question of open housing, there was a "small but significant positive relation with education" (1988b, p. 278). Again, however, Whites were much more likely to reject government enforcement "regardless of the group involved" than they were to oppose a Black family living next door to them (p. 288; see also Sniderman, Tetlock, Carmines, & Peterson, 1993).

Another suggestive result from Schuman and Bobo's survey experiment was the fact that education was found to be a better predictor of support for neighborhood integration when a qualification (in italics in the following) was added: "If a black family *with the same income and education as you* moved in next door, would you mind it a lot, a little, or not at all?" With the qualifier, the percentage answering "not at all" went up from 73% to 79%. More important for our purposes, the association with education was stronger when the social status of the potential neighbors was specified (1988b, pp. 290-291). Without the qualifier, the more educated respondents were somewhat more likely to volunteer the answer, "It depends." This suggests that some potential White opposition to Black neighbors stems from worries about social status as much or more than concerns about race; this is especially true among the better-educated third of the population. In sum, by the mid-1980s, three-fourths of Whites claimed that they would not be at all troubled by a Black neighbor, and less than 5% said they would "mind a lot." Interpreting such facts raises the half-empty, half-full problem. When only 4-5% say that they would "mind a lot," one can take heart. On the other hand, in a country with as large a population as the United States, 4-5% is around 10 million people. If only 1% of those are confirmed racists willing to act on their beliefs, they can cause considerable trouble for neighborhood integration.

Different kinds of beliefs need to be distinguished if we are to make progress in our understanding of how education affects them. One very useful categorization has been introduced by Apostle, Glock, Piazza, and Suelzle (1983), who divided the attitudes of 500 interviewees into perceptions, explanations, and prescriptions. For example, a White person might believe (perception) that Blacks are more likely to get into trouble with the police than Whites are, but he or she could offer many different explanations for that belief. The key to deciding whether the perception is racist or not lies in the explanation. For example, one person might say that Blacks get into trouble with the police because Blacks have criminal genes; another may say that Blacks get into trouble because the police discriminate against Blacks. The perception takes on a sharply different meaning depending on the explanation. Furthermore, prescriptions for change can differ dramatically depending upon the explanations—genetic engineering versus sensitivity training for the police, for example. Apostle et al. organized their interviewees' explanations for Black-White inequality into six broad categories: supernatural, genetic, cultural, individualistic, environmental, and radical. Some explanations were combinations of two or more of these categories.

The kinds of explanations offered by Whites in this study differed sharply by education level. People with college educations, especially those who had graduated from college, were much more likely to give environmental, radical, or combined radical-environmental explanations—such as Blacks get into more trouble with the police because their poverty rate is higher (environmental) and/or because the police are prejudiced against Blacks (radical). About 60% of college graduates, 28% of nongraduates with some college, and 11% of those who had never attended college used one of these "modern" or structural explanations of Black-White inequality. Younger people were also more likely to do so, but controlling for age did not reduce the percentage of variance explained by education a great deal—the eta-squared moved from .24 to .18 (Apostle et al., 1983, p. 157).

Differences among Whites and differences between Blacks and Whites in the explanations they offer for inequality between the races have been studied extensively in recent years. Like Apostle et al., Kluegel and Bobo (1993, p. 144) found that "structural" (social and institutional) attributions were positively associated with education, whereas individualist attributions and old-fashioned prejudiced explanations were negatively associated with education level. Education tended to increase structural explanations much less than it reduced prejudice, but both relations were statistically significant and conform to the patterns found in other studies. The same authors also point out that support for income equalization is often negatively associated with education for both Whites and Blacks (Bobo & Kluegel, 1993, Tables 3-5). Egalitarianism among the educated, it has repeatedly been found, does not generally extend to income equality. College-educated people are somewhat less likely to blame the poor for being poor than are those with less education, but they are still very likely to do so, and there are no big differences between Blacks and Whites in their tendency to attribute poverty to individualistic rather than social (structural) causes once education level is controlled.[7]

This handful of qualifications to the generalization that education promotes tolerance indicates the sort of refinements we need in order to try to specify how education might lead to tolerance. For example, do women and Blacks become more liberal as a result of higher education because they take different kinds of courses than do White males (Kluegel & Smith, 1986), or because of other experiences in college, or because their different backgrounds lead them to interpret the "same" experiences differently? Answering this kind of question requires that we look more closely at variety in the predictor variable (education); that will be done in Chapters 4 and 5. For now, we will continue to examine differences in the outcomes, because these raise important questions to be addressed later in this book.

Moral Tolerance

If moral tolerance concerns acts in private, one might wonder how tolerance or intolerance even comes up in relation to these acts. Why should anyone care what others do in private? But everyone does care about at least some of the things that others do in private. Privacy does not necessarily erase illegality. It certainly does not eliminate immorality. Very often moral intolerance involves "victimless crimes." For example, although there is no direct victim other than the person who smokes marijuana, smoking marijuana is nonetheless a crime and is considered morally wrong by many Americans. Participating in premarital or homosexual intercourse, practicing Satanism or witchcraft, and viewing pornographic videos are not crimes, but most Americans are not indifferent to such acts. Most believe they are wrong whether or not they are illegal, and many believe that they should be prohibited by law—perhaps because they think such acts have public consequences even if they are done mostly in private. At the minimum level of intolerance, many people might show their intolerance of persons who do "immoral" things by refusing to associate with them.

The "harm" that is done by "immoral" acts, apart from any harm to the immediate participants, usually takes the form of indirect injury, often a symbolic challenge to a way of life or to a moral or religious value. But many moral values are imposed by criminal law. Most crimes are also considered sins; most sins are also crimes. We talk of *imposition* mainly when an issue is contested, when some people think there "ought to be a law" and others think the "government ought to mind its own business." Below, I use three such contested issues to examine moral tolerance and its relation to education: abortion, homosexuality, and atheism. There is a fair amount of research on each of these and some evidence that many Americans, particularly those who think of themselves as conservative, consider all three to be violations of a related cluster of values (Miller, 1994).

Abortion

Hardly anyone *likes* abortion, any more than they like appendectomies. In that sense, almost no one is "pro"-abortion, even people who think that abortion is often desperately needed and ought to be a legal right. Legalization versus criminalization is the choice about this last-resort method of birth control. Should abortion be a private (im)moral act or should it be a crime and therefore public? Although the rhetoric of the main organizations on either side of the issue tends to be "simplistic" (Dillon, 1993), the issues surrounding abortion can be more complicated than many we have dealt with in this book. One of the complications in measuring abortion attitudes is that the survey questions on abortion have remained constant while important changes in abortion law have occurred. Most people do not have a very good understanding of the law. Many think it is much more restrictive than it in fact is. One study found, for example, that nearly half the persons surveyed did not know that in the first trimester of pregnancy, abortion is simply a matter of choice. Survey after survey has shown that the majority of respondents think abortion should be legal in some circumstances, most importantly for medical reasons, such as when a pregnancy endangers a woman's health; but most abortions are not performed for such reasons (Adamek, 1994). Another complication is that abortion law, like most legal bases for tolerance, is negative. The often-used phrase "shall make no law" pertains. But when abortion gets mingled with entitlements such as Medicaid, the issue is transformed. The government is no longer merely prohibiting prohibitions, it is paying for procedures (Khushf, 1994). Arguments have swirled around this issue. How can one be entitled to medical care but not to a particular, legal, procedure? Because it is immoral? Because it is elective? Is it permissible to elect to be immoral as long as one pays for it oneself? Can the state legally deny access to a legal procedure by refusing to pay for it? This is not the place to settle or even list all the arguments—I mean only to suggest how complicated they are.

Because of these complications, survey questions tend to give a partial picture of the range of people's attitudes on abortion. Granted these limitations, what do we know about people's attitudes and the association of those attitudes with education? First, people differ not only in what they believe, but in how strongly they believe it. "Abortion is not ranked as the 'most important problem facing the country' by very many people," but people who oppose legal abortions are much more likely to see it as an important issue (Scott & Schuman, 1988, pp. 787, 791). This is an example of a general phenomenon: Conservatives tend

TABLE 3.9 Percentage of the Population Supporting Legal Abortion,
by Education Level, 1962-1975

	Grade School		High School		College	
Age	1962-1965	1974-1975	1962-1965	1974-1975	1962-1965	1974-1975
25-36	37	55	49	75	59	83
37-48	51	58	51	76	59	82
49-60	47	63	54	73	64	77
61-72	42	65	53	78	57	84

to be more passionate in their beliefs than liberals; advocates of intolerance are more likely to act on their beliefs than are advocates of tolerance (Marcus et al., 1995).

Depending on the survey question or questions asked about abortion and on the statistical techniques used, education has been found to have effects ranging from modest to strong on attitudes about abortion. For example, in three National Fertility Studies in 1965, 1970, and 1975, women's approval of legal abortion increased sharply; by 1975, education was the most important predictor of attitudes out of a list of six, even after the other five were controlled for (Beniger, 1984). The fact that education increased in importance as a predictor from 1965 to 1975 indicates that women with more education changed their beliefs more quickly than did women with less education, a fairly common finding (to be discussed as one of the indirect effects of education in Chapter 4).

To get a broad picture of the relation of education to attitudes in the years when abortion was debated and ultimately legalized (or decriminalized) by Supreme Court decision in 1973, we can use Hyman and Wright's (1979, p. 123) summary of results from the General Social Survey. Table 3.9 reports how many people favored legalizing abortion a decade before this was done and a year or two after it was. The table allows us to see the change over a decade and how support was influenced by the age and education levels of people answering the survey. Reading down the columns in the table, we see that in contrast with many other issues, age did not have a much of an effect on support for legal abortion. On the other hand, the change over the decade was substantial; approval changed from a bare majority to a substantial majority. And reading across the rows, we see that in both the early 1960s and the mid-1970s, education was clearly related to support.

More variables can be taken into consideration using different statistical techniques. For example, Legge (1983), using data from the National Election

Survey of 1980, found that education was fourth on a list of 12 variables in its ability to discriminate among categories of attitudes toward legalized abortion. Education was well behind some religious variables and respondents' scores on a "women's equity scale," but it was well ahead of race, income, political party, and number of children under age 6. Although the National Election Study asked different questions from those on the General Social Survey (GSS), the results were about the same: About 12% thought that abortion should always be illegal, about 37% thought it should always be legal, and slightly over half said it should be legal under various circumstances (Legge, 1983, p. 485). Similar results have been found in nearly every study. For example, using 1990 survey data and predicting abortion attitudes in separate regressions for men and women, Walzer (1994) found that education was a significant predictor after controlling for 15 other variables. Its effect was not notably different for men and women. However, race was a more significant predictor of women's attitudes about abortion than of men's. Black women were more likely than White women to favor legalized abortion.

The race issue has received quite a bit of attention—more than it deserves, probably, as the gap between Blacks' and Whites' support for abortion rights has never been very large. Race hardly ever explains more than 2% of the variance in attitudes about abortion. But researchers have found race interesting, in part no doubt because race is a national fixation, and in part because it raises a paradox. Although Blacks on average are slightly less supportive of legalized abortion than are Whites, they are approximately twice as likely to have abortions. The approval or attitude gap between the races is not large—not nearly as large as the behavior gap. In 14 surveys using a 6-point approval scale between 1972 and 1988, Whites scored around 3.9 and Blacks around 3.3. The gap has become smaller in the more recent surveys. When a dozen or so demographic and religious variables were controlled for, it shrunk to statistical insignificance in 1987 and 1988 (Wilcox, 1990). In a related study, Wilcox (1992) has provided more direct evidence about education's effects. Education was the only variable that was a significant predictor for all four of the groups he studied: Blacks and Whites living in the South and in other regions of the United States.

Looking a bit deeper, one can uncover some interesting relations. Although neither race nor gender by itself is very important as a predictor of abortion attitudes, taken together they become more significant. Black women are more likely to support legal abortion than are White women, but Black men are less likely to do so than are White men. Also, the variables associated with abortion attitudes for the four gender-race groups differ.

Using a 1980 Roper Survey that provided an unusually rich measure of related moral attitudes—and an unusually poor measure of abortion attitudes—Dugger (1991) found differences between the attitudes of Black and White women. First, using standard background variables, it was easier to predict White than Black attitudes on abortion (see also Wilcox, 1992). More interesting, White women's attitudes were best predicted by their views on other moral issues, such as premarital sex, homosexuality, sex education, and liberal divorce laws. For Black women, however, this was not true. For them, education was the best predictor. Education was a significant predictor for both, but it was about three times as strong a predictor for Blacks as for Whites. A last refinement was introduced by Lynxwiler and Gay (1994), who compared the attitudes of women of childbearing age. There were many fewer differences between Black and White women in their childbearing years than between women past those years. But again, for all groups, education had a significant if modest positive effect on attitudes toward the legality of abortion.

Abortion is an important religious issue, so it is not surprising to find that religious variables (denomination and intensity of religious belief) often predict abortion attitudes better than education does. Using GSS data for 1973-1988 and the same 6-point scale measuring approval of abortion's legality, Granberg (1991) found religion to be a very strong predictor. For example, Catholics with Catholic spouses had a low average approval score (3.3), and former Catholics turned fundamentalist Protestant were even more opposed. Jewish respondents were most consistently in favor of legality, around 5.0 on the 6-point scale. Respondents' other moral views—especially if they constituted a coherent morally conservative worldview including religiosity, "motherhood, sexuality, and the proper place of religion in society" (Spicer, 1994, p. 115)—often predicted attitudes about abortion better than did years of schooling.

The views of the people with whom an individual interacts can also be very important. A person's attitude toward abortion can be greatly influenced by frequent interactions with close friends or family members whom he or she respects—even when the other kinds of variables we have been discussing are controlled for (Kenny, 1993). But education almost always has a role. I will mention one last example, one that is particularly interesting because it concerns not only attitudes but behaviors. Using data from the National Longitudinal Study of Youth, Plotnick (1992) found that teenage girls who got pregnant were more likely to have abortions if they liked school and had high educational expectations. This is a striking confirmation of the association of education (not even education level, but attitudes toward education) and attitudes toward the legality of abortion, if, that is, it is reasonable to deduce attitudes from behavior in this instance.

A final note: Although the evidence is clear that education is likely to be associated with a person's favoring legalized abortion, one astute reader (Dan Levy) of an early draft of this book noted that he does not believe the issue of abortion is a fair test of tolerance. On the other hand, I think that the legality of abortion is a particularly good test of tolerance. Our disagreement hinges on the status of the fetus (unborn child) as a potential object of tolerance. Although that fundamental disagreement is hard to resolve, we can agree when the issue is put as follows: If legalized abortion is an example of tolerance, it is also an example of an issue where substantial disagreement exists over whether, in this instance, tolerance is a good or a bad thing.

Homosexuality

Since AIDS emerged or was discovered in the early 1980s, attitudes of Americans about homosexuality have been closely tied to the disease. There is evidence both that people are more hostile toward homosexuals because they blame homosexuals for the scourge of AIDS and, more significant, that people are less willing to support medical programs for persons with AIDS because they believe that those who have the disease are homosexual sinners who deserve the punishment that God has visited upon them (Ezekiel, 1995; Jelen & Wilcox, 1992; Stipp & Kerr, 1989). Homosexuals, like atheists, are widely disliked in the United States. Hostility toward Blacks and Jews appears to be less common. As Gibson and Tedin (1988) note, "For most Americans, gays may well be among the groups they like the least" (p. 587). Gays certainly have fewer legal protections than do members of most other groups. In many places in the United States, for example, a landlord may legally refuse to rent to someone on the grounds that he or she is a homosexual. There may be state and local protections against this sort of discrimination, but federal prohibitions of discrimination against homosexuals are few at best.

Even among college students, usually a fairly liberal group, a large minority (20-24% of women and 42-45% of men in 1994 and 1995) think "it is important to have laws prohibiting homosexual relationships" (Shea, 1995, 1996). This is only a slightly smaller proportion than the percentage of the general population who think homosexuality should be illegal (Smith, 1990). Opposition to homosexuality perhaps occurs because, as Britton (1990) puts it, any "violations of prevailing norms threaten the collectivity" (p. 425). More than half the respondents in one survey saw gays as a "threat" (Gibson & Tedin, 1988). Of course, any threat coming from this group would almost have to be symbolic or normative, given that, for example, gays are not known for "straight bashing."

Trends in the direction of liberalization of attitudes toward Blacks, Jews, atheists, and legal abortion are very clear. By contrast, almost no movement has occurred in the public's attitudes about whether homosexuality is "always or almost always wrong"—around 75% annually from 1973 through 1989 (Smith, 1990). On the other hand, roughly 60% would favor open housing laws for gays (Stipp & Kerr, 1989). These two facts yield a pretty good measure of tolerance in the sense in which we have used the term here. Only 15% say homosexual relations between consenting adults are "not wrong" (Smith, 1990), but about four times that many favor laws protecting homosexuals' rights in housing.

When attitudes toward gays become confounded with worries about AIDS—a much more direct threat, to life, not merely to a way of life—willingness to suspend civil rights can be quite strong. In surveys conducted in 1985 and 1987, about half the respondents thought that people with AIDS should have to carry special identification cards and/or be quarantined. A significant minority (about one-fifth) favored tattooing people with the disease for easy identification (Price & Hsu, 1992). How closely related to level of education are such attitudes? The two studies with the best samples, largest numbers of controls, and most advanced estimation techniques have come up with roughly the same results we have seen for our other groups. In the first study, the dependent variable was willingness to suppress the political rights of gays (Gibson & Tedin, 1988).[8] Education came in third in a large field of variables, in both the bivariate and multivariate estimates of the effects on attitudes toward gays. People with higher levels of education were significantly less likely to support repression of gays' political rights. The two variables with effects bigger than education were how strongly the respondent believed in the "norms of democracy" and how threatened he or she felt by homosexuals. But "the direct and indirect effects of education . . . while not large in magnitude, are pervasive. . . . Virtually every variable in the model is affected at least to some degree by level of education" (pp. 599-600). In the second study, Price and Hsu (1992) also found that education strongly reduced (directly and indirectly) subjects' willingness to restrict the liberties of people with AIDS (by quarantining and tattooing them).

In these two studies and many others, the strongest predictors of tolerant attitudes are related attitudes, such as commitment to the norms of democracy. In such studies education usually finishes at the top of the list of the second group of variables including demographic characteristics such as sex, age, income, race, and region of residence. The size and rank of the effects of such characteristics vary with the issue and sometimes with the era being studied. For example, region of residence (South versus non-South) was much more important than any other variable in predicting racial attitudes in the 1950s. By the 1990s, people living in the South had attitudes largely indistinguishable from those of people living in other regions, and when differences remained, they usually did not persist after controls were introduced for education and religious fundamentalism. For attitudes toward homosexuality, as for several other issues, education's place in most lists of predictors remains firm, even while regional, racial, and gender differences are fading. This is all the more remarkable because the variance in education levels in the population has declined considerably in recent decades. In other words, even though on average people are getting increasingly similar amounts of education, differences in amounts of education still produce significant differences in beliefs and attitudes.

Atheism

Atheists are also a widely disliked group in the United States, but unlike homosexuals or disputants in the abortion issue, to say nothing of Blacks and Jews, atheists tend to be invisible. Probably no one has ever said, "Funny, he doesn't look atheist." Atheism just doesn't come up very often. Except for those few who have organized politically—for example, to work for the removal of the motto "In God we trust" from American currency and coins—atheists constitute an abstract social category for most people, not a recognizable social group. Atheists are more similar to the category of, say, men uninterested in football. It surely exists, but it does not cause much concern. However, when survey researchers ask people about atheists, they give very negative responses.

Atheists are not a large group. The "nones" on the General Social Survey 1972-1986 (those who responded with "none" when asked about their religious affiliation) have been around 6% to 7% of the total. Among college students in the 1990s, about twice that proportion (13-15%) claim no religious affiliation (NORC, 1986, 1994; Shea, 1995, 1996). Despite atheists' marginality, many citizens are, when asked, very willing to deny to atheists normal rights of citizenship. Serious issues are behind this willingness to deny rights, most of which have to do with the separation of church and state, for example, the legality of prayer in public schools. For citizens with theocratic tendencies, atheists (or "secular humanists") represent a fundamental challenge.

Most of what we know about attitudes toward atheists stems from the fact that they were associated with communists in most people's minds in the 1950s and thus have been studied in replications of the famous Stouffer (1955) tolerance questions ever since. Religious tolerance is probably the form of tolerance that is most firmly rooted in U.S. society. Irreligious tolerance is a separate matter, of course, but it is often covered in laws and principles protecting religious differences. Religious tolerance is a part of the national history and mythology that most Americans know; it is a civil liberty that enjoys high levels of support. But for "strange" new religions, the historical record is more mixed. The Mormons are the best-known example of a group whose religious and moral practices, polygamy in particular, have not been legally tolerated. More recently, groups such as Hare Krishna, the Unification Church, and the Branch Davidians have not had their rights enthusiastically supported by most Americans. But when it comes to predicting support for such groups, education has routinely been the most important variable (O'Donnell, 1993).

A similar pattern emerges for atheists. They are not widely liked or tolerated, but highly educated people are most likely to favor atheists' being covered by the First Amendment. Although support for atheists' rights and liberties has increased sharply since the 1950s, it can still be quite low. For example, people willing to allow an atheist to give a speech in their community against churches and religion went up from 37% in 1954 to more than 60% in the 1980s. Still, in the 1990s, approximately one-fourth of the population has been found not to favor First Amendment rights for atheists (NORC, 1994). Although the increase in support for the employment rights of atheists has been dramatic, in the most recently available survey barely half the population would allow an atheist to teach in college: 12% in 1954, 45% in 1985, 52% in 1994 (NORC, 1986, 1994; Stouffer, 1955).

How strongly are these attitudes related to education? As strongly as, or more strongly than, most we have reviewed in this book. The associations (gammas) between tolerance for atheists and education have been large and significant ever since the relations were first measured, and they were larger and more significant in the 1970s than they had been in the 1950s and 1960s (Hyman & Wright, 1979). As a concluding example, we can use the 1987 General Social Survey free speech question: 40% of respondents with less than 9 years of education thought that an atheist should be allowed to speak in their community; 58% of those with 9 to 11 years of school thought so; 66% of high school graduates favored free speech; and 84% of those with postsecondary educations did so (Corbett, 1991; see Whitt & Nelson, 1975, for a discussion of other variables). Of course, free speech is a political right even when the group claiming it is, like atheists or homosexuals, morally defined. Political rights tend to cut across other sorts of group boundaries (ethnic, racial, religious, or moral), and it is to political tolerance that we now turn.

Political Tolerance (Civil Liberties)

One of the reasons political tolerance is primary, first in importance among all forms of tolerance, is that it applies to all groups, to all potential objects of tolerance and repression; it transcends social and moral boundaries. For example, when a lesbian wishes to give a speech, she has a constitutional right, like anyone else, to do so; it is a matter of political tolerance. However, if she wishes to adopt a child, the situation is much less clear. No one has a right to adopt a child. On the other hand, all persons are supposedly guaranteed equal protection under the law. The Fourteenth Amendment does not say "except for homosexuals." Denying homosexuals access to adoption is moral intolerance. If homosexuals wish to do something about that intolerance, however, their main recourse is to actions protected by constitutionally guaranteed political tolerance, such as freedoms of speech, press, and assembly. These rights and freedoms have been widely studied, mostly by political scientists, who have often believed support for them is crucial to the maintenance of a democratic polity. A lack of widespread support, most political scientists agree, should be cause for concern. (But compare the "elitist theory of democracy" discussed briefly in Chapter 2.)

Since the mid-1950s, the study of political tolerance has largely consisted of increasingly elaborate footnotes to Samuel Stouffer's *Communism, Conformity and Civil Liberties: A Cross-Section of the Nation Speaks Its Mind* (1955). In the early 1970s, Stouffer's survey was replicated by Nunn et al. (1978), and many of Stouffer's questions have been repeated, sometimes in expanded or modified form, by the General Social Survey in most years since 1972. The result is a massive archive that has been used by many researchers. We will quickly review some of their work here. The first finding of note is the proportion of citizens willing to afford civil liberties to their fellow citizens and how that has changed over time. Table 3.10 provides a sample of some of the relevant data. The change over time has been substantial; for example, only 6% of Americans in 1954 would allow a communist to teach in a college, but that percentage had increased by a factor of nine four decades later. Still, on the issue of allowing "outsiders" to teach, one gets a solid tolerant majority only for homosexuals; approximately half of Americans would deny the right to teach in college classrooms solely on the basis of individuals' political and social beliefs. Although support for freedom of speech has increased, still today around a quarter to a third of the population would deny this fundamental liberty to at least some of their fellow citizens. For both speech and college employment, the evidence in Table 3.10 is striking. We see dramatic increases—except for

TABLE 3.10 Percentage of the Population Giving Politically Tolerant Responses, 1954-1994

Issue	1954	1977	1987	1994
Allow a speech by				
Communist	27	56	60	67
Atheist	37	62	70	73
Racist	—	59	62	61
Militarist	—	51	58	64
Homosexual	—	62	70	79
Allow to teach in college				
Communist	6	39	48	55
Atheist	12	39	48	52
Racist	—	41	45	42
Militarist	—	34	41	46
Homosexual	—	49	59	71

SOURCES: Corbett (1991) and National Opinion Research Center (1994).

tolerance of racists. For them, tolerance peaked in the late 1980s and leveled off or declined slightly in 1993 and 1994 (NORC, 1994).

Our specific question is whether these beliefs about who is entitled to constitutional rights and liberties vary by education. They do, and strongly. There are several ways to measure and report these relations (see Davis, 1982), but they have always been robust, and they have generally grown in strength since 1954 (Nunn et al., 1978). Among the variables studied by Stouffer, Nunn et al., and Davis, education "is clearly the most pervasive net predictor" (Davis, 1982, p. 569). Table 3.11 shows the relation of education to the scores on Nunn et al.'s 5-point tolerance scale, after adjustments for other variables. The tolerance scores of all education groups increased from the 1950s to the 1970s, but they went up most for the three most-educated groups; that made the overall association with education stronger. It is also important to note that the relation between tolerance and education did not change as a result of the "degree of perceived threat," a variable that we shall later see is often a very important predictor of tolerance (Williams, Nunn, & St. Peter, 1976b, p. 414).

Examples such as these could be reported at great length, but this is unnecessary to make the main point about the strong association of education with political tolerance. The effects are not universal, of course. Few effects are. Education's effects can often be countered by (or strengthened by) the action of

TABLE 3.11 Adjusted Mean Tolerance Scores, by Education Level, 1954 and 1973

Education	1954	1973
College graduate	3.6	4.2
Some college	3.4	4.1
High school graduate	3.0	3.6
Some high school	2.7	3.0
Grade school only	2.3	2.4

SOURCE: Williams, Nunn, and St. Peter (1976a, p. 398).

other variables.[9] The influence of education can be blocked by more powerful sources of social identity, such as ethnicity, but when the effects of education are not thus blocked, education is one of the strongest predictors of tolerance (Alba, 1978; compare Isaac, Mutran, & Stryker, 1980, on Blacks' and Whites' attitudes).

Further specifications about both the tolerators and the "toleratees" help sketch in some of the complexities in the education-tolerance relationship. McCutcheon (1985) used a latent class analysis to conclude that respondents to the General Social Survey could be categorized into four broad groups: 22% were tolerant of all groups, 56% were intolerant of all groups, 11% were intolerant only of the political Right, and 10% were intolerant only of the political Left.[10] The majority of respondents, the first two groups, were consistent in their views and did not switch them according to the political leanings of the "target." For those consistent respondents, the education-tolerance hypothesis held. But for the remaining fifth of the population, it did not: There was no linear effect of education on tolerance of the political Left, and increased education was associated with decreased tolerance of the political Right.

Using a somewhat parallel approach, Lawrence (1976) found that education's effects were much greater on hard than on easy issues—hard issues being those on which the population as a whole is most divided and least tolerant. For example, on the question of support of the right of one's neighbors to circulate a petition against crime, the link with education was quite small, in part because hardly anyone challenged this right. On the other hand, on a hard issue such as support for the right to demonstrate in favor of Blacks' rights to buy or rent housing in White neighborhoods, the effect of education was much stronger. Although most respondents were strongly in favor of freedom of assembly and the right to petition the government, in particular when these were stated as general principles, "consistency in applying a general norm . . . increase[d] with

education" (Lawrence, 1976, p. 94). This means that people with higher educations were more likely to give the same answer to questions about the general
principle and to questions about its application in a specific situation. (On the
relation of consistency to education, see also Sniderman & Piazza, 1993, p. 83.)

Lawrence's work on who will be tolerant, and of whom or what, is often
cited as adumbrating the biggest development in research on political tolerance
since Stouffer's survey in the 1950s. In the late 1970s and early 1980s, a new
element was added to studies of political tolerance by John Sullivan and his
colleagues (1982, 1985). Sullivan and his coauthors insisted on a more rigorous
definition of political tolerance, one that, in essence, is what I have been using
in this book. Sullivan's results challenged those of many other scholars on two
issues, both related to the effects of education: (a) whether the changes over time
on the Stouffer measures really meant that people were becoming more tolerant
as they became more educated, and (b) whether the size of the link between
education and tolerance was as large as had been estimated.

Political tolerance may be defined as extending to an opponent the same
political rights and liberties as one would extend to an ally. According to Sullivan
et al. (1985), "Individuals can be said to be tolerant of a group only if they
actually object to, or dislike, that group" (p. 77). Given that this is true, to
measure tolerance, one first has to ask respondents who their opponents are, and
then ask them whether they would allow those opponents to make a speech, to
run for office, to publish a book, and so on. This two-step method is necessary
to ensure that a survey is measuring tolerance rather than level of support for or
opposition to various groups. If more-educated people are more likely than
less-educated people to support the political rights of communists, socialists,
and atheists, that may be because they are less opposed to (or perhaps even
support) these groups. That is a real difference between more- and less-educated
people, of course, but it is not, strictly speaking, a difference in tolerance. The
need for the two-step, "content-controlled" method is clearest in comparative
studies. Suppose one took Stouffer-like tolerance questions to France and asked:
"Would you allow socialists and communists to teach in a university, give a
speech, run for political office . . . ?" Vastly more French than U.S. respondents
would answer yes to such questions. The reason is not necessarily that the French
are more tolerant than Americans, but that there are vastly more people who
identify as communists and socialists in France, where those parties routinely
win national and local elections.

To get around this kind of problem, Sullivan et al. first asked respondents
which group they disliked the most—that is, what was their "least-liked group."
Respondents were then asked whether they would extend civil liberties to

TABLE 3.12 Percentage Selecting Various Target Groups, by Education Level

	Grade School	High School	Some College
Communists and socialists	50	43	28
Radical Right groups	15	20	39

SOURCE: Sullivan et al. (1985, p. 151).

persons in the "target groups" thus identified. When asked to choose, people with different levels of education tend to pick different target groups. As Table 3.12 shows, the differences in the United States by education level are strong. Sullivan et al. propose that people with more education feel more threatened by right-wing groups, whereas those with less education feel more threatened by left-wing groups. There are several reasons this might be so, but the main point is that a survey in the United States that asks respondents only about left-wing groups would tend to make people with more education look more tolerant. If the same respondents are asked about right-wing groups, they might not give such tolerant answers.

The least-liked, content-controlled, target group methods of Sullivan et al. have generated quite a lot of controversy. Despite whatever criticisms may have been leveled at the approach, its fundamental conceptual correctness means that it is rarely ignored. Problems have occurred with how Sullivan et al. implemented their idea that it makes sense to say that you tolerate someone or something only when you have negative attitudes or beliefs about that person, group, or thing. One response to Sullivan et al.'s work has been the General Social Survey's addition of some right-wing groups (militarists and racists) to the list of groups respondents are asked about. This is not quite the same as the two-step method, but it is pretty close. Left-wing target groups have been balanced by target groups on the right in the GSS.

Sullivan et al.'s method, in brief, is to ask two questions: (a) What is your least-liked group? (b) Would you tolerate it? The general idea is sound, but it overlooks several subtleties.[11] There is more to target group selection than first meets the eye. First, it matters whether the target group selected is itself tolerant or intolerant. It seems reasonable to say that people who least like intolerant groups are more tolerant than those who least like tolerant groups. "Least liking" is not politically neutral; that is, it is not a matter of personal taste, with no political consequences. Equally important is whether the "perceived threat" that leads one to dislike and/or to be intolerant of a particular group has any basis in reality. There is a difference, after all, between feeling threatened by armed terrorists and fearing an imaginary conspiracy (such as that laid out in "The Protocols of the Learned Elders of Zion"). Furthermore, the number of disliked groups an individual selects has an important bearing on his or her level of tolerance. If one individual dislikes virtually all "outsiders" and another dislikes only a few groups, this says something about their levels of tolerance, even if both persons are equally negative about the groups they dislike the most. In sum, there is a crucial difference between someone who is intolerant of a few really dangerous, intolerant groups and someone who is intolerant of many groups, especially when those groups are tolerant and objectively nonthreatening (e.g., men with beards).

There is also the question of the *intensity* of disliking. Two people might pick the same least-liked group but dislike it with different levels of intensity. For example, I might pick the KKK as my least-liked group, but because I am not a member of any of its target groups, I might dislike the KKK with much less strength of feeling than might someone who is directly threatened by its practices. Intensity of disliking may be behind Sullivan et al.'s findings that tolerance levels are lower than had been thought and that the association of tolerance level with education level is smaller than previously estimated. Sullivan et al.'s two questions may come close to the following two questions: Who are you intolerant of? Would you tolerate them? Respondents are asked to seek "their own threshold of tolerance" (Weil, 1984, p. 965). It is not surprising that upon doing so, they become intolerant.

Other critics have claimed that Sullivan et al.'s approach magnifies small differences. People are not really all that selective about the groups they will or will not tolerate. People who oppose a speech by one group will also tend to oppose a speech by another, even another at the opposite end of the political spectrum (Corbett, 1991). Sniderman, Tetlock, Glaser, Green, and Hout (1989) have noted that there is "little evidence that the expression of underlying tolerance . . . differs across groups or acts" (p. 31). Most respondents are generally and consistently tolerant or intolerant. They do not act as Aquinas recommended (see Chapter 1, this volume) and as Sullivan et al. imply that they act: Be tolerant only when it serves the interests of "truth." Finally, because of the tendency of people to be fairly consistent, "it is not true that people must dislike a group in order to be intolerant of it. . . . it is the racial bigot, not the person committed to racial tolerance, who is the more likely to oppose free speech for racists" (Sniderman et al., 1989, p. 41).[12]

Gibson (1992a) has also found that political intolerance is so stable and consistent for most people that "it is relatively easily measured, even with techniques that are on their face quite dissimilar" (p. 576). The two main techniques are Sullivan et al.'s and Stouffer's (as continued by the General Social Survey). The latter is a good measure of intolerance, even if it is not strictly a measure of tolerance. The Stouffer and Sullivan et al. measures are fairly highly correlated ($r = .61$), but they are distinct. Despite their differences, when we turn to studying the causes of intolerance, it does not matter which measure we use for the dependent variable. The predictive power of the independent variables, including education, is very similar regardless of how the dependent variable is measured: "Our understanding of the etiology of intolerance is not dependent on the particular measure" of tolerance we use (Gibson, 1992a, p. 571). So, how important is education as a predictor of political tolerance, however measured? In Gibson's regressions with nine independent variables, education comes in third or fourth—behind commitment to general and procedural norms of democracy and open/closed-mindedness, and ahead of social class, age, gender, ideological self-label, and self-esteem.

In conclusion, when we remember that education in these regressions is nothing more than "time served," third or fourth is an impressive showing. It is even more impressive if we consider that when education comes in third or fourth in such regressions, it is usually bested only by measures of related attitudes. Education is usually at the top of the list of demographic or background measures. Often the related attitudes are better predictors because, on the face of it at any rate, they imply or are implied by tolerance. For example, it is hard to see how one could be open-minded and intolerant or how one could be committed to democratic norms without also supporting political tolerance, given that tolerance is a democratic norm.

Measures of attitudes and traits are highly imperfect. The debate over how to improve them has been valuable and will surely continue. Our interest lies mainly in the fact that no aspect of the debate calls into question education's importance to our understanding of the origins of tolerance.

Conclusions About Opposing Evidence

If by *opposing evidence* we mean reliable data showing that education and tolerance are negatively related—or that education and prejudice are positively related—there are few or no such data. It is clear that the effects of education can vary: All levels of education are not always related to all kinds of tolerance to exactly the same degree. But there are *no studies whatsoever* that show on balance a negative association between education level and tolerance level. It is not even easy to find studies that show no relationship one way or the other. There are a few studies that are sometimes cited as showing these things, but upon examination, one finds that they do not really do so. The examples to be examined here all meet the criteria mentioned earlier: large, representative samples, building cumulatively on prior research, and/or examining issues over time. The three best known of such studies are Remmers's 1963 book *Anti-Democratic Attitudes in American Schools,* a study of political tolerance mostly among high school students; Stembler's 1961 book *Education and Attitude Change,* which summarizes nearly all the valid surveys of Whites' attitudes toward Blacks and Jews before 1960; and Jackman and Muha's 1984 article "Education and Intergroup Attitudes," which I have discussed briefly in Chapter 2.

What Remmers (1963) shows is that high school students from the late 1940s to the early 1960s were not very politically tolerant on questions roughly like those Stouffer asked his respondents in the same period. For example, in 1951 and 1961, about two-thirds of students did not "think that members of the Communist party should be allowed to speak on the radio" even in peacetime (p. 66). There were few changes over time in a tolerant direction. On the other hand, high school students' support for religious freedom was much stronger. Between 84% and 90%, depending upon the year, disagreed with the statement, "Some religious groups should not be allowed the same freedom as others" (p. 66). Interesting though this may be, Remmers does not really address our question about the relation of level of education to tolerance, because there were generally no differences in education levels of the students he surveyed. Remmers's work has probably been cited as an example of negative findings because he uncovered few differences between ninth and twelfth graders. Also, and more important, he found support for First Amendment rights to be lower among students who had taken a course in civics. This surprising result has been discovered several times.[13] I will address this finding more fully in Chapter 5; here I need only note that the topic of this chapter is amount of education, not specific courses that students may have taken. Remmers does note, by the way, that students whose mothers had more education were more likely to be politically tolerant, as were students who had taken what we would today call a multicultural course (see Chapter 5).

Stembler's (1961) work has been even more frequently cited than Remmers's as demonstrating no effect or a negative effect of education on tolerance. It is easy to see why one could get that impression, but the impression lasts only if one reads Stembler's text casually and pays little attention to his evidence. Stembler discounts data showing that educated people are not more prejudiced by saying these data may all be due to social desirability bias, though he provides no evidence whatsoever to support this claim. And Stembler does not always play fair with his adjectives, sometimes using the same words to describe large and small relationships, so as to make his text support an argument that his data do not. But Stembler's study, in which he reviewed 26 important opinion surveys conducted between 1944 and 1959, was broader and more comprehensive than anything that had previously appeared on the subject; it was probably the most thorough work that had been done in this area when it appeared in 1961.

I read Stembler's findings (not his text) to be overwhelmingly supportive of the general thesis that education reduces prejudice and increases support for other people's rights. For example, my count of his summaries (pp. 42-44, 70-71) on attitudes toward Jews indicates that education had a positive effect on 11 attitudes and beliefs, made no difference on 5, and had a negative effect on 4. A similar count of attitudes toward Negroes is 8 positive, 3 no difference, 0 negative. And the positive relationships Stembler summarizes are strong and unmistakable, and they persist when other variables are controlled. Stembler's data are quite clear. The relationship of education to attitudes toward minority groups is not pure, nor is it always of the same magnitude. For example, people with higher educations were more likely to support legal measures banning discrimination against minority groups, but less likely to seek intimate contact with members of those groups. But when Stembler is driven in his closing pages to admit that education actually does have positive effects, he concludes that *"the positive effects of education are real and not spurious.* None of the other variables examined accounts for the correlations observed. Where democratic values show gains with increased education, the cause lies in some aspect of education itself" (p. 180). He suggests that "formal learning" is not that aspect. Perhaps he is right. (See Chapters 4 and 5.)

Finally, we need to examine the results from Jackman and Muha's 1984 article reporting on a 1975 survey of a national sample. It is particularly important to scrutinize these results because this article is the most commonly cited work purporting to show that education does not improve intergroup attitudes and beliefs. I have already presented my argument against Jackman's broad line of interpretation in Chapter 2. Here I want to point out that her data do not support the widely repeated conclusion that education has little or no effect. Jackman and Muha examined the attitudes of men toward women, Whites toward Blacks, and the nonpoor toward the poor. One point that Jackman has made that seems unquestionable (discussed briefly above) is that although education may lead to egalitarian beliefs and attitudes in the political, moral, and social realms, it does not necessarily lead to economic egalitarianism. A quick count of Jackman and Muha's 45 measures of the economic attitudes of the three highest education groups (some college, college graduates, postbaccalaureate studies) reveals that 31 of those measures were not statistically significant, that there were no positive attitudes attributable to education, and that there were 14 statistically significant negative relationships. These illiberal economic attitudes were expressed on questions addressing such issues as support for welfare benefits for the poor and feeling close to poor people.[14] Other scholars have noted that higher education levels do not lead to a desire to take from the rich and give to the poor (Kluegel & Smith, 1986; Lipset, 1981). This is well established, but our topic is support for social, political, and moral tolerance, not advocacy of income redistribution.

For men's attitudes toward women, we find that of 48 attitude/belief comparisons, education made a positive difference only on 7. The other 41 were all statistically insignificant. However, there were no negative results. Education made a fairly small positive difference on some aspects of gender equity. The best case in Jackman and Muha's data for the positive influence of education on attitudes concerns Whites' attitudes and beliefs about Blacks. Of the 45 comparisons for the highly educated groups, 25 were not significant, but there were no negative relationships, and there were 20 statistically significant positive ones. The differences by education were not large. Only rarely did the variance explained by education (after controls) approach 10%. But *all* statistically significant differences by education among Whites' attitudes and beliefs were positive. Whites with more education were more likely to support Blacks' rights and less likely to believe stereotypes about Blacks.

The evidence about the education-tolerance link from this one often-cited survey is not as strong as it is on surveys conducted before and since 1975. But even on this survey there are no negative associations between education and tolerant social attitudes and quite a few positive ones. So, what can we conclude about this strongest "opposing" evidence? Surprisingly, that it is not in fact opposing evidence; rather, the relationship is in the same direction as that found in all other studies, but it is somewhat smaller.

Conclusion

After reviewing all these studies, what can we conclude? Education's effects on political, social, and moral attitudes and beliefs are somewhat varied. They are not uniformly large, but the overall pattern of results is absolutely unmistakable: Education increases tolerance and reduces prejudice and stereotyping of political, social, and moral groups. This review of dozens of important studies—some of which themselves reviewed dozens of other studies—involving many thousands of people responding to hundreds of questions clearly demonstrates a robust pattern of significant statistical associations between education level and positive intergroup attitudes. The fact of the statistical association is beyond reasonable doubt. It persists after controlling for just about every imaginable variable that might otherwise explain the association.

It seems justifiable to conclude that the burden of proof is upon those who might wish to claim that education does not promote tolerance. Yet much remains uncertain. *That* education encourages positive intergroup attitudes and beliefs is clear. *How* it does so is much more open to question. And until we can explain the "how," there are still grounds for skepticism about the "that." More important, until we understand the "how," any attempt to use our knowledge of the "that" will amount to groping in the dark.

So how *does* schooling foster tolerance? I have found that most answers to that question can be categorized into one of four main types: (a) personality development, (b) cognitive development, (c) intergroup contact, or (d) civic, moral, and multicultural instruction. Each of these is considered in turn in the next two chapters.

CHAPTER 4

How Does Education
Promote Tolerance
Indirectly?

▨ Introduction to Chapters 4 and 5

There are four broad theories of schooling's influence on attitudes and beliefs, or four ways I have categorized such theories. To introduce this chapter and the next, it is useful to highlight a few features of those four theories. As can be seen in Figure 4.1, two of the theories, intergroup contact and personality development, stress the importance of processes of socialization. These often unintentional processes may occur in ways that nourish tolerant beliefs and behaviors. The other two theories or clusters of explanations—civic education and cognitive development—focus on the ways formal instruction might increase tolerance.

Another axis, distinguishing direct from indirect effects, can be drawn through the four explanations of how education promotes tolerance. It is this

	Directly	**Indirectly**
Socialization	intergroup contact	personality development
Instruction	civic education	cognitive development

Figure 4.1. How Tolerance Is Taught/Learned in Schools

second axis that I will use initially to organize the discussion in Chapters 4 and 5. First, Chapter 4 looks at the indirect ways education might influence students' social, moral, and political values. What do I mean by *direct* and *indirect*? I can best explain this by giving more details about the four explanations of how tolerance is taught and learned.

Intergroup contact and civic education are *direct* approaches to instruction in or socialization to tolerance. Contact occurs when people who are members of different social groups interact with one another and, in the process, learn quite directly (by doing) how to interact more harmoniously. Civic education also implies direct instruction. Civic education in tolerant attitudes and beliefs occurs when curricula are designed and teachers explicitly strive to teach principles of tolerance such as constitutional provisions guaranteeing civil liberties. By *civic education,* in this context, I also mean courses in multicultural education, moral education, and other areas that try to help students learn tolerance by fostering intergroup knowledge and understanding.

In contrast, personality development and cognitive development are *indirect* in respect to teaching and learning tolerance. They describe processes of socialization and learning that may predispose or enable individuals to become more tolerant, but personality and cognitive development do not result in toleration directly. For example, if intolerance is based on ignorance and superstition, schoolwork that promotes cognitive development may foster tolerance indirectly—by providing students with knowledge and encouraging rational thinking. Similarly, if intolerance and the urge to discriminate stem in part from a lack of social skills and low levels of self-esteem, then to the extent that schooling helps students develop social skills and healthy personalities, it may contribute to the likelihood that students will also become more tolerant.

Educational researchers very often assume that values are most effectively taught indirectly and perhaps unintentionally. Values and attitudes are, in the old phrase, best "caught, not taught." At this point in my argument the presumption in favor of the indirect means of learning tolerance is only a presumption. Many educators, sociologists, and psychologists make that presumption; they find claims about the efficacy of indirect learning more persuasive than claims that we can teach such things as tolerance directly. And there is much to justify that view. But evidence will never be sound enough for us to know for certain whether direct or indirect effects are more powerful. Indirect techniques are difficult to evaluate. They must often be judged using indirect, high-inference evidence. It is less difficult to figure out ways to test the effectiveness of direct approaches.

It is fairly easy, for example, to design a quasi-experiment to test the effects of direct teaching, in part because direct effects can be assumed to occur in a period of time short enough to study. By contrast, indirect learning that one "catches" can take years, and it is difficult to tell whether other variables produced the outcome in question. Of course, the comparative ease of measurement of either direct or indirect effects is not evidence of their actual importance. There is no reason to assume that because something is easy (or hard) to measure it is more significant. Such assumptions are actually fairly common, but they are probably based more in the psychological roots of the needs of researchers than in the evidential roots of the nature of the phenomena being studied.

One caveat about the system of categories used in this chapter and the next: Ultimately we will see that our four categories of explanations, handy though they might be for organizing our thinking, can often result in somewhat arbitrary divisions in what are actually better described as continua—between direct and indirect learning or between education and socialization. The distinctions the categories make are real, but they are differences of degree. Ultimately, processes of learning are too intricate to fit neatly under such rubrics.

General Discussion of Indirect Approaches and Effects

We begin with the indirect approach, if for no other reason than it is probably what many readers will find most familiar. An excellent example to open this discussion is Jackson, Boostrom, and Hansen's *The Moral Life of Schools* (1993). Although this intensive observational study deals with moral learning generally and not specifically with tolerance, it provides a superb introduction to our topic and to the view that the indirect and the "unintentional outcomes of schooling . . . are of greater moral significance—that is, more likely to have enduring effects" (p. 44). Jackson et al.'s most central point is that morality (defined generally as judgments about good and bad and about how people treat one another) pervades schooling. Jackson and his colleagues identify two clusters or types of moral learning in schools. First is the group of direct, intentional means of instruction, such as catechism classes in Catholic schools or values clarification and other direct attempts at secular moral education in public schools. A more frequent occurrence in the category of direct moral instruction is the moral lesson within the regular curriculum, as when discussion of a literary work leads to moral commentary on a character's choices and actions. Perhaps the most frequent type of direct moral teaching mentioned by Jackson et al. is made up of little moral asides that occur in the course of ordinary classroom activity—for example, "Robert, you know that it's important to take turns and not interrupt; we can't work together as a group otherwise."

The second and, according to Jackson et al., more important cluster of forms of moral instruction is indirect and perhaps unintentional. It includes school and classroom rules, which, because they regulate interpersonal relations, are moral. The way the curriculum is structured and delivered also is an indirect source of moral lessons. A good example might be frequent quizzes; these may or may not be pedagogically sound, but they carry a moral message: They are "emblematic of distrust" (p. 21). Finally in the indirect, unintentional category is what Jackson et al. refer to as "expressive morality." For instance, "teachers smile and frown a lot when they teach and . . . this can often be read as a kind of moral commentary on the activity in which they are engaged" (p. 31). We will examine these aspects of moral education in more detail in this and the next chapter. Here I wish mainly to repeat that, like many other writers on the subject, Jackson and his coauthors conclude that indirect, unintentional instruction is most important. Much of what they have to say on the subject falls within what I call the *personality development* group of explanations. To the extent that personality development can be thought of as a kind of learning, it is a kind that is usually both indirect and unintentional.

We can also make another kind of case for indirection in education. Not only are *approaches* to education often indirect, so too are the *outcomes*. Indirect pedagogy can produce "sleeper effects." The seeds are planted in school, but the attitudes emerge only later. Long after they have left school, people with higher levels of education tend to develop new attitudes and beliefs in ways that differ from those of people with lower levels of education. More-educated people often adjust their beliefs to changing circumstances more quickly. This effect persists even after other variables that might influence attitude change (such as age) are controlled. Two examples can illustrate.

Women's attitudes toward legalized abortion became sharply more favorable in the early 1970s. Three national surveys showed a weak relation between education and attitudes in 1965, a slightly stronger association in 1970, and a much stronger link in 1975. In 10 years, education moved from third to first place in a list of variables predicting abortion attitudes. The standardized coefficient tripled (Beniger, 1984). But women's average education level grew very little in those 10 years. Rather, the change occurred because women with more education altered their beliefs more quickly than did those with less education.

A second example comes from surveys in the mid-1980s concerning attitudes toward people with AIDS. Although education about the causes and dangers of AIDS is quite common today, it was not common when most of the people responding to the surveys were getting their educations—for the simple reason that AIDS was unknown when most of them were in school.[1] Respondents with higher levels of education were much less likely to favor restrictions on the civil liberties of people infected with AIDS (Price & Hsu, 1992). A good part of the reason for highly educated respondents' tolerance was that they were more informed about the comparatively modest threat the disease poses to the general population. They had learned how the virus is actually transmitted (e.g., not by shaking hands). Although they could not have learned this directly in their formal studies, given that the disease was unknown when they were in school, they were probably more able to learn about the disease outside of school due to their higher levels of education.

This example is very important. Through it, we *know* that any educational effects must have been indirect, because they could not have been direct; it was impossible for most respondents to have learned directly about AIDS in school, as AIDS did not exist while they were in school. Nonetheless, their level of schooling was associated with their attitudes about people with AIDS. Although this example makes a very strong case for the indirect effects of education, it does not specify what kind of indirect effects produced the outcome. Perhaps additional schooling helped people acquire cognitive skills that enabled them to absorb and evaluate new information. Or perhaps schooling helped people develop their personalities in ways that made them less susceptible to irrational fears. It is to the second type of explanation that we now turn.

Personality Development

What is personality? How is it related to attitudes and beliefs such as tolerance? These are difficult questions, because personality is one of the more contested concepts in psychology. We can hardly hope to settle any of the issues dividing scholars of personality here. Rather, I will make a few remarks that will help to introduce our particular questions. Most researchers would agree that *personality* refers to "internal dispositions" and "stable attributes" (Knutson, 1973, p. 29). But it is hard to narrow things down much beyond "internal" and "stable." Many aspects of personality, or traits, have been studied. Indeed, just about any adjective that can be used to describe a person can be thought of as a personality trait, and odds are that a psychologist has constructed a scale to measure it. When one begins to list examples, the breadth of the subject becomes clear. A person(ality) might be said to be introspective, creative, energetic, aggressive, conformist, ambitious, pragmatic, optimistic, compassionate, anxious, idealistic, spiritual, greedy, reclusive, inquisitive, and so on. In fact, one research tradition in the 1930s involved combing dictionaries for such terms and then boiling down the thousands found into related groups—ultimately, just short of 200 groups were formed (Knutson, 1973).

What about tolerance? Is it a personality trait? Or do personality traits make people more or less likely to have tolerant attitudes and beliefs? Are ambitious people (high in "n-Ach") more or less likely than creative people (high in "divergent thinking") to tolerate people with whom they disagree? Are attitudes part of a person's personality, or are attitudes best thought of as influenced by deeper personality traits? What about a person's values—that is, his or her beliefs about right and wrong—are they part of personality? Many students of such questions would agree that what are called traits are more general and more permanent than attitudes and beliefs. For example, if dogmatism is a trait, it could show up in a person's religious beliefs or political attitudes. The person might change religious beliefs, but the change would probably be from one dogmatic creed to another. If there are "internal" and "stable" traits, it seems likely that they would influence attitudes and beliefs, but the influence would be general, not specific.[2] Dogmatism could as easily accommodate itself to Muslim, Christian, or Jewish fundamentalism.

Our last and most important question has to do with the stability of traits. Are they malleable enough to be influenced by education? In other words, can education influence tolerance indirectly, by influencing personality?

Several types of evidence will be pertinent to our investigation of the associations among education, personality, and tolerance. Many of the surveys used in Chapter 3 to establish the link between education and tolerance (such as the General Social Survey) also contain scales designed to measure personality traits. In addition, some major studies of personality "syndromes," or clusters of related traits, are important for our purposes because they include measures of social, political, and moral tolerance. Among the best known of these syndromes are the "authoritarian personality," of which dogmatism is a variant (Rokeach, 1960; Sanford, 1973); "individual modernity" (Inkeles & Smith, 1974); and "postmaterialism" (Inglehart, 1990). There is a large psychometric literature about each of these, especially authoritarianism. We will focus only on how the syndromes are tied to theoretical and empirical investigations of education's influence on personality development and tolerance.

When these personality syndromes are affected by education, most theorists have claimed, the formal curriculum is much less important than the social structures of schooling. By *structures* here I mean any regular patterns of social interaction in educational settings.

The Influence of School Structures

Formal education's institutional structures and the procedural norms schools follow (or sometimes only pay lip service to) may indirectly and unintentionally foster tolerance. This happens through socialization—the process of learning the values and norms of one's society. All socialization effects need not be indirect or unintentional, of course. School desegregation (see Chapter 5) is a well-known case of a purposive social policy meant to change attitudes and beliefs through socialization. But personality development is not usually approached in this direct way, even when educators believe or hope that schooling will aid in personality development. Most of the evidence for personality development is indirect and theoretical, given that direct, short-term data are nearly impossible to obtain.

Classical Sociological Theory

The classic source for this line of theorizing is Emile Durkheim's turn-of-the-century lectures for students planning to become elementary teachers, later published as *Moral Education* (1961); most subsequent work on the socialization effects of school structures has built upon that book. Morality, according to Durkheim, is a set of rules or norms that make life in common possible. Students learn social rules in school. That is how they develop the spirit of self-discipline that makes it possible for them to conform to the norms of the broader society. The particular school rules are not especially important. What is important is that the child develop the sense of limits and constraints that is the basis of any sound personality. The main thing the school teaches is the positive value of group norms, which makes it possible for groups to function. Because ultimately the child must be able to *understand* the need for social rules, not merely conform to them, the preschool years are not crucial in moral development. Moral character must be developed through the kinds of reasoning about social experience of which preschoolers are cognitively incapable. Thus, according to Durkheim, personality development depends upon cognitive development, an insight later built upon by Piaget and Kohlberg (see below). This cognitive component of moral growth is the reason that the basic elements of character that make social life possible are best developed in school. The family, too, has a crucial role to play. However, by its very nature, with members bound together by ties of affection, the family is not well equipped to teach the *impersonal* rules that are crucial to the maintenance of modern society.

Durkheim's conceptions of moral education are expanded upon by Robert Dreeben in *On What Is Learned in School* (1968). Dreeben also stresses the ways in which the functions and structures of families and schools are distinct. Schools, he notes, provide "a much larger pool of individuals within which a pupil establishes relationships" (p. 21). This diversity of relationships with people to whom children have no kinship ties aids in the "formal and prolonged process of separating children from the family" (p. 35) and readies young people for economic and political life. Schools, in other words, prepare pupils for public life; they introduce children to the norms that govern public life. These norms, learned first in school, can then be transferred to other social realms. To function in the public sphere, individuals need to know how to relate to persons to whom they do not necessarily have affective ties but with whom they must have dealings (fellow pupils, teachers, and so on). Schools bring about "changes in the state of mind that enable men to participate in a public life outside the circle of the family" (p. 107). From the perspective of how schools teach tolerance, the most important of the norms students often learn in schools are the two parts of the apparently opposed pair that Dreeben calls "universalism and specificity."

Dreeben's basic contention regarding these norms is that all persons in a particular category (specificity) are expected to be treated the same way (universalism). Identical performance on a school exercise, for example, should result in identical grades for all students in the same class. The category that matters is "student," or "third grader," not female, or African American, or Catholic, or middle-income. Parents naturally treat their children as special and focus on their individually distinguishing characteristics. Teachers, at least in some of their work, are not expected to do this. Teachers who do not treat students as identical members of the same category for the purposes of grading, for example, and who pay attention to individual characteristics (gender, race, and so on) are violating key societal norms, norms that "seem to contribute . . . to a sense of tolerance, fairness, [and] consideration" (p. 148). The kind of thinking in which individuals' special distinguishing features are ignored on principle so that they can be treated equally is new for most children. They first encounter its systematic use in school.

The school, then, is children's most important introduction to the broader life of the society. Schooling is usually the first and most extensive context in which children move out of the affective sphere of the family and into a more impersonal world, where they must associate with people with whom they have no friendship or kinship ties. To traditional bonds of family are added a new set of formal social relations—rules and procedures that purportedly apply to all students with equal force. There is no reason to assume that schools and teachers always live up to such "universalistic" ideals, but there is every reason to assume that they do so more than do students' families and friends. The ideals taught, if sometimes only in the breach, by schools include the norms of procedural equality and rights that are such important constituents of tolerance, especially political tolerance.

An argument similar to Dreeben's and Durkheim's is made by Jackson et al. (1993) in their ethnographic study. According to these authors, schools and teachers are highly influential moral agents, more than they often realize. How is this influence exerted? Jackson and his colleagues, who observed classroom interactions intensively, substantiated many of Durkheim's claims about how schools influence the moral development of students. Durkheim noted that schools and classrooms are "small societies." (John Dewey made the same observation at about the same time.) Like all societies, schools need rules of interpersonal conduct. Schools and classrooms certainly have plenty of these. The content of the rules may be less important than the lesson that in order for groups of comparative strangers to function there must be some rules, and rules that make it possible to live together in groups are what is meant by moral rules and by norms such as tolerance.

Even more subtle than the official rules are the "substructural elements" that Jackson et al. point out are essential to the functioning of a school. These may also be thought of as culture or shared understandings. One is "the assumption of truthfulness" (p. 18), without which student-teacher interchanges would be pointless. Another curricular substructure is the set of assumptions about justice, which includes "the assumption that teachers will ask fair questions and give reasonable exams, that turns will be taken when it comes time to speak, that speakers will be given sufficient time to compose their thoughts, that others will listen to what they say, and that everyone will face similar standards of judgment when it comes to grading and evaluation" (p. 28).

The three works briefly reviewed above all come to essentially the same conclusion: Schools have a profound influence on students' general orientation toward life in society. In particular, schools shape students' notion of right and wrong in public, impersonal encounters. Most important is the norm of procedural fairness, which is learned in schools through a kind of socialization and personality development. The lessons learned are needed if one is to live in a society in which the people with whom one interacts may have interests and values quite different from one's own. It does not take children long to learn the norm of procedural fairness for all persons who fall into the same category. A child usually resorts to it in the first instance to make certain that he or she is treated fairly. Students learn quickly to keep a sharp eye on teachers for signs of favoritism and inequality of treatment. The concept of equal rights is a natural extension of this vigilance. A school can hardly function without it, nor can a modern diverse society. The principle of equal rights leads inevitably, at least on some occasions, to forbearance, to putting up with others who are different from oneself. Schools and societies may get by without ecumenical, multicultural values, but "functional tolerance" (Serow, 1983), or mutual forbearance, is an indispensable minimum.

Individual Modernity

What I have been calling personality development conducive to tolerance has also been studied as personality "modernization." Much of the interesting research based on the concepts of Durkheim and Dreeben has been conducted by scholars studying personality modernization processes in less developed countries. These researchers have identified a "modernity syndrome" (Inkeles, 1973)—a cluster of personality traits and attitudes that are more common in modern (rich, industrialized) societies than in traditional (poor, agricultural) societies. Individuals need to have these traits if they are to function well in modern societies and, conversely, such societies need at least a certain minimum of modern individuals in order to thrive. Tolerance—or its close relatives, such as openness to new experience—always has an important place on lists of traits constituting individual modernity, along with such characteristics as "freedom from absolute submission to received authority . . . and the concomitant granting of more autonomy and rights to those of lesser status and power, such as minority groups and women" (Inkeles & Smith, 1974, p. 109).

Because Inkeles and his various coauthors and followers have contributed importantly to our understanding of how education influences personality in ways that foster tolerance, we will examine their work with some care. Their most important general finding is that personality, as they define it, is not necessarily set or fixed in early childhood. Indeed, some personality changes can occur in adulthood as a consequence of the environments in which men (Inkeles did not study women) are employed.

So what is "individual modernity"? It is, say Inkeles and Smith (1974), "a complex of qualities rather than a single trait" (p. 17); it is a syndrome, of which tolerance is an important part. In a traditional agricultural society, modernity of personality consists of "new ways of thinking and of feeling" (p. 19). Inkeles and Smith identify 19 of these; they are the "themes" that emerge in the Overall Modernity (OM) scale (p. 108). What is modern man like? Most important, he is informed about the world in which he lives (p. 117), he is interested in it, hopes to participate in it, and is aware of its diversity, especially its diversity of beliefs and values. He tends to be open to new experience, to think about the future, and to be ready for change. He has a secular understanding of how things work (such as the weather or machinery) and a belief that one can figure things out and, therefore, that it makes sense to plan ahead. Not only does he believe he can get things done (personal self-efficacy), he thinks other people can do so too. He is likely to hope to accomplish things by improving his education, and he has high occupational aspirations. He is universalistic in his values (see the discussion of Dreeben above) and respects the human dignity of others. In traditional agricultural societies, such individuals are quite rare, but if they are exposed to modern institutions such as factories, bureaucracies, and schools, some people change. "In place of fear of strangers and hostility to those very different from themselves, some have acquired more trust and more tolerance of human diversity. From rigidity and closed-mindedness, they have moved toward flexibility and cognitive openness" (pp. 4-5).

Inkeles and Smith have an unfortunate tendency to talk of modernity as a categorical variable, but it is important to remember that their scale is a continuous measure. They also stress how social structure influences the personality traits making up overall modernity, but they further claim that one cannot have modern structures without modern individuals to man them. This looks like a contradiction or an impossible regression: No modern individuals without modern institutions, no modern institutions without modern individuals. But the contradiction can disappear if one remembers that the modern personality themes are continuous variables that covary with structure. A small increase in personality modernity can modestly influence the modernity of social structures, which can affect personality, and so on. Also, the relation of individuals to structure need not involve the same individuals. For example, some "traditional" individuals may have experience with modern institutions, perhaps by working for foreigners. This experience gives them the know-how to set up, say, a small manufacturing firm. They then hire traditional individuals, who in turn become more modern through contact with a modern institution, in this case a factory. The factory workers send their children to school, something they would not have done had they continued traditional agricultural pursuits in their remote village. Those children seek employment in the modern sector of the economy, and so on.

When modern traits and attitudes can be shown to have developed through exposure to modern institutions, the most important of such institutions is always education. Inkeles and Smith originally studied 6 nations—Argentina, Chile, East Pakistan, India, Israel, and Nigeria. In each of these countries a strong linear relation was found between level of education and modernity score. Even after the effects of 10 other variables were partialed out, the correlations of modernity score with years of schooling ranged from .24 to .52—very high correlations indeed for this kind of research (see the discussion in Chapter 2, this volume). Applying the scale to the study of 6 additional populations, researchers have achieved comparable results; the mean correlation for all 12 nations was .47 (Holsinger & Theisen, 1977, p. 327; Suzman, 1973).

Why do schools have this effect? Modernity theorists generally look to the social-structural characteristics of schools rather than at curricula to explain how children's experiences in schools lead them to adopt modern attitudes and values. As Inkeles and Smith put it, when people change because of the influence of institutions such as schools, "they do so by incorporating the norms implicit in such organizations into their own personality, and by expressing those norms through their own attitudes, values, and behavior" (p. 307). Inkeles and Smith came to this conclusion about the effects of schooling after analyzing data about differences among adults with different levels of schooling.

To substantiate this conclusion, studies of various kinds of schools and pupils were necessary. Such studies were particularly important to distinguish what schools do to students while they are in class from what schools do for students after they leave school (Inkeles & Holsinger, 1973, p. 158). If schools influence students' attitudes while they are in school, this needs to be distinguished from, for example, the tendency of school credentials to open job opportunities. These employment opportunities, in turn, could influence the attitudes of former students after they leave school; even if schooling has no direct effect, it could have an indirect influence on modernity through access to employment.

Because Inkeles's basic description of how schooling influences personality is parallel to Dreeben's, we need not examine it in detail here. I want only to emphasize that, in this interpretation, "learning in the school [is] incidental to the curriculum" (Inkeles, 1973, p. 175). For example, students who develop their personal self-efficacy are likely to do so by generalizing from experiences, not through direct instruction. Succeeding at one thing, such as reading or long division, can lead students to think that they can succeed at other things, and this encourages the growth of their self-efficacy. Self-efficacy, like most of the other traits that make up individual modernity, is not usually taught directly, it is "picked up" through experience. Take another key component of modernity: valuing justice. The grade school teacher does not typically produce a pedagogical unit on justice. Rather, if students learn to value justice, they are more likely to do so by patterning their values and behaviors after those exemplified by the teacher.

Several detailed studies of school experiences help to specify how the lessons of modernity and tolerance are learned in schools. Their importance is increased by the fact that these studies, unlike the original modernity research, gathered data about females as well as males. In one key study of elementary students in Brazil, scores on the OM scale increased sharply with each additional year of school. This was not an aging effect—the scores of children not in school remained unchanged (Holsinger, 1973). On the other hand, in a study of high school students in Puerto Rico, it was found that the link between years of schooling and modernity was comparatively weak at the secondary level. The strong effects in previous studies had mostly been found at the elementary level (Cunningham, 1973; Holsinger, 1973). There may be something of a ceiling effect in the relation between years of schooling and modernity: Schooling increases modernity, but not nearly so quickly after the first 6 years or so (see also Sack, 1973).

This kind of ceiling, I should note, does not seem to limit the growth of tolerance. In fact, as we saw in Chapter 3, the effect is often just the opposite: A threshold effect appears to be at work; not until an individual had already completed quite a few years of schooling (around 12) does an additional year of study have a major effect on tolerance. I suspect, and other evidence to be reviewed below suggests, that the effect of years of school and type of schooling varies by level to produce a U-shaped relation: Growth can be fairly rapid in the elementary years, tends to be slower in secondary years, and occurs more rapidly again in higher education.

In general, parental attitudes have been found to be much less important than schooling in determining individuals' modernity. Indeed, it has been found that in societies such as traditional Tunisia, parents usually oppose any modernizing tendencies by their children, especially by their daughters. Thus, the lessons that schools teach tend to be of greatest importance to individuals who have little opportunity to learn them in other contexts, such as females in Islamic countries. On the other hand, if a school's lessons are actively opposed by a traditional society, its effects can be close to nil. In fact, very quickly after leaving school, Tunisian students' gains in modernity were lost. Without the support of other institutions, the attitudes of students (especially females) reverted to what they were before the individuals attended school (Klineberg, 1973). This finding is, of course, very powerful evidence of the causal impact of school: The effect persisted and grew with schooling, but it quickly faded once the independent variable (schooling) was removed.

Two findings in the studies just reviewed are especially important, because they place almost beyond any reasonable doubt the influence of schooling on children's modernity. First is Klineberg's evidence that students' modernity declines when schooling stops; second is Holsinger's demonstration that children who were not in school did not gain in modernity as they aged. Neither of these studies, nor both of them together, constitutes "proof" of the effects of education, certainly, but each provides very strong evidence. Modernity research is not immune to criticism, of course. Psychometric questions about the scales used (Armer, 1976) and a reemphasis on the continuing importance of traditional, "primordial" ethnic ties (Greeley, 1974) both suggest that any conclusions must be tentative. But the link between education and individual modernity (including tolerance) is at minimum a highly reasonable working hypothesis.

On the other hand, there is growing evidence that the development of modern institutions does not always reduce all traditional attitudes. Ethnic hatred, for example, can flourish in modern societies. Modern economic development can reduce communications barriers, thereby increasing the arena of interethnic competition, which in turn can lead to increased ethnocentrism and other forms of traditional thinking (Hodson, Sekulic, & Massey, 1994). Looking at things the other way around, modern attitudes and personalities do not always require modern economic institutions and industrial production in order to emerge. Crenshaw (1995) has found that even agricultural societies can support political democracy, presuming that they have a sufficient level of social complexity. The aspect of Crenshaw's social complexity that most interests us is, of course, schooling. Education (measured as percentage of the population in secondary school) was found to be a significant predictor of a nation's score on Crenshaw's "political democracy index" in 11 of his 12 models. Education had this effect regardless of the level or type of economic development.

The lessons of modernity can, of course, be learned in other settings besides schools. The home is one obvious place, but schools and teachers operate in a public context in which modernity plays a bigger role than in the private milieu of the family. Individuals may learn either traditional or modern values at home, but families lack the structural characteristics of public institutions (such as the interaction of large numbers of strangers), and these structures are among the main "teachers" of modernity. Still, while schools are institutions in which the development of individual modernity is fostered, there are other public arenas in which modern personality development can occur and in which tolerance may be learned. Indeed, Inkeles and his colleagues originally set out to demonstrate the importance of the workplace for the development of values and attitudes, but they found that although the work environment mattered, it did not match early schooling in its ability to influence personality development (compare Sack, 1973).

Self-Direction and Conforming to Authority

In a study of the occupational conditions that encourage and discourage conformist attitudes in the United States, Kohn (1969) reached similar conclusions, through a different route, about the effects of modern institutions, including schools, on personality. Like Inkeles, Kohn went looking for occupational effects, and he found them, but he also found educational effects that were much larger. Kohn's outcome variable, "conformity," is strongly, but inversely, related to Inkeles's "individual modernity"; that is, someone who is modern would be nonconformist. Kohn cites Inkeles's evidence that "everywhere the movement of peasants into industrial occupations results in changes in attitudes, values and beliefs . . . that are *altogether consonant* with the effects we attribute to occupational self-direction" (p. 194; emphasis added). "Conformity," as defined and measured in Kohn's work, is "necessarily anti-civil-libertarian"; it is necessarily politically intolerant. But Kohn meant his concept to be broader than politics and to include social and moral (in)tolerance, and "even beliefs about proper dress and deportment" (p. 201). Kohn was looking, then, for something that pervades the personality, not merely a few isolated attitudes. However, he distanced himself from the idea of a depth psychology authoritarian personality structure; he was unwilling to accept the psychodynamic assumptions of Adorno, Frenkel-Brunswick, Levinson, and Sanford (1950) that authoritarian prejudice arises from, and serves the function of maintaining, a sick personality. Psychodynamic theories tend to assume that personality is formed quite early in life and that little fundamental change is possible. Kohn, like Inkeles, was more interested in individuals' postchildhood experiences, especially in how people's occupations influence their personalities.

Kohn's book is titled *Class and Conformity* (1969). His basic idea is that socioeconomic class influences parents' beliefs about good child rearing in ways that affect their children's political, social, and moral values. Kohn's thesis, in a nutshell, is that working-class parents emphasize conformity to external authority, whereas middle-class parents stress internal self-direction. Given that education level is one of Kohn's two main components of "class" (the other is occupational position), and that education is the component that predicts most of the variance in conformity, a more accurate title for Kohn's book would be *Education and Conformity*. Kohn dealt with education mostly as a proxy for class. That is similar to the mistake Inkeles made. Kohn treated the most powerful explanatory variable (education) as a measure of something else (class). Inkeles treated education mostly as an annoyance to be controlled so that one could look more closely at the influence of working in factories. But both authors have reported their data in such a way that it is possible to get at the evidence about education. Besides, in later work, both Inkeles and Kohn have examined education and its effects.

Initially, Kohn's emphasis was on the effects of the characteristics of an individual's work. Certain types of jobs, particularly those in which the work is complicated and demands independent judgment (high in "occupational self-direction"), were found to be related to intellectual flexibility, tolerance, and nonauthoritarianism. The correlations between (non)conformity and class (defined as years of school plus occupational self-direction) were not large. In fact, working-class people and middle-class people had many more values in common than they had differences of beliefs about topics such as the most important aims of child rearing (Kohn, 1969, pp. 85-86). The relation of class to such values was even smaller when education was not part of the definition of class. But the relation of occupational self-direction to conformity to external authority has been confirmed several times in cross-national studies as well as with U.S. samples (Kohn, 1971; Korman, 1975; Sack, 1973; Slomczynski, 1989). For our purposes, the key fact is that for most individuals, occupational influences are considerably less significant as determinants of authoritarian conformity than are the effects of numbers of years of schooling.

Because schooling is the important variable, it would seem reasonable to look at it more closely to see what aspects of the school experience most influence tolerance and related attitudes. In the mid-1980s, Kohn and colleagues addressed the problem of identifying "the mechanisms by which education affects personality" (Miller, Kohn, & Schooler, 1986, p. 372; see also Miller, Slomczynski, & Kohn, 1985). They took the idea of occupational self-direction and applied it to the structure of the curriculum. They examined "educational

self-direction," which is "the use of initiative, thought, and independent judgment in schoolwork" (p. 372). Their conclusion, in brief, is that educational
self-direction in schooling has the same kind of effect as occupational self-
direction in the workplace: It leads to more intellectual flexibility and reduces
authoritarian conformity.

We can conclude, then, that one reason increases in tolerance result from
increases in education is the fact that the higher up the educational ladder
students go, the more likely they are to encounter complex, self-directed
curricula. Complex schoolwork that demands educational self-direction fosters
personality development conducive to the development of tolerant attitudes.
And, not incidentally, the more education students have, the more likely they
are, upon leaving school, to acquire employment involving complex, self-
directed work. Hence, there are both direct effects of schooling on tolerance
(specifically in Miller et al., 1985, on "ideational flexibility") and indirect effects
through occupational opportunities.

To disentangle the direct from the indirect effects of education, we need
studies of students in schools. There are some such studies. Among the more
interesting of these is Nielsen's (1977) comparative work on 14-year-old West
German and U.S. high school students. He found that students who had experienced a democratic, nonauthoritarian school climate, where they believed they
were rewarded for independence of thought and felt free to ask questions, were
more likely to favor tolerating political dissent. Nielsen's specification of school
climate closely parallels Miller et al.'s (1985) discussion of educational self-
direction: "School social climates which encourage independence of thought
[and] emphasize concept (as opposed to rote) learning" (p. 11) were more likely
to produce students who were tolerant of dissent. As we shall see below,
however, climate thus defined had less influence than students' political knowledge; further, the influence of climate was often indirect, through knowledge.
Nonetheless, climate and structure did have small independent effects. In sum,
although different studies have assigned different ranks to the importance of the
variables, there seems little doubt that schools influence individuals by their
structures, not only by their curricula, and that schools' social rules and academic
procedures can have effects quite apart from the content of studies.

Conclusions on Dreeben, Inkeles, and Kohn

The key ideas in the works of Dreeben, Inkeles, and Kohn emerged at about
the same time, in the 1950s and especially the 1960s. Their concepts are all
related, and there is enough mutual citation that we can be sure that they were

aware of the family resemblances among their works. We might want to call the set of research traits they share a scholarly "syndrome." In any case, the works of Dreeben, Inkeles, Kohn, and others fit quite nicely with what I am trying to demonstrate here: that education promotes tolerance partly by its effects on personality. Many researchers would disagree with these authors, however, and see personality as less variant, less open to influence from organizational structures. Some of the debate between those who see personality as largely unchanging and those who see it as alterable reflects a definitional difference. Those who think of personality as changeable tend to include in their definition of personality things that everyone agrees actually change (such as attitudes and beliefs). However, as we have seen in Chapter 3, even here there is a basic divide between those social psychologists and others who see short-term individual attitudes as almost impossible to change and sociologists, political scientists, and others who spend much time documenting long-term aggregate change and explaining it by reference to characteristics of the social structure. These are not mutually exclusive positions, of course.

Be that as it may, for us, at present, the question is whether tolerance is set in a person's makeup earlier rather than later, whether there is more rather than less possibility for change. One camp is formed by those who say that personality and attitudes are late-fixed/more-changeable, the other by those who say they are early-fixed/less-changeable. Perhaps the best-known advocate of the early/less camp is Gordon Allport, whose work we shall examine briefly here and more extensively in the next chapter.

More Psychologically Oriented Approaches

The psychologically oriented researchers working on our subject generally claim that the burden of proof, and it is a heavy burden, is on those who would say that tolerance is not deeply embedded in individual personality. They tend to stress that a person's tolerance or intolerance is rooted in personality traits, which is very hard to change through the manipulation of the individual's environment.

The Nature of Prejudice and
The Authoritarian Personality

Few works have shaped social psychology as importantly as Allport's *The Nature of Prejudice* (1954). Allport firmly contends that prejudice "is ultimately a problem of personality formation and development" (p. 41); it is a "trait of personality" (p. 73). As such, it is not susceptible to piecemeal efforts to change it. But if one combs carefully through *The Nature of Prejudice,* one finds that Allport was fundamentally ambiguous about whether one can reduce prejudice by manipulating situational variables to induce personality change. On the one hand, he claimed that "since the home is the chief and earliest source of prejudiced attitudes, we should not expect too much from programs of intercultural educa- tion in schools." On the other hand, he noted that the "cumulative effects" of "extra-familial influences" seem to be effective in reducing prejudice (p. 296).

But Allport's guarded optimism about the possible benefits of social inter- vention never quite overcame his psychodynamic beliefs. People who have prejudiced personalities, he said, seem more open to frustration but less able to tolerate it. Rather than "meeting their frustrations head on," they respond with "infantile anger and displacement" (p. 348). They also tend to feel easily threatened, to be assailed by an "insecurity that seems to lie at the root of the personality." The prejudiced person has "a weak ego unable to face its conflicts squarely and unflinchingly" (pp. 396-397). Such an individual needs therapy more than education.

There is a second, more cognitive, strand in Allport's thinking, and this, I believe, is ultimately at the root of his optimism about the possibility of reducing prejudice through intergroup contact (see Chapter 5) and through education. Because "ethnic prejudice is an antipathy based upon a *faulty* and inflexible generalization" (p. 9; emphasis added), the identification of a prejudice must involve a factual or empirical judgment about whether the belief is "faulty." Although prejudice is a feeling, an antipathy, it originates in and is maintained by cognitive failings that promote faulty generalizations. It seems reasonable to suggest, therefore, that one possible treatment for prejudice could be to teach rules of rational generalization, particularly rules that are flexible enough to accommodate new information. Allport claimed that the discovery of the cog- nitive element in prejudice is the "most momentous discovery of psychological research in the field of prejudice." That discovery, in brief, is that "the cognitive processes of prejudiced people are in general different from the cognitive processes of tolerant people." Prejudice is "likely to be a reflection of . . . [a person's] whole habit of thinking about the world he lives in" (pp. 174-175; compare Ezekiel, 1995).

A survey of personality researchers dealing with prejudice and tolerance would yield a very high percentage who include a cognitive element as key to understanding prejudice and intolerance. However, what that element is called varies. It varies mainly according to researchers' tastes—or their disciplines' academic cultures. For example, one might call a person's tendency to solve problems rationally a personality trait, a cognitive characteristic, or a cognitive (versus affective) aspect of personality. In the first half of this chapter I have discussed researchers who view a preference for reason as a personality trait, as part of a person's emotional makeup. In the second half, we will examine research by those who stress the cognitive side of cognitive-cum-emotional characteristics such as prejudice, stereotyping, tolerance, and intolerance. But, as I shall note repeatedly, the differences between the two sides are often small.

More important differences exist on the question of whether education can influence these traits and characteristics, whether they be cognitive, emotional, or some combination of the two. Some well-known traditions of scholarship are based on the assumption that personality traits are too fundamental to be influenced much by schooling. Inglehart's (1990) work on "postmaterialism" is an important example. His measures of postmaterialism include items dealing with tolerance (especially free speech), and he is firm about the inconsequential role of education in fostering postmaterialism. He admits that there is a strong statistical association between education level and level of postmaterialism. The question is whether the variance of education with tolerance (or postmaterialism) is due to something that happens to students in schools or whether schooling and postmaterialism are each caused by a third variable. Inglehart thinks that third variable is wealthy parents. Being raised in an economically secure setting provides an individual with psychological security during his or her formative years, which leads to postmaterialism; and, of course, having wealthy parents also increases the likelihood that a person will obtain more advanced education. There is considerable debate about this interpretation, even among those using Inglehart's own evidence. Given the quality of the data, it is not possible to settle this question, but in my view, those who contend that Inglehart's outcome variable is importantly determined by (not merely associated with) education have the stronger case (Duch & Taylor, 1993, 1994).

The role of education has also been very important in later studies of *The Authoritarian Personality* (Adorno et al., 1950). This book and its various scales have been reanalyzed extraordinarily often. Here I can say only a few words about its basic ideas before turning to the question of the effects of education. According to Adorno and his coauthors, social attitudes such as prejudice, anti-Semitism, and ethnocentrism have personality functions. Hating Jews, for example, might make it easier for some personalities to deal with feelings of insecurity brought about by the way they were raised. An important mechanism for authoritarians is projection: "Impulses which cannot be admitted to the conscious ego tend to be projected onto minority groups" (Sanford, 1973, p. 145). For example, a person preoccupied with sex, but who finds this difficult to admit, might claim that others (such as Blacks or gays) are preoccupied with sex. The most outrageous, and the clearest, example of such projection was the Nazi claim that Jews were sadistic. The kind of person most likely to engage in projection and to resort to ethnocentrism and anti-Semitism to protect his or her own weak ego is the authoritarian personality. The main measure of the authoritarian personality is the famous F scale, which was designed to measure "potential fascism [F] in the personality" (Sanford, 1973, p. 149).

Our two-part question is as follows: If the authoritarian personality is a valuable way to look at the origins of tolerance and intolerance, then is this personality syndrome open to the influence of education? The only kind of personality theory we cannot accommodate in this book would be one that claims that social, political, and moral attitudes and beliefs are exclusively determined by personality traits and that those traits are wholly fixed before school age. The Freudian roots of the authors of *The Authoritarian Personality* led them to place their greatest emphasis on the kind of child rearing to which individuals were subject as the source of authoritarianism. But the theory is compatible with interpretations that do not insist on outcomes wholly determined by the infancy/toddler years. Indeed, Nevitt Sanford, one of the original authors of the study, claimed that a low level of education "is a major factor in authoritarianism." This is the main reason low socioeconomic status is tied to authoritarianism—working-class people have lower levels of education (Sanford, 1973, p. 159; note that this interpretation is the exact opposite of Inglehart's, discussed in Chapter 3). Sanford also did extensive subsequent research showing that college education reduces authoritarianism.[3] Like Allport and Kohn, Sanford too saw the emotional needs and cognitive characteristics that lead to prejudice, ethnocentrism, and authoritarianism as linked: "Which comes first, the cognitive failings or the inner conflicts? Is it necessary to ask this question about processes so intimately bound up together?" (p. 163).

Work on authoritarianism has been extensive. Much controversy has surrounded so-called working-class authoritarianism, or the tendency of members of the working class to be as attracted to extremist right-wing political movements as to left-wing ideologies such as communism and socialism. Lipset's *Political Man* (1981), originally published in 1960, first laid out the general argument. His thesis seemed to many critics to involve a political agenda (e.g., Miller & Riessman, 1961); the theory of worker authoritarianism appeared designed to thumb the nose at Marxists. Be that as it may, the main conclusion of interest for our purposes is the importance of education. There is little if any correlation between occupational status and authoritarianism once education has been controlled. Any tendency of working-class people to be attracted to the extremist political right is not easily attributable to what they do to make a living; it has much more to do with their level of education (Gabennesch, 1972; Grabb, 1979; Lipset, 1981).

Further developments in the measurement of authoritarianism also occurred in the 1950s and 1960s. Most important of these was work by Rokeach (1960), who developed what can be thought of as a general, content-free variant of the F scale, one that identifies left- as well as right-wing authoritarianism. Rokeach calls this "dogmatism," a key measure of which is "closed-mindedness." A version of either authoritarianism (F scale) or dogmatism has been used in many subsequent studies of tolerance. Authoritarianism was very prominent in Kohn's studies of class and conformity, discussed above (see also Rose, 1969), and dogmatism has had a prominent place in Sullivan et al.'s studies of political tolerance. It is to these that we now turn, because they most fully explore the personality development explanation of the origins of tolerance.

The work of Sullivan and various colleagues has sometimes been viewed as a challenge to the idea that education fosters political tolerance. However, the findings of these researchers are more accurately seen, I believe, as supplying causal links between years of education and tolerance; they identify how education is associated with tolerance. The research of Sullivan and his colleagues presents a challenge to the idea that education has an effect only if one believes that mere time served in schools or years logged in the education system in and of themselves foster tolerance. But surely any changes in important attitudes and values due to schooling—that is, any changes that are not maturation effects—have to be attributable to something that occurs in schools, not simply to the passage of time. Sullivan and colleagues specify what occurs, and their specifications fall largely into the personality development strand of explanation. Three works by this research group are most important for a review of the potential links of education, through personality, to tolerance: Sullivan, Marcus, Piereson, and Feldman's "The Development of Political Tolerance" (1979); Sullivan, Piereson, and Marcus's *Political Tolerance and American Democracy* (1982); and Marcus, Sullivan, Theiss-Morse, and Wood's *With Malice Toward Some* (1995).

These three studies take somewhat different approaches. The configuration of the personality variables studied and the way they are measured varies among them, but the general pattern of conclusions is very consistent. One major personality psychology variable Sullivan and colleagues use is Rokeach's (1960) "dogmatism" (or rigidity of thought or closed-mindedness scale), discussed briefly above. They also build importantly on Maslow's (1954) concept of a "need hierarchy." According to Maslow, people have a series of needs that are arranged in stages; that is, a person cannot move to the higher levels until his or her lower-level psychological needs are met. The arrangement of needs in this hierarchy, from lowest to highest, is as follows: physiological, safety and security, affiliation and love, self-esteem, and self-actualization. The highest of these is rather vague, or abstract. Self-actualization seems to be the level attributed to anyone who does not say to a researcher that one of the other levels is very important. The research technique is basically to ask people what matters most to them. If they say, for instance, "having enough money" or "living in a safe neighborhood," they fall at the low end of the needs hierarchy. If they say "feeling as though I make a contribution" or "creativity," they are at the high end. This does not mean, of course, that people who value creativity do not also value having enough money. Typically, according to Maslow, it means that they do not need to worry overly much about money so that they can "afford" to try to be creative. Later theorists have suggested that some people may "skip" or reorder stages—starving artists, for example. But starving artists usually do not actually starve (rather, they eat cheap food), and such individuals are, in any case, quite rare. For most people, the needs hierarchy provides an accurate description.

What does all this have to do with tolerance? Basically, people who fall at the high end of the needs hierarchy tend also to score high on tolerance scales. People who score low on dogmatism usually score high on measures of tolerance. One might suspect, and I have suggested as much in Chapter 3, that open-mindedness is tolerance. No wonder there is a correlation between the two. If open-mindedness and tolerance are actually the same thing, the only reason the correlation between them is not perfect is measurement error. However, as there are some people at the rigid end of the dogmatism scale (closed-minded) who score high on tolerance, this is not likely (Sullivan et al., 1982; see also Zalkind, Gaugler, & Schwartz, 1975, for a brief discussion). In sum, self-esteem, self-actualization, and (lack of) dogmatism are all related importantly to tolerance (see Staub, 1989). These relations hold in complicated path models with many controls for other variables. Are self-esteem, self-actualization, and low dogmatism, in turn, related to education? Briefly, yes.

The paths by which education influences personality and thereby tolerance are sometimes complex. The simplest path routinely encountered in the literature is that mentioned by Sullivan et al. (1979):

Education → Self-Esteem → Tolerance

The more education one has, the higher, on average, is one's self-esteem; the higher one's self-esteem, the greater one's political tolerance.

These links are called into question, however, by longitudinal research on a large, nationally representative sample of the high school graduating class of 1972. Although self-esteem level had a strong bivariate association with education level when subjects were reinterviewed in 1986, this association was reduced to statistical insignificance once controls for other variables were added. The association of education with self-direction, however, did seem attributable to students' college experiences (Knox, Lindsay, & Kolb, 1993). In their extensive review of the literature, Pascarella and Terenzini (1991) found at best modest effects of advanced education on self-esteem. They conclude that there are "probably small, and to some extent indirect, effects of college on self-esteem" (p. 181).

Using a more complicated model, Sullivan et al. (1982) summed self-esteem, self-actualization, low dogmatism, and faith in people into one composite variable, which they call "psychological security." The pattern was the same as with their simpler self-esteem measure: Education was associated with psychological security, which, in turn, was associated with tolerance. More interesting still is a set of two intervening variables:

$$\text{Education} \xrightarrow{\ .28\ } \begin{matrix}\text{Psychological}\\ \text{Security}\end{matrix} \xrightarrow{\ .51\ } \begin{matrix}\text{General Norms}\\ \text{of Democracy}\end{matrix} \xrightarrow{\ .33\ } \text{Tolerance}$$

In this model (Sullivan et al., 1982, p. 221), education leads to psychological security, which leads people to be more likely to support general norms of democracy, which support is associated with a higher likelihood of tolerance. (The numbers above the arrows are the path coefficients.)

The direct association between years of education and tolerance is nil in these models.[4] Some have interpreted this as a challenge to the importance of education, but I would argue that the lack of a direct association is, rather, a sign of progress in inferring causation. The more we know about *how* education fosters tolerance, the smaller the direct association between years of schooling and tolerance will be. The bigger the direct association, the more there is for us to explain. Once we have done the explaining, and have found the paths of education's influence, the direct association of years of education and tolerance should shrink to nothing. If these arguments are correct, perhaps supporters of education dismayed by Sullivan et al.'s finding that education has no direct association should reconsider. Explaining an association with intervening variables is not the same as explaining it away.

In their most recent work on tolerance, Sullivan and colleagues have added one more important personality need to their list of explanatory variables—the "need for cognition" (Marcus et al., 1995), a psychological need that naturally leads us to the next section.

Cognitive Development

Of the four clusters of theories accounting for the links between schooling and tolerance, what can be called *cognitive sophistication theory* (Nunn, Crockett, & Williams, 1978, p. 65; Quinley & Glock, 1979, pp. 34-35) is surely the oldest and one of the most frequently cited. But, in the last analysis, it is less fully developed than any of the others. The general argument is as follows: In the growth of tolerance, cognitive maturity may be more important than the psychological maturity emphasized by most modernization theories—admitting, of course, that it is not easy to separate the two sorts of maturity. Although certain personality traits are undoubtedly conducive to (but not necessary for) the development of social and moral tolerance in individuals, cognitive capacities of a somewhat advanced nature are necessary for individuals to acquire the beliefs and commitments that constitute some kinds of tolerance. Without the ability to imagine broad social or temporally distant consequences, for example, a person cannot understand the reasons for tolerating political nonconformists or opponents. Preadolescent children are too developmentally immature to understand such consequences (Adelson & O'Neil, 1966; Jones, 1980; Owen & Dennis, 1987; Zellman, 1975; Zellman & Sears, 1971), and many, perhaps most, adults have not developed the needed cognitive capacities either.

Selznick and Steinberg (1969), in their study of the roots of anti-Semitism, made what is still one of the most forceful arguments ever offered for the cognitive sophistication approach. And they made it specifically to challenge the thesis of the authoritarian personality. In attempts to understand persons who hold manifestly irrational anti-Semitic beliefs, there are two main approaches: One is based in the belief that such persons have psychological inadequacies; the other is based in the belief that they have intellectual deficiencies. The debate between adherents of these two approaches can be harsh. For example, some people still believe that Jews drink the blood of Christians. Are people who believe this, to put it colloquially, crazy or stupid? Do they have personality disorders and psychological needs that lead them to accept absurd beliefs, or do they lack the intellectual wherewithal to reject superstition? Selznick and Steinberg favor the second kind of explanation. They say that most people with anti-Semitic views have a "lack of intellectual sophistication," not "personal psychopathology." Because anti-Semitism is widespread in the population, they argue, it can be learned through ordinary "processes of socialization. The more pertinent question is why . . . some people reject anti-Semitic beliefs." The cognitive capacities that enable people to reject prejudice, they conclude, are "transmitted mainly through the educational system" (pp. 168-169).

A related version of the cognitive sophistication approach contends that political tolerance is uncommon because it is hard to learn. This view has been most thoroughly expounded by McClosky and Brill (1983), who argue that the principles upon which political tolerance and civil liberties rest "are highly complex and recondite" (p. 28). At least, they maintain, "defending the civil liberties of outcasts, dissenters, criminals, or other marginal members of society ordinarily entails a more difficult and complex decision process than is involved in suppressing them" (pp. 18-19). Granting this, is the ability to handle complex decision processes fostered in schools? McClosky and Brill say that education is an important variable, but they conclude that social learning by adults outside of schools does more to generate tolerance.[5]

Be that as it may, the case for the significance of education, particularly higher education, has often been made by university apologists. Tolerance of diverse opinions is a pedagogical ideal virtually as old as higher education (but one that has less often guided primary and secondary school educators). As Robert de Sorbon put it seven centuries ago, "Nothing is perfectly known until it has been masticated in the jaws of debate" (quoted in Durkheim, 1969, p. 165), and one cannot have debates without tolerating opponents. From Abelard's *sic et non* (for and against) to Aquinas's contention that "men who look for the truth without considering their doubts first are like people who do not look where they are going" (quoted in Kors, 1990, p. 83), it was believed by the earliest university scholars that higher education *is* disputation. This belief that advanced education requires tolerance of intellectual diversity dates back to ancient Greece and was most explicitly stated by Aristotle in the *Topics,* where he concluded that "if we have no one else with whom to argue, we must do so with ourselves" (Kors, 1990, p. 82). Whenever advanced education has flourished, so has this ideal that divergent opinions must be available—at least to "responsible" scholars.

Seen thus, tolerance, particularly freedom of expression, is part of the professional ethics of scholars and intellectuals.[6] Their work is made difficult if not impossible without it. It is not surprising, therefore, that institutions that intellectuals (partly) control should foster one of their key values. Historically, tolerance has been most developed in societies with relatively strong and autonomous intellectual classes, often with an institutional base in universities. In such societies, university students, in addition to developing their general cognitive abilities and acquiring occupational credentials, may be introduced to the ways intellectual disciplines can encourage criticism and debate. In this manner, even the most formal academic subjects—if they familiarize students with the professional ethics of scientists and scholars and if these principles are generalized—could easily have important sociopolitical consequences for the development of tolerance, more important perhaps than courses explicitly intended to teach it. For example, Nevitt Sanford (1973) tells about a student "whose system of primitive, right-wing authoritarian ideas was changed through a class in psychological statistics." The student could not adhere to her narrow beliefs "in the face of knowledge about variability, probability, and so forth" (pp. 162-163).

Although the above arguments seem reasonable enough and have often been repeated, what evidence do we have for them? There are two steps in the argument, two stages in the demonstration, which I will investigate by turns below: (1) Education increases cognitive sophistication; (2) cognitive sophistication fosters tolerance.

Does Education Increase Cognitive Sophistication?

Many studies of the relation of cognitive sophistication and tolerance have simply assumed a causal relationship between cognitive sophistication and years of postcompulsory schooling. This assumed relationship, in turn, is said to explain the link between education and tolerance. A causal link between cognitive development and years of schooling could be due to a tendency of years of schooling to increase cognitive development, or it could be due to the fact that cognitively sophisticated individuals seek out additional years of schooling—or both, of course. Fortunately, some fairly direct studies help forge this first link in our chain of argument. Usually, the more important studies that have assessed education's effects on cognitive development have focused on higher education (but see Goodrich, 1996).

Studies of College Effects

A fairly large body of research exists regarding the influence of higher education on students' attitudes and beliefs. Most of the conclusions, whether the studies have been based on convenience samples at single institutions or on broad national surveys, point in the same direction: Higher education has a liberalizing influence; the more exposed students are to it, the more they are likely to be tolerant; and seniors are more tolerant on average than are freshmen (Feldman & Newcomb, 1969; Nunn, 1973; Pascarella & Terenzini, 1991; Perry, 1970). Also particularly worthy of note for the cognitive sophistication hypothesis is that the higher students' grades, the more likely they are to be tolerant, a result that has appeared in studies of high school students as well (Cunningham, 1973; Nielsen, 1977).

But university students, who are central to the cognitive sophistication hypothesis, have been less well studied than one might expect. Rich (1980) has introduced some important methodological criticisms of many earlier research efforts. He contends that, by not controlling simultaneously for other variables, many studies have attributed an effect to college education that actually originated in students' backgrounds. In his own study of students' support for civil liberties, Rich found that when college made a difference, very often it did so by facilitating students' "initial proclivities" (p. 27). That is, students who started out fairly supportive of civil liberties tended to become more so, whereas those who entered college conservative about civil liberties often became more conservative. But even Rich, in his caution and after introducing several controls, found two college variables that had significant effects on support for civil liberties: the students' grades and the selectivity of the institution they were attending. He notes that the "better students become more tolerant, while poorer students do not change at all" (p. 28). Good grades and academic selectivity, it can be argued, constitute fairly accurate proxy measures for cognitive sophistication.

Even better for identifying college effects than cross-sectional studies with multivariate controls, such as Rich's, are longitudinal studies with such controls. Longitudinal studies are quite rare, which makes work such as that of Funk and Willits (1987) particularly important. These researchers surveyed high school sophomores in 1970 and conducted a follow-up study in 1981. Although not a study of tolerance per se, this research is very convincing about the liberalizing influence of education on attitudes, including attitudes often related to tolerance: low traditionalism about sex roles and low religiosity. Because their study was truly longitudinal, Funk and Willits could control for the prior attitudes of their subjects. They also used a comparison group of people who did not go to college. Their findings, in brief, were that the liberalizing influence of higher education persisted even when selection effects, prior attitudes, and several other important variables (e.g., gender and geographic mobility) were controlled for. The higher the respondents' educational attainment, the lower their scores on scales measuring religiosity and traditionalism in sex role attitudes. The authors did not directly investigate how college exerted this influence, but they concluded that their evidence is consistent with an interpretation that college stimulates cognitive development by bringing about exposure to new ideas.

Pascarella and Terenzini (1991) conducted an extensive review of the effects of higher education on general cognitive skills and intellectual growth. The outcome variables were variously labeled in different studies; "reasoning skills, critical thinking, intellectual flexibility, reflective judgment, cognitive complexity" (p. 114) were among the more common terms. The results of the many studies reviewed by Pascarella and Terenzini make it plain that college seniors are more advanced on measures of these cognitive outcomes than are freshmen. However, the advanced cognitive skills of seniors may be due to many things other than the influence of higher education. Most important, less-able students might flunk out or drop out before their senior year, leaving only the more-able students to be measured. But there have been enough longitudinal studies with good controls to permit confidence in the conclusion that "freshman-senior differences on various measures of critical thinking" (p. 129) cannot be attributed only to the fact that seniors are 4 years older and that less-able students are more likely to leave college.

Schommer (1993) examined high school and college students' epistemological beliefs. She particularly studied three naive epistemological beliefs: *quick learning,* the belief that learning happens quickly or not at all; *simple knowledge,* the view of knowledge as a basket of unconnected facts; and *certain knowledge,* the idea that knowledge does not change (p. 357). Among her high school student subjects the unsophisticated view—that knowledge is simple, quick, and unchanging—was fairly widespread. In the first year of high school, there were no differences between gifted and nongifted students. But by the senior year of high school, the gifted students were less likely to believe in simple and quick learning. Among college students, Schommer discovered somewhat parallel differences in beliefs about knowledge: 2-year college students were more likely than 4-year college students to believe in simple, quick, unchanging knowledge. Some of these differences were "eliminated" when parental education level was controlled for. Specifically, parents with higher levels of education had children who were less likely to have naive epistemological beliefs. Hence, students' giftedness, their parents' education, and the type of college they attended all seemed to have important effects on whether or not they held beliefs that were "barriers to higher-level thinking" (p. 366).

Studies of the influences of different kinds of institutions (2-year, 4-year, public, private, and so on) on cognitive development do not usually yield strong effects. Effects are particularly weak after the fact that different kinds of students go to different kinds of institutions is controlled for. The association of students' major fields of study with their attitudes and values are generally stronger (contrast Rich, 1980; Stembler, 1961), but we have the same interpretive problem with these studies: We cannot tell whether tolerant students are more likely to be found in certain fields because of the ways those disciplines influence them or because tolerant students choose tolerant disciplines—or, most likely perhaps, both. A frequently found association of field of study and attitudes is the liberalizing effect and tolerance-inducing effect of higher education in the social sciences (Guimond, 1989).[7]

One of the few longitudinal studies investigating this relation between academic discipline and political doctrine examined the attitudes of 1969 graduates of the University of Michigan 10 years later (1979) to assess the effects of postbaccalaureate study (Hoge & Hoge, 1984). Postgraduate education was found to have a strong influence on attitudes, and the patterns of influence were similar to those found in several other studies. For example, support for free enterprise values went up among those who had advanced degrees in fields such as accounting, medicine, and engineering, whereas education in the social sciences and humanities weakened commitment to capitalism. However, support for free enterprise and conservative economic beliefs did not predict hostility toward deviant social groups among this sample of university graduates. This fits with a finding I have noted several times: Well-educated people are more likely to show tolerance of political, social, and moral nonconformists than they are to have left-wing views about the economy or to show compassion toward the poor (see Gans, 1995).

If different kinds of institutions and different fields of study influence students' attitudes and beliefs, this may be because the faculty members in those institutions and fields have different beliefs. Such faculty could attract students with similar views or could persuade students of their views—or, again, most likely both. Studies of faculty political and social values have generally revealed the same patterns by institution and by academic discipline as have studies of students' values. Examples from the most extensive of such studies, based on a national sample of faculty, are presented in Table 4.1.

The top part of the table lists the three types of institutions with the most and the three with the fewest faculty members who identify themselves as either "liberal" or "left." Selective liberal arts colleges (liberal arts I) and research

TABLE 4.1 Political Self-Identification of Faculty, by Type of Institution and Academic Field, 1984 (in percentages)

	Left	Liberal	Total
Type of college			
Liberal arts I	13.6	45.6	59.2
Comprehensive university and college II	8.9	38.0	46.9
Research university I	6.4	39.0	45.4
Liberal arts II	2.9	30.3	33.2
2-year college	3.9	27.8	31.7
Doctoral university II	4.5	35.2	39.7
Field of study			
Sociology	29.8	48.6	78.4
Social work	19.3	48.1	67.4
Political science	17.8	48.3	66.1
Psychology	8.1	56.9	65.0
History	10.0	46.0	56.0
Agriculture	0.0	13.4	13.4
Business	0.7	15.9	16.6
Physical education	0.0	17.6	17.6
Home economics	0.0	21.8	21.8
Industrial arts	0.0	26.7	26.7

SOURCE: Hamilton and Hargens (1993, pp. 614, 624).

universities had the most left-leaning faculty members, whereas 2-year colleges and less selective liberal arts colleges (liberal arts II) had the fewest. Although these differences are substantial, there was considerably more variety among academic fields than among institutional types (and much of the difference among types is probably due to the distribution of fields across the types). Table 4.1 also lists, in the section on field of study, the five most and the five least liberal/left fields. The social sciences (with the exception of economics) have dramatically more faculty on the left of the political spectrum than do vocational fields such as agriculture and business. Whether these characteristics of faculty members influence their students is impossible to ascertain with these data, but were there no such differences among faculty, one promising explanation for the effects of college on students' values would be eliminated. The correlation of faculty and student political values in the same disciplines means that it is possible that faculty beliefs influence students' beliefs, although this has not been studied directly.

As we saw in Chapter 2, Astin (1993) found similar patterns in students' self-identifications. Also, like Astin, Hamilton and Hargens (1993) found conservative trends: The proportion of professors calling themselves conservative increased about 7% from 1969 to 1984. Concerns about the influence of left-wing professors, sometimes voiced in the press, are perhaps exaggerated. The exaggeration is especially obvious when one considers the number of students majoring in fields such as business and when one remembers that about 20 times as many students attend the most conservative institutions, the 2-year colleges, as attend the most liberal/left institutions, the liberal arts I colleges. On the other hand, there is no doubt that professors are on the whole rather more liberal and tolerant than the general public.[8] They probably transmit some of their values to their students—but this still leaves open the question of how they do so.

In this section, I am suggesting that of the many higher-education variables that could foster tolerance, the development of cognitive abilities may be among the most important. Practically by definition, tolerance requires interposing thought between affect and act, between feelings and behaviors. To tolerate, one usually needs to calculate, to weigh costs and benefits. "Democratic self-restraint" and "sober second thoughts" are terms that have often been used to describe the process. Other virtues, such as friendship and altruism, are corrupted when one introduces balance-sheet thinking. But some forms of tolerance entail calculations of self-interest—farsighted calculations, to be sure—usually in the form of putting up with a lesser evil to preserve a greater good. A typical example would be deciding that tolerating the dangers and inconveniences of extremist speech or offensive religious cults or flag burning is the price we have to pay for the greater values of liberty and democracy. If the cognitive development hypothesis is correct, higher education increases the likelihood that people will be more able and perhaps more willing to engage in such calculations.

How Does Cognitive
Sophistication Lead to Tolerance?

There have been several attempts to link cognitive development directly to tolerance. These have differed on the question of the origins of cognitive sophistication—whether it arises from genetic inheritance, education, social learning, or some combination of the three. They have been alike in that they have used a measure of intellectual maturity and related it to a measure of tolerance. I have already mentioned McClosky and Brill's (1983) study in this regard. These researchers attribute the generally low level of political tolerance displayed by the American public—especially the contradiction between belief in a principle and failure to apply it in specific cases—to a lack of understanding. Thus, "many members of the public lack the skill or awareness to perceive that the particular forms of tolerance they oppose are linked to rights they claim to favor" (p. 259). McClosky and Brill attribute low levels of tolerance to a shortage of the knowledge and skills needed to be tolerant, which in turn is caused by a shortage of opportunities for social learning.

McClosky and Brill tested this learning-tolerance link by giving respondents to their political attitude survey a little quiz on facts about law and politics. They found consistently high correlations between respondents' scores on the test of political knowledge and their scores on the measure of support for civil liberties. This finding is more an example of civic education (see Chapter 5) than of cognitive sophistication. But McClosky and Brill often discuss civics knowledge and cognitive skills together, and, indeed, it is often difficult, and sometimes inappropriate, to separate the two. For example, Selznick and Steinberg (1969) claim that information can foster cognitive skills:

> The acquisition of knowledge about the world permits a realistic problem-solving attitude toward it. For the cognitively naive, the world is often baffling and inexplicable, and this is an invitation to fantasy and magical explanations. One aspect of a primitive cognitive style is that it assigns blame and searches for scapegoats precisely because it fails to comprehend impersonal and abstract causes. (p. 191)

Tolerant people not only tend to know more, they also more often value knowledge, appreciate intellectuality, and respect the life of the mind. McClosky and Brill come to this conclusion by analyzing responses to such questions as whether subjects would rather trust their fates to "thinking people who have lots of ideas" or to people with much practical experience, such as businessmen. Of those who received high tolerance scores, 70% said they would prefer to rely on "thinking people" such as "professors and intellectuals," whereas only 6% of those who received low tolerance scores would do so (pp. 315-316). Note, however, that McClosky and Brill were not measuring cognitive sophistication as much as they were recording attitudes toward the life of the mind. Presumably an individual could have these attitudes even if his or her own cognitive capacities were quite limited.

Marcus et al. (1995), in their studies of political tolerance, have come to three findings significant for the case I am building here. First, political knowledge leads directly to political tolerance, a finding discussed at greater length in Chapter 5. Second, subjects expressing a high "need for cognition" were more tolerant. Third, subjects asked to focus on their thoughts when responding to a political tolerance problem were more tolerant than those who were told to pay attention to their feelings. The three influences were related, but they also had separate effects. Knowledge influences *how* one thinks about political tolerance, not only *what* one thinks (see Chapter 5).

Similar to McClosky and Brill's measure of subjects' *preference* for intellectual solutions is the construct "*need* for cognition" discussed by Marcus et al. Using a scale developed by Cacioppo and Petty (1982), Marcus et al. asked for agreement or disagreement with such statements as "Thinking is not my idea of fun" and "I find satisfaction in deliberating hard and for long hours" (p. 248). Subjects who scored high on a need for cognition were more tolerant than those who expressed "less interest in a cognitive approach to life" (p. 167) and were more influenced by "their own thoughts, which in turn . . . [made] them more tolerant" (p. 175).

When responding to hypothetical tolerance dilemmas, some subjects were told to pay attention either to their thoughts or to their feelings. Following these directions influenced subjects' level of tolerance. Specifically, "subjects who are told to pay attention to their feelings are significantly less tolerant than those who are told to pay attention to their thoughts" (p. 80). Presumably, people who paid attention to their thoughts without being told to do so would also be more tolerant. Marcus et al. stress that "it is not affect that increases expressions of tolerance, it is cognition" (p. 223), and "attending to thoughts will lead to greater tolerance, whereas attending to feelings will lead to greater intolerance" (p. 63). Although this conclusion is well supported by their evidence, it is important to remember that it pertains only to *political* tolerance.[9] I will argue briefly below (in the section on Kohlberg's theory) that *feelings* of empathy might be important for social or moral tolerance. But Marcus et al.'s general point is clear and clearly correct. The reason for the link between thought and tolerance is the well-known tendency for people to be more likely to *act* on their feelings than on their thoughts. Tolerance is precisely *not* acting on one's feelings, but controlling them with one's thoughts. Not surprisingly, therefore, people who think and who like to think are more likely to be tolerant.

One very direct test of the links among education, cognitive sophistication, and tolerance was conducted by Bobo and Licari (1989). Using data from the General Social Survey, they argued that "education changes cognitive style in ways that increase the likelihood of recognizing the importance of extending civil liberties to those we dislike" (p. 291). Their approach differed from McClosky and Brill's in two ways: First, they used a general measure of verbal intelligence (a 10-item vocabulary test) and not a measure of specific political knowledge to assess cognitive sophistication; second, they were interested in discovering how much of the relation between education and tolerance was mediated by the cognitive sophistication thus measured. Bobo and Licari concluded that "education is the single most important variable" accounting for differences in respondents' tolerance levels, and "the cognitive sophistication measure accounts for a large share (approximately 33%) of the effect of education on tolerance" (p. 298).

Cognitive sophistication can be ideologically neutral. Although it is usually associated with social, political, and moral tolerance, and more broadly with liberal or left-wing values, cognitive sophistication affects the shape of conservatives' values too. Sidanius, Pratto, and Bobo (1996) found that people with conservative values were more likely to be consistent in their beliefs if they had advanced educations. The higher the subjects' education level (their "intellectual sophistication"), the better their conservatism could be used to predict their racism, and the better conservatism and racism together could be used to predict their opposition to affirmative action. Basically, this means that higher levels of education tend to promote intellectual consistency in a person's political and social views. Unfortunately, Sidanius et al. did not use an independent measure of intellectual sophistication, but used education level as a substitute. Nonetheless, the results are exactly what one might predict if education leads to cognitive sophistication: Individuals' political views are more logically coherent the more education (cognitive sophistication) they have (see Sniderman & Piazza, 1993, for further evidence on the same point).

What this suggests is that people with higher levels of education are more likely to have principled beliefs (see the discussion of Kohlberg's theory, below); their views are more likely to form a consistent whole, regardless of their particular ideological positions.[10] This coherence of beliefs is equally likely for conservatives and liberals. Sidanius et al. did not find that education was completely neutral, however. People were less racist, had fewer anti-Black feelings, and less "generalized antiegalitarianism" the more education they had. But those racist anti-egalitarians who escaped the egalitarian influences of education had a more coherent cluster of beliefs the more educated they were.

Why does cognitive sophistication encourage tolerance in particular? Why does it not encourage intellectual consistency in any view, including consistent intolerance? It probably does. *Intellectual consistency* refers to the form of a set of beliefs, not their substance. In the United States, however, that form often leads to substantive support for tolerance. I believe one reason for this is the fact that the United States is founded upon principles that logically imply tolerance (freedom of religion and speech, equal political rights, and so on), and those principles are supported, at least viscerally, by the vast majority of the population. People who think about the principles they support are often led, through simple logical consistency, to tolerance.

This sort of link among principles, consistency, and tolerance is nicely illustrated in Chong's (1993) interviews on political tolerance. Chong found that in discussing whether a group ought to be protected by a right, respondents with more education tended to focus on the right, whereas those with less education tended to focus on the group. Specifically, when asked about free speech for Nazis, most of those who had not graduated from college talked about how they felt about Nazis, whereas most college graduates talked about democratic rights. Chong then "examined whether respondents could be nudged from their original frame of reference [group or rights] by any additional considerations" (pp. 891-892). He found that it was easier to get the less educated to alter their approach. The more educated stuck with their principled argument (see also Bassili, 1996, for the effects of counterarguments on issues of tolerance).

The studies reviewed thus far provide considerable evidence that cognitive sophistication encourages tolerance and may even be an important component of tolerance, especially political tolerance. This means that the role of cognitive psychology could be central in explanations of the kind of political attitudes and behaviors that add up to tolerance (see Bar-Tal & Saxe, 1990; Lau & Sears, 1986; Torney-Purta, 1990). The notion, once widespread, that personality traits determined in infancy can explain most adult political behavior is being increasingly challenged as evidence accumulates that a great deal of political learning takes place in adulthood (Sigel, 1989). Data indicating the role of higher education in individuals' forming significant attitudes such as political tolerance further weaken the credibility of what we might call the *infancy ideology,* which is an important component of at least some of the personality theories reviewed in the previous section.

Further research is needed to clarify the relations among the educational variables that foster tolerance. Cognitive sophistication may be as much a matter of intellectual values as it is of knowledge, skills, and logical consistency. One of the things that students may be taught in higher education is something like intellectual or cognitive "manners." Among the lessons that higher education may convey are, for example, that a prejudice does not count as a good argument (and an essay based on one will justly receive a low grade), that being persuaded by emotional rhetoric rather than evidence or reasoning is not the mark of an educated person, and that intellectual integrity is more important than the particular conclusions one reaches. These lessons are not part of some "hidden" curriculum; they are often taught quite consciously and figure prominently in the official objectives of institutions and programs of general or liberal education. It probably does not matter whether we think of such lessons as education or as socialization to the role of educated person. In either case, these parts of the higher-education experience could be important means through which social and political attitudes are formed in colleges and universities. To see whether and how higher education actually has such consequences, through the teaching of "cognitive manners," we will probably need more longitudinal studies specifically designed to test the effects of particular curricula. The best of such studies, the classic work of Perry (1970), is quite old and was confined to a narrow demographic range of students. (See Perkins, 1995, 1996, for more recent investigations.)

Some studies show that the cognitive "climate" of schooling, or the general environment of learning, can have important direct effects on tolerance. Climate can also have indirect effects on tolerance by promoting cognitive sophistication. The basic idea is that the pattern of "activities . . . in an organization (e.g., whether they are rigid or flexible) can have an influence on the pattern of individual thinking and behavior" (Nielsen, 1977, p. 64). This is parallel to what we have seen earlier in this chapter in the discussion of Melvin Kohn's theories. Kohn and his colleagues have concluded that when students do substantively complex schoolwork—particularly when they have some autonomy to decide how they will do that work—they become more intellectually flexible and are thereby less likely to be authoritarian and intolerant (Miller et al., 1985).

Among the several explanations for how higher education increases tolerance by influencing cognitive development, one of the least elaborated, but quite suggestive, focuses on what one might best call *secularism,* or a preference for nonmagical and naturalistic thinking rather than reliance on supernatural explanations—a subject touched upon briefly above in the discussion of the modern personality. One indication of the importance of secularism is the fact that people answering "none" when asked on surveys about their religious affiliations are almost always more tolerant than those in any other group, whereas those who attend religious services frequently are less tolerant, regardless of their denominations (Beatty & Walter, 1984). Occasionally, on the odd question, Jewish respondents are slightly more tolerant than the "nones" (Corbett, 1982, p. 143), but the tolerance scores of the nones are routinely stronger, and when one uses the stringent Sullivan et al. "least-liked group" test, the nones' comparative tolerance advantage over other groups is larger (Piereson, Sullivan, & Marcus, 1980). The nones also tend to be the most highly educated group in the population. Because they have not been well studied, we cannot be sure whether the nones' higher tolerance scores would persist if their education level were controlled for.

One way that higher education might foster tolerance is by increasing the ranks of the nones. Attempts to investigate this would, again, be plagued by problems of selection effects. Earlier we saw that entering freshman are about twice as likely as the general population to be nones. This may mean that those with no religious affiliation are more likely to choose advanced education. Advanced education may not influence them to be nones; rather, they may already be secular-minded when they arrive at higher education. In either case, we might wish to argue that there is an "elective affinity" between secularism and higher education, whatever the direction(s) of causation. As Pascarella and Terenzini (1991) conclude, college education brings about a decline in "students' traditional religious affiliations . . . and in their general religious orientations. . . . Religious beliefs become more individual and less doctrinaire, and tolerance for the religious views of others appears to increase" (p. 326). It is easy to think of possible paths of influence among tolerance, secularism, education, cognitive sophistication, and related variables. At this point, path diagrams such as the two in Figure 4.2 are largely guesswork, but these are the two hypotheses I suspect would be most likely to be substantiated by research. As usual, longitudinal evidence, although difficult to collect, would be most useful for testing these hypotheses.

According to one study, education reduces church attendance, dogmatism, and belief in the devil, and, in so doing, increases tolerance (Gibson & Tedin, 1988). Many studies have confirmed the unsurprising finding that people are less tolerant of groups they believe to be threatening. Although this effect is sometimes less strong among highly educated respondents (Green & Waxman, 1987), it exists for them too. One possible effect of education, through cognitive sophistication, is to enable people to make more realistic appraisals of dangers they face, perhaps especially to discount threats coming from supernatural sources. It is probable that more-educated people are less likely than less-educated people to feel threatened by imaginary dangers, which are very often the most frightening kind. Real threats from real dangers can also stimulate magical thinking, particularly among individuals with low tolerance of ambiguity (Keinan, 1994). People with high ambiguity tolerance, which, like other forms of tolerance, is promoted by advanced education, are better able to handle the stress of real or imagined dangers without sacrificing their rationality.

Education → Cognitive Sophistication → Secularism → Tolerance

Secularism → Education → Cognitive Sophistication → Tolerance

Figure 4.2. Possible Causal Paths Linking Tolerance, Cognitive Sophistication, Secularism, and Education

Another possible way education fosters cognitive development is through its curricular structure or form. Schools' main avenue of instruction is written language; this is what separates the way schools instruct from information transfer in most other settings. Literacy, according to Goody (1986), is qualitatively different from speech and other nonwritten forms of communication. Literacy, he asserts, is an "important technology of the intellect," one that is crucial "for the development of what we think of as reasoning" (p. 167). Literacy "increases the analytic potential of the human mind" (p. 142). In the terms used in this chapter, schools, by introducing and fostering literacy, promote cognitive development, which in turn promotes tolerance. Basil Bernstein (1975) makes a related point. He demonstrates that schools teach students to use language "universalistically," in much the same way that Goody says literacy enables them to think more systematically. Leaving aside Bernstein's main interest (social class differences in language use), his insight is helpful for the construction of my general argument. Learning to speak (Bernstein) and to write (Goody) in ways that outsiders can understand is a kind of cognitive competence that is probably an important stimulant to tolerance. Tolerance can often involve taking the view of another. So does writing universalistically. For example, even such an apparently minor tendency encouraged by education as the use of more nouns and fewer pronouns can have important consequences. Nouns are more universal because people who do not know the particular context may understand a message if it contains nouns; pronouns are more particular—they can be understood only by someone familiar with a specific context. For example, the phrase "Education increases tolerance" requires less context (is more universal) than "It increases it." Whether the use of universal codes is a cognitive or a personality tendency, schooling tends to promote it and, in so doing, fosters tolerance indirectly.

Perhaps the simplest way to link education and cognitive sophistication to tolerance is through intelligence, as measured by IQ tests. IQ could increase the propensity for all three: education, cognitive sophistication, and tolerance. Or intelligence could be the mediating variable between educational level and attitudes (see Wagner & Schonbach, 1984). Depending upon how one views the origins of IQ, one would place it differently in a causal model, for example, either preceding education and attitudes or between them. A recent example of an argument for the importance of IQ concerns the Defining Issues Test, an instrument designed to measure moral development based on Kohlberg's theory. Sanders, Lubinski, and Benbow (1995) claim that the Defining Issues Test "is simply another way of measuring verbal ability" (p. 502). Be that as it may, there is no doubt that Kohlberg's theory of moral development, the highest stages of which lead to principled tolerance, is a heavily cognitive theory, which is why it is discussed in this section.

Kohlberg's Stage Theory

Few researchers have had as strong an impact on values education as Lawrence Kohlberg. Thomas (1992), for example, claims that Kohlberg's theory "remains the most stimulating and potentially the most fertile model of children's moral growth in current psychological and philosophical circles" (p. 514). Research on the theory of moral development, by Kohlberg himself as well as by numerous others, has been very extensive. I shall present the briefest of overviews here—just enough to describe the theory and to establish that, to the extent the theory is valid, it provides very strong support for the cognitive development explanation of how education can foster tolerance.

Kohlberg sees moral development as a function of cognitive development. The way a researcher determines a child's moral stage is by analyzing the cognitive criteria the child uses when making a moral judgment. Let us begin with three structural or formal properties of the stages postulated by the theory. First, Kohlberg (1982, 1984) claims that the stages of moral development are universal: They exist in all societies and in all groups within any particular society. However, the distribution of individuals across the stages varies by culture: Different societies and different groups within a society may have different proportions of its members in the various stages. Second, as with most stage theories, the sequence of the stages is invariant; that is, one cannot skip a stage. Third, an individual's moral reasoning about all issues will tend to be at the same stage.

The content of the stages is summarized in the following list (see Kohlberg, 1984, pp. 174-176). The six stages, which are divided into three levels, are based on the ways that individuals think about moral problems. In parentheses following the descriptions of the stages in the list are factors that motivate individuals at the given stages; for example, children at Stage 1 are mainly interested in avoiding punishment.

■ Level I: Preconventional morality

  Stage 1: Heteronomous morality (avoiding punishment)

  Stage 2: Individualism, instrumentalism, and exchange (serving one's own interests while recognizing those of others)

■ Level II: Conventional morality

  Stage 3: Interpersonal expectations and conformity (being seen as a good person; maintaining social rules)

  Stage 4: Social system and conscience (upholding group and institutional duties, not only individual duties)

■ Level III: Postconventional or principled morality

  Stage 5: Social contract and individual rights (rational calculation of overall utility)

  Stage 6: Universal ethical principles (personal commitment to universal principles)

Tolerance, as I have described it in this book, is mostly a Level III, Stage 5 phenomenon, which means that it is at the highest level but not the highest stage. In later works, however, Kohlberg and colleagues have wondered whether anyone truly attains Stage 6 (Power, Higgins, & Kohlberg, 1989).

What influences an individual's stage of moral reasoning? Aging has a lot to do with it. As a child ages, he or she usually moves to higher levels of Piagetian logical reasoning. Moral reasoning, however, usually lags somewhat behind logical reasoning. The logical level is necessary but not sufficient for moral development. Other influences on moral levels and stages include the opportunities a child has to learn social roles and the forms of justice prevalent in the child's social groups and institutions, such as family and school. It is here that the social climate of the school, discussed briefly above, can be important.

Moral education, based on Kohlberg's theory, involves helping the student to move to the next higher level of thinking about morality. Were children "systematically exposed to moral reasoning one stage above their own, they would be . . . attracted" to it (Power et al., 1989, p. 11). The main method of accomplishing this exposure to the next higher level of moral reasoning is rational discussion of and argument about moral issues. The method thus requires (and probably teaches) a minimum degree of procedural or functional tolerance, because one cannot rationally discuss controversial issues without putting up with people whose views differ from one's own.

Our main questions are as follows: (a) Does Kohlbergian moral education work to foster tolerance? (b) Does advancing one's level of education increase the odds that one will advance to the higher stages (4 and 5) of moral development, more so than if one stops one's education at an earlier point? The answer to both questions is, briefly, yes. On the first point, it is clear that Kohlberg considers the rights and liberties guaranteed by the U.S. Constitution, which he believes to be a "moral document," to be located at the highest stages of morality. Much evidence supports the second point as well. For example, Pascarella and Terenzini (1991) conclude that the research in many studies of U.S. higher education "clearly indicates that college is linked with statistically significant increases in the use of principled reasoning [Level III, Stages 5 and 6] to judge moral issues" (p. 364).[11] Considerable international findings demonstrate that the same set of stages can be applied to moral reasoning in other countries, and that moving up the stages increases as a function of additional schooling (Breslin, 1982; Gallatin & Adelson, 1971; Tapp & Kohlberg, 1971). But it is the issue of the universality of the stages that has most divided contemporary researchers. The universality of Kohlberg's stages has been disputed rigorously, not on grounds of national or cultural diversity, but on grounds of gender differences.

The best-known challenge to the idea of the universality of Kohlberg's stages comes from Carol Gilligan in her book *In a Different Voice* (1982). Gilligan claims that although Kohlberg's stages may describe the moral development of males accurately, they are inadequate to describe females' moral universe. In contrast to the increasingly complex ratiocinations about rules and principles that characterize boys' growth, girls' conceptions of morality have more to do with empathy, understanding, and helping behavior. Gilligan is surely right to point out that Kohlberg and others err when they assume that the experience of members of one gender (Kohlberg originally used only male subjects) is the universal experience of all humans. On the other hand, I think she tends to overemphasize gender differences almost as much as Kohlberg ignores them. It may be the case that in the future increasing gender equality will yield growing similarity in moral reasoning between the sexes. Even older research does not indicate dramatic differences between the sexes. One extensive review of the literature concludes that "the moral reasoning of males and females is more similar than different" (Walker, 1984, p. 687; compare Umberson, Chen, House, Hopkins, & Slaten, 1996). And Gilligan herself points out that as males and females mature, their moral reasoning becomes more similar.

What does all this mean for our topic? If school encourages the development of higher levels of moral reasoning (defined by either Kohlberg or Gilligan), and if higher levels of moral development promote tolerance, then the broad category of Kohlbergian research (both mainstream and revisionist) supports the general approach taken in this chapter. Gilligan's version may be more in tune

Cognitive Model

Negative Emotion → Cognitive Override → Action Checked

Emotional Model

Negative Emotion → Emotional Override → Action Checked

Figure 4.3. Cognitive and Emotional Models of Tolerance

with a personality development approach and Kohlberg's with a cognitive development approach, but both give us insights into how education can facilitate the growth of tolerance.

Gilligan's work calls attention to a very important dimension of tolerance and interpersonal relations that has not been emphasized so far in this book. In this section on cognitive development, and throughout this work, I have stressed that tolerance involves interposing reasoning between emotions and acts. In the cognitive model of tolerance, negative affect is checked by "sober second thoughts" so that negative feelings do not lead to hostile action. But there is another model, suggested by Gilligan's work. It may be more commonly used by one gender, but like the cognitive model, it is available to, and employed by, both. In the emotional model of tolerance, an initial negative emotion, such as repulsion, is overcome by another, more positive emotion, such as empathy. This "second feeling," like the second thought, checks the impulse to hostile action. The two models are depicted in Figure 4.3. The models are identical except that the initial negative emotion is overridden in the one case by thought and in the other by feeling. The outcome is the same in both cases, but the middle link in the causal chain suggests different ways in which education advances tolerance and how pedagogies might be designed to further it.

Although we have little direct evidence at this point, I would guess that the cognitive model provides a better description of how individuals usually arrive at *political* tolerance (Marcus et al., 1995). The emotional model, to the extent that it can be demonstrated, would more often come into play in questions of *social* and *moral* tolerance.

Merely to state these differences between emotion and cognition is probably to overstate them. At least it is the case that, except in brain-damaged people who have lesions separating parts of their brains, emotion and cognition usually accompany each other (Goleman, 1995). "Empathy," in addition to being an emotion, can be a rational procedure used, for example, by historians in their research (Ringer, 1969, pp. 98-99). And if, as I shall suggest below, chimpanzees can be said to exercise tolerant restraint, all forms of tolerance probably do not presume the use of the very highest cognitive functions.

Conclusion

There is considerable room for dispute between those who take a personality approach to attitudes and those who prefer a cognitive approach. Quinley and Glock (1979), for example, argue that once one controls for education level, the effects of personality are minimal. Like Selznick and Steinberg (1969), they think that education's effects are very important and that they are mainly cognitive. Sullivan et al. (1982; Sullivan, Shamir, Walsh, & Roberts, 1985), on the other hand, claim that education's effects occur mostly through their influence on personality.

It is not always easy to distinguish between traits of personality and traits of intellect. Dogmatism, referred to by both the personality and the cognitive camps, is a good example. Dogmatism is a way of (not) thinking, but it can be so integral to a person that it is as much a strong personality trait as a weakness in cognitive capacity. One way to divide the labor between the two camps is to say that a tendency to use one's intellect is a personality trait, but actually using it is a cognitive activity. Even such distinctions can occasionally be somewhat arbitrary, however. For example, Pascarella and Terenzini (1991), in summarizing several effects of college on personality, come to the following conclusions. Even after important variables such as IQ and socioeconomic status are controlled for, "people who complete college show significant gains in their tolerance for ambiguity, flexibility of thought, and preference for reflective and abstract thought, as well as for logical, rational and critical approaches to problem solving" (p. 259). This list of college's effects on personality is also manifestly a list of cognitive characteristics.

The debate between the personality psychologists and the cognitive psychologists is to some extent a nominal dispute, a debate over labels. Those in the personality camp tend to see characteristics such as rationality as *preferences*—or, perhaps, compulsions. Those in the cognitive camp, on the other hand, are more likely to think of intellectual flexibility, rational problem solving, and the rest as *abilities*. It makes greatest sense, I think, to say they are both abilities and preferences. When a person uses logic to solve problems, for example, it is usually because he or she is able to do so and prefers to do so. On the other hand, for most people most of the time, using or not using a logical approach to problem solving is probably not a conscious choice; it is more a habit shaped by past experience. In any case, the types of personality development and cognitive development that foster heightened levels of cognition in persons dealing with social, political, and moral issues tend also to foster tolerance. And such personality development and cognitive development are often encouraged by education. The two types of development usually go together. Indeed, it is hard to see how educational practices could teach one without influencing the other. When instructors teach logical approaches to social problems, they usually not only teach skills, but also encourage students to have positive attitudes about using the skills.

I want to conclude this chapter on personality and cognitive development by briefly discussing two recent studies, each the best in its field. One examines the effects of college experiences on students' attitudes; the other investigates the "morality" of apes and monkeys. These two studies provide radically different types of evidence, but they converge on a few main points that lead us naturally to the topics of the next chapter.

The best and most recent study of college students relevant to our subject focuses on students' openness to diversity in questions of race, culture, and values as well as their openness to challenges to their beliefs (Pascarella, Edison, Nora, Hagedorn, & Terenzini, 1996). Although that openness is not exactly the same as tolerance, it is at least a first cousin, perhaps even a parent. An 8-item scale was constructed on the basis of subjects' agreement or disagreement with statements such as, "I enjoy taking courses that challenge my beliefs and values" and "Contact with individuals whose background (e.g., race, national origin, sexual orientation) is different from my own is an essential part of my college education" (p. 179).[12] Pascarella ct al. examined the effects of 30 predictor variables on students' openness to diversity and to challenges to their beliefs. Their findings allow us to weigh the kinds of results we have been examining in this chapter and introduce us to some of those we will investigate in the next. We find some evidence in support of not just a few, but many of the hypothesized relations examined in this book. That evidence buttresses Pascarella and Terenzini's (1991) earlier conclusion that the effect of higher education on students is the "cumulative result of a set of interrelated experiences sustained over an extended period" (p. 610); it is not attributable to only one feature of higher education.

Altogether, the 30 variables predicted about half of the variance in students' openness to diversity and challenge ($R^2 = .49$). Not surprisingly, the best predictors by far of students' scores on the openness scale in the spring were their scores the previous fall. But the effects of several other predictors were impressive, particularly given the fact that they had less than a year to exert an influence. They are also very impressive because they persisted after the researchers controlled for precollege variables, including prior attitudes. Differences due to courses taken were not large. Surprisingly, given earlier studies, no significant relation was found between openness and the number of social sciences taken; however, a negative effect of math courses on openness was discovered. Several outcomes that fit under the rubric of "cognitive sophistication" were found. Students' academic ability, the number of hours per week they spent studying, and their participation in serious discussions and in discussions on a wide range of topics were all related to their openness to diversity and challenge. Such openness is, by most accounts, as much a personality variable as a cognitive measure. Hence, we again see the mingling of personality and cognitive domains, both of which are changed by higher education in ways that encourage tolerance.

Although cognitive variables had important influences on personality traits that foster tolerance, so too did the variables of the sort we will examine in Chapter 5: intergroup contact and direct instruction. Before moving on to those topics, however, it is instructive to look at a very different kind of study, one that examines a much more basic level of personality and cognitive development than that occurring among college students.

Much evidence indicates that, among nonhuman primates, the "function of intellect" is social. The evolutionary advantage of big brains in human prehistory was not so much that they fostered tool making or more sophisticated modes of hunting, but rather that they made possible more intricate and advantageous patterns of social interaction (Byrne & Whiten, 1988). This is a line of reasoning most recently pursued by Frans de Waal (1996) in his work on social cognition among apes, monkeys, and other primates, including humans. His assumption is that the social interactions of humans have enough in common with those of other primates that studying those other primates can be instructive for scholars whose main interest is *Homo sapiens.*

Frans de Waal sees one type of tolerance among chimpanzees as an early form of sharing. "Food tolerance" is the most obvious instance: Stronger individuals routinely allow others access to food that they could monopolize for themselves. Adults put up with teasing from juveniles and ignore behaviors they would not tolerate from peers. Larger, stronger males could seriously injure younger, smaller males who show an untoward interest in the females—and sometimes they do. But sometimes they exercise a good deal of forbearance. Why? Because consistent intolerance would weaken the group.

The social interactions among chimpanzees can be more complicated and their group ties stronger because their dominance hierarchies are tempered by tolerance. Bonds more intricate than mere dominance can hold the group together better. The chimpanzee group cannot function unless its members tolerate differences of interest. Because of "the reliance of social primates on each other for defense against outside threats and for finding food and water . . . they can ill afford to be at war with companions on whom they depend" (p. 206). Tolerance is one of a repertoire of social skills that make community life possible. Some species have much more cognitive capacity to develop these skills. Within a species or a group, some individuals are much more adept than others. Individuals who have those skills serve not only their own interests, but those of the group.

By observing the interactions among relatively simple societies of a few dozen nonhuman individuals, animal ethologists have uncovered insights about social relations among humans as well as other primates. For example, chimpanzees display what de Waal (1996) calls "community concern," which is brought about by "the stake each individual has in promoting those characteristics of the . . . group that increase the benefits derived from living in it" (p. 207). It is also clear that chimpanzees direct a very large percentage of their intellects toward understanding social relations among their number. In human societies, that number can be much larger and the possible social interactions much more intricate because of humans' greater cognitive capacities. As the boundaries of the group are enlarged, the need for social skills such as tolerance becomes more pressing. Tolerance is a way to expand moral inclusion beyond the relatively narrow group with whom one has direct ties of kinship and positive emotional bonds to individuals and groups toward whom one has negative affect. For better or worse, these skills constitute one of the main resources we humans have at our disposal as we overrun the globe.

The common thread uniting works as different in scope and method as the two just reviewed—the one on first-year college students, the other on chimps— is social interaction, as well as the processes of learning that occur as a result of such interaction. Hostile, negative learning is possible—perhaps common. But so too is learning ways of relating to others that improve the lives of individuals by enriching their social environments. Certain dispositions and cognitive capacities make learning social skills easier and more likely. Chimps and college freshmen learn social skills by doing. They learn how to interact peacefully with others by coming into contact with them. But the frosh, thanks to their greater intellectual capacities, have another approach open to them: systematic instruction in civics, morality, and intergroup relations. Both intergroup contact and systematic instruction are examined in the next chapter.

CHAPTER 5

Can We Teach
Tolerance Directly?

N THIS CHAPTER we turn from the fairly subtle
and indirect ways education promotes tolerance,
discussed in Chapter 4, and examine the more direct
means through which curricula and the social settings of schooling advance tolerance. These direct
means of teaching tolerance are often consciously manipulated by educators
seeking particular outcomes, and so it is easier to assess success in reaching those
educational outcomes than it is to measure the effects of more indirect stimulants of
tolerance such as those addressed in Chapter 4. Here I group the ways tolerance
may be directly taught and learned in schools under two main rubrics: (a)
intergroup contact and (b) civic, moral, and multicultural (CMMC) education.

▨ Intergroup Contact

The most extensive studies of the effects of intergroup contact have been carried out by researchers testing what is usually called *contact theory* (or the contact hypothesis). The basic idea is simple: If you bring together members of different social groups in settings such as schools, increased harmony among the groups is likely. The idea is old (it was part of the rationale behind the 19th-century common school movement, for example), and it accords with common sense. Yet it is also clear that contact may lead to conflict, or "attitude change in the wrong direction" (Sampson, 1986, p. 182; see also Henderson-King & Nisbett, 1996; Livingston & Berger, 1994). The big task for the researcher or the practitioner is to determine when contact among groups is likely to contribute to improved intergroup relations—and when it is not.

The list of conditions that need to be specified is long and complicated. A few examples illustrate the magnitude of the problems involved in identifying when contact works and when it does not. One specification has to do with timing: First or early contact between groups may increase their tendency to stereotype one another, but in the long run, exposure of people to members of different groups more often reduces antagonism (Reed, 1980). Thus, an inter-vention may well "backfire," but mainly in the short run. Another important qualification to the contact hypothesis is one version or another of the "power-threat" or group-threat hypothesis, discussed more extensively below. The basic theory, which is fairly well substantiated, is that the greater the size of the minority group, the greater the likelihood that the dominant majority group will feel threatened by it and act toward it in a hostile way. However, it is also true that the greater the size of the minority group, the greater the potential for intergroup contact and its beneficial effects. Hence, the effects of growth in the size of a minority group can be contradictory and may appear on balance to be minimal as one effect negates the other. As a final example of how complicated the contact theory can be in application, consider situations in which there are real differences of interest (not just ignorant prejudices) between groups or factions. In such circumstances contact may serve to highlight the differences and lead to worsening relations. This has apparently occurred with liberal and conservative Christian groups (Wuthnow, 1988; see also Dubey, 1979; Hewstone & Brown, 1986). As they have gotten to know one another better, they have come to realize just how far apart their values are.

Such qualifications remind us that it is crucial to specify the conditions under which contact is likely either to reduce or to increase intergroup antagonisms, or when tolerance is likely to be a response to intergroup conflict. When Williams (1947) and Allport (1954) initiated contact theory, they were fully aware that not just any contact would improve relations among people and the groups to which they belonged. They and subsequent researchers (e.g., Amir, 1969) have largely agreed on several criteria for a successful "contact situation":

1. The change must be introduced quickly and thoroughly by respected authorities who enforce it consistently.
2. Intergroup contacts must be frequent enough and close enough that it is possible for people to become acquainted with members of the other group as individuals.
3. The groups brought together must have equal status within the contact situation.
4. Competition has to be avoided and cooperation fostered between members of the desegregated groups.

These criteria have always been part of the contact hypothesis, and that hypothesis has an extensive history. The best-known document in that history contains strong claims about the beneficial consequences of interracial contact; these claims are featured prominently in the *amicus curiae* brief, the "Social Science Statement," prepared for the 1954 desegregation case *Brown v. Board of Education* (Allport, 1953).

Because contact theory has been so fundamental to most justifications for desegregation policies, a huge amount of research has been undertaken to validate the criteria outlined by Williams and Allport. Reviewing some of that research will help us get a better understanding of how education, by promoting intergroup contact, might also promote tolerance, as well as other positive outcomes.

Most of the research reviewed in this chapter actually focuses on outcomes other than tolerance. The most commonly studied outcome is reduction of prejudice. If we define prejudice as *a negative attitude toward someone based on insufficient or erroneous information,* we see that prejudice is not the opposite of tolerance, despite the tendency for it to be thus defined in much research (e.g., Martire & Clark, 1982). As I have suggested in Chapter 1, tolerance is a second-order attitude; it is an attitude that is a reaction to an attitude, particularly a negative attitude, such as a prejudice. *Discrimination,* not prejudice, is the opposite of tolerance. Discrimination is *acting* against someone toward whom one has a negative attitude, such as a prejudice. Tolerance is having a negative attitude but *not acting* against the "attitude object." Of course, there is an important relation between prejudice and tolerance: If prejudice were eliminated, one of the occasions for tolerance would also be removed. But there are other occasions besides prejudice when tolerance is an option, such as realistic conflicts of interest.

Another good example of tolerance that illustrates my repeated point that tolerance is much harder to measure than intolerance or discrimination is found in Schelling's (1971) "integration tolerance schedules" (p. 167). These refer to individuals' upper limits to the presence of members of other groups in their residential area before they decide to leave for elsewhere. Some Whites, for example, might move from their homes if only a few Blacks move into the area in which they live. Others might not move even if Blacks become a substantial majority. As we shall see below, Blacks and Whites tend to have different preferences, or tolerance schedules, and this makes desegregation (and therefore contact) quite complicated. My main point here, however, is that it is intolerance that causes action or movement. Those who are tolerant stay as they were. Because the tolerant are less active, they are also usually less visible.

Stereotyping

Another often-measured outcome of increased intergroup contact is the reduction of stereotyping. As I have noted in Chapter 2, reducing stereotyping has a family resemblance to increasing tolerance, but it is not the same thing. In one very well designed study of contact on a university campus, Rothbart and John (1993) studied the same group of White subjects over 4 years and measured their stereotypes about and their contacts with African Americans and Asian Americans. In general, they found a low level of intimate personal contact, and the level did not go up over the 4 years. Also, the amount of contact did not predict changes in individuals' perceptions: The subjects had as many stereo-typical beliefs at the end of the study as at the beginning. But what does this tell us about tolerance? Well, actually, nothing, because that is not what was studied. Of course, one form of discrimination might be said to be avoidance of contact, and using that definition, Rothbart and John found continued discrimination, or no increase in tolerance. More generally, however, we cannot judge trends in tolerance from data about trends in stereotyping. It is quite possible for a person's stereotypes to change little, but for that person to learn to cease discriminating on the basis of those stereotypes. People can maintain their stereotypes even while becoming more tolerant.

In brief, much of the research used in this book, from which I argue and draw conclusions, is not about tolerance in the strict sense of the term—even when the researchers say they are studying "tolerance." This complicates our task. We need to pay close attention to what is actually being studied. When we use research that is not directly concerned with tolerance, but only related to tolerance, we must do so with great care.

Let us return to the conditions under which intergroup contact is likely to foster better intergroup relations—including tolerance. These conditions are particularly important because intergroup contact often does not have positive effects on students' attitudes, mostly because these conditions have not been met (Stephan & Brigham, 1985).

Criteria for Effective Contact

Firm Enforcement

Among the criteria for successful intergroup contact, probably the most controversial is the idea that contact must be introduced briskly by respected authorities—what we might think of as the "quick and firm" approach. This seems to contradict common sense as well as some impressive social theory about the wisdom of piecemeal, muddling-through approaches to complex social experimentation (Lindbloom & Woodhouse, 1993). But when it comes to school desegregation, "they'll never know what hit 'em" policies have, more often than not, led to trouble-free transitions to compliance with the law. That conclusion is supported by an impressive amount of evidence. After reviewing that evidence, Hochschild (1984) concluded that Americans face a dilemma: "The more perfect the means of popular control, the worse for racial equity" (p. 144). When a White community controls democratically the way desegregation is implemented, it usually opts for pilot studies and extensive community consultation. This often panics Whites who are uncertain about desegregation; they conclude that it must really be bad if it has to be approached in such a cautious, roundabout way. Further, moving slowly to eliminate illegal segregation indicates a lack of resolve on the part of public officials. This apparent uncertainty of authorities raises doubts in parents' and students' minds and makes them less open to the effects of intergroup contact. And, of course, gradualism gives confirmed bigots more time to organize. Hochschild reviewed evidence from hundreds of communities undergoing desegregation and concluded that Allport (1954) was right when he stated that most Americans would be willing to go along with desegregation when presented with "a forthright *fait accompli*" (p. xxi).

Educators need to do more than "go along" with desegregation, however. There is also good research indicating that it is unwise for educators simply to ignore intergroup relations in contact situations and hope for the best. Educators, too, must firmly and consistently enforce the new ethical and legal guidelines. For example, Schofield (1993) emphasizes that school officials must take responsibility for the success of desegregation to bring about tolerance and not merely have faith that school desegregation will work its magic without any further intervention. She states that "teachers can make a very important contribution to the success of desegregated schools by clearly articulating their expectation that students will respect each other's rights and by backing up their stated expectations with disciplinary measures" (p. 310). Furthermore, teachers' attitudes are important because teachers who favor desegregation are more likely to organize their classes in such a way that they meet other criteria for a successful contact situation, such as cooperation and equal-status interactions (Epstein, 1985).

Meaningful Interaction

The importance of "meaningful" interaction is also clear. Individuals usually need more than superficial contact with others in order to change their attitudes and behaviors toward them, especially if they are to change their attitudes in a positive direction. School desegregation that leads to little more than students brushing past one another in the halls is not likely to be effective at much of anything. The doleful consequences of resegregation in desegregated schools have often been noted (Schofield, 1982). One cause of such resegregation is tracking, whether by ability, achievement, or aspirations. Because different ethnic groups have, on average, different levels of academic achievement, tracking tends to resegregate. But tracking does not lead to complete resegregation. Whereas the proportions of each ethnic group in the academic, vocational, and general tracks rarely match the proportions in the general school population, it is even more rare for the color line between tracks to be as rigid as, for example, in the cafeteria, where students self-segregate at high levels. Although resegregation stemming from tracking is only partial, and is probably less extensive than students will bring about themselves if not discouraged by school policies (such as random seating assignments in classes), it is a serious concern among educators who wish to promote intergroup harmony through contact (Hallinan & Williams, 1989).

Reducing tracking may not have as large an effect as some have hoped (Oakes, 1985), but it is something that educators can do to increase contact. The same is true of seating arrangements in classrooms, tracked or not, which Patchen (1982) has found to be just as important as the proportion of each race in a school or classroom. Other strategies for increasing contact that might be

more effective, such as desegregating neighborhoods and reducing job discrimination, are obviously not within the purview of teachers, school principals, or
superintendents.

We have mixed evidence about the importance of different kinds of contact.
Whereas one important neighborhood study indicates that even the most casual
contact can improve relations,[1] other research has come to different conclusions.
For example, whereas Martire and Clark (1982) found that social contact
between Jews and non-Jewish Whites was associated with lower levels of
anti-Semitism, this relationship did not pertain between Jews and Blacks. That
is probably mostly because Black-Jewish contact tends to be more superficial
and mostly economic (at work, in stores, at the doctor's office)—a kind of
contact that does little to influence Blacks' or Whites' levels of anti-Semitism.
The key difference was that Whites tended to have more personal contacts with
Jews than did Blacks (pp. 49-52). A similar finding from a local study of Blacks
in Los Angeles allows us to look more closely at Black-Jewish contact. This
study provides strong support for the contact hypothesis in some circumstances.
The influence of contact on Blacks' attitudes toward Jews was found to be
positive, but only among those who had had intimate neighborhood contact, and
only among older Blacks (Tsukashima & Montero, 1976). Of course, the authors
may have the cause backward or, at least, the causation may have been reciprocal
in this local sample, as well as in Martire and Clark's national study. The origins
of the statistical association may have been that Blacks who were less anti-
Semitic were more likely to come into contact with Jews, rather than contact
making them less likely to be anti-Semitic. Thus, in these studies, we discern
what is a persistent pattern in research on intergroup contact: partial and
ambiguous findings. Some kinds of contact among some individuals improve
intergroup attitudes—or, more positive attitudes make some kinds of contact
more likely.

In other words, most studies of the impact of contact on attitudes are
bedeviled by the problem of *self-selection bias* or, more simply, *selection effects.*
Statistical associations between contact and tolerance may be present because
tolerant people seek contact and intolerant people avoid it. The possibilities are
depicted in Figure 5.1. The top part of the figure suggests that contact reduces
prejudice, but this does not happen very often, because prejudice reduces
contact. The bottom part of the figure puts the relationship differently, and
indicates there may be a self-sustaining loop. Positive attitudes may lead to
contact, and contact then leads to further positive attitudes. There is empirical
evidence for both of the relationships sketched in Figure 5.1. For example,
Wagner and Machleit (1986) point out that the positive feedback loop is

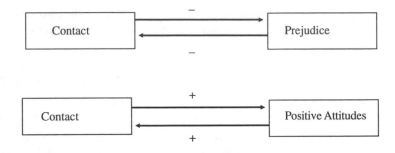

Figure 5.1. Contact and Attitudes: Directions of Causality

especially evident for contact involving voluntary leisure-time activities. For such activities, the direction of causality is unclear. On the other hand, when the contact is not voluntary—as in most school or work settings—selection effects are very unlikely to have come into play, because the individuals in the contact situation did not select to enter it. Thus, if contact is associated with attitude changes in nonvoluntary circumstances, then the contact is very likely to have been the causal agent.[2]

Powers and Ellison (1995) have directly addressed the problem of self-selection bias in a study of Blacks' attitudes toward Whites in which they used especially sensitive methods. They conclude that the odds that self-selection will bias results are smaller than many researchers have assumed. After controlling for selection bias, Powers and Ellison were able to substantiate what the previously reviewed studies have said: The contact hypothesis holds up, but, again, some specific forms of contact have more influence than others. Casual contact of Blacks with Whites makes little difference, but for Blacks close friendships with Whites can "counter negative images and stereotypes of whites" (p. 220). The only time these researchers found casual contact to have positive effects was among Blacks who had both close and casual contacts with Whites. Finally, they found that education interacted with the degree of closeness of the contact to influence Blacks' attitudes about interracial dating. More-educated Blacks were more tolerant of interracial dating, but only if they had close, friendly contact with Whites. For those who had not had such contact, education made no difference.

Equal Status

The most difficult criterion to meet for educators seeking the ideal contact situation is that of equal status among the groups coming into contact. Equal-status contact is important, the theory goes, because interaction among individuals of unequal status can easily reinforce the stereotypes and prejudices of the dominant group. But although equal status may be key, it is not easy to bring about. After all, desegregation is to a large extent motivated by the fact that minority groups do not have equal status outside the contact situation—how can it be easy to bring about such equality within the contact situation? Students cannot shed their social status at the schoolhouse door. Because of this, desegregation can often lead to increased stereotyping and ill will among groups (Cohen, 1984; Henderson-King & Nisbett, 1996). Teachers often require special training to learn how to implement appropriate interventions to counteract such potentially negative effects of intergroup interactions (Cohen & Lotan, 1995). The heroic efforts that Cohen and Lotan (1995) describe as needed to make equal-status contact work must be comparatively rare. This leads one to think that equal status, although certainly helpful, may not always be necessary. There is some evidence to this effect. Patchen (1982) found that inequality of status (whether measured by parents' socioeconomic status or students' academic ability and achievement) in desegregated high schools did not make it more difficult for Black and White students to get along. Patchen's findings, then, do "not support the proposition that equal status is an important prerequisite for intergroup contact to have positive results" (p. 205). This is encouraging because it means that the modal case of desegregation (Black and White students with different socioeconomic backgrounds and levels of academic achievement) can occur without "necessarily making it difficult for students of the two races to get along with each other" (p. 341).

Academic tracking also tends to make the equal-status criterion hard to meet, as well as making the meaningful interaction criterion more difficult to attain. To see how tracking can subvert equal-status contact, we do best to turn to ethnographic work, the most systematic of which on our topic remains Schofield's (1982) 6-year study of a magnet middle school. The racial atmosphere in the school sometimes bordered on the surreal, particularly when it came to what Schofield calls the "pretense awareness context" (p. 67) of students and teachers. All teachers and students knew they were racially different from others in the school, and knew that all others knew, but they all acted as though they were unaware of the differences, or they *said* they acted as though they were unaware of the differences. The consequences of steadfastly "ignoring" race were often quite negative. One example is the way students were assigned to academic tracks. This was done in a "color-blind" manner, using only cognitive criteria. Grouping students according to academic criteria, however, led to partial de facto segregation by social class, which, in turn, also meant partial de facto racial segregation. And "students tended to see race, rather than social class, as the causal variable" (p. 109). Given that many students, like many adults, are easily persuaded by explanations that attribute individual differences to race, contact can bring about a change in attitudes in just the opposite direction of what is hoped. A quotation Schofield (1982) presents from an interview with a student makes this startlingly clear:

> *Interviewer:*   Do you think that being in a school like Wexler has changed white kids' ideas about blacks?
>
> *Mary:*   It changed mine. It made me prejudiced really. . . . You know, it is just so obvious that whites are smarter than blacks. My mother keeps telling me it's socioeconomic background. (p. 93)

This sort of reaction highlights the possible negative effects of contact between unequal groups. Although equal-status contact may not be crucial to changing students' behaviors, it is something that should be aimed for whenever possible. Cohen and Lotan (1995) provide helpful suggestions about how teachers can work to provide equal-status contact when students' status is not equal. For instance, a teacher can find something that a low-status student is good at and incorporate that into his or her teaching. The teacher can call attention to this special talent and use it to help the class—or, better yet, the cooperative learning group—to complete a task. This can be enough, even if it involves only a relatively brief incident, to loosen stereotypes and foster positive interactions among students.

Cooperation

We conclude with the importance of a cooperative setting for the groups coming into contact. In such a setting, individual and group competition is reduced. The validity of the cooperation criterion (or noncompetition criterion) has been more thoroughly demonstrated than that of most of the other criteria discussed above. Indeed, it is as close as we are ever likely to come in the social sciences to a conclusion that can win general acceptance among researchers (Johnson, Johnson, & Maruyama, 1984). The evidence is clear that if groups are brought together in situations of competitive stress, they can quickly become highly antagonistic (Tajfel, 1978). The converse is equally clear: When cooperation extends across group lines, stereotyping and hostility decline. For example, one of the strongest findings in Patchen's (1982; Patchen, Hofmann,

& Brown, 1977) extensive study of some 5,000 high school students in Indian-apolis is that cooperative work on projects of mutual interest, in extracurricular activities as well as in the classroom, had positive behavioral and attitudinal outcomes: It led not only to friendly interactions but also to actual friendships across racial lines. Although academic achievement is not our major focus here, it is worth noting that the kind of cooperative group approaches some people favor on social grounds also tend, much more often than not, to boost student achievement as well (Epstein, 1985; Slavin, 1985). Hence, there is no need to sacrifice academic for social goals. Quite the opposite—cooperation is most often a win-win situation for students.

A particular methodological issue arises more often in regard to the study of cooperation in contact groups than in regard to any of the other topics discussed in this book. That issue concerns the relative merits, or advantages and disadvantages, of quasi-experiments, natural experiments, and "true" (or artificial) experiments. Each of these methods has its strengths and weaknesses. I bring up the issue here mostly because true experiments on cooperation are possible and have been conducted. The strength of true experiments is also their weakness: They isolate variables in a way they are rarely otherwise isolated. Although this allows researchers to study interactions in a pure state, that purity may have limited relevance to actual, "impure" social situations. Conversely, nonexperimental methods look at the sociopolitical world using statistical controls rather than control groups; this results in much higher levels of uncer-tainty about causal relationships. The advantages and disadvantages of the two methods leave us with a difficult question: Is it better to be certain about something that doesn't matter or to be uncertain about something that does? Given this unfortunate choice, the only rational approach is a rigorously plural-istic methodology incorporating all flawed methods in hopes of combining the advantages of each while not forgetting the limitations. For our purposes, it is most important to note one general finding: Cooperation usually improves relations among individuals in a contact situation, often regardless of the methods used to study it.

When we examine more detailed and applied questions, however, the different methods sometimes produce different results. This is one of the important causes of some of our most significant remaining areas of uncertainty about the effects of contact. For example, say that one's general goal is to encourage people to revise their assessments of ethnic and racial groups, and that the way to bring this about is to enable people to get to know others as individuals. What is the best way to accomplish this? Should students be clearly assigned to cooperative groups on the basis of race or ethnicity, thus using the firm approach (the first criterion)? Cooperation is good, but should each cooperative group compete with the other cooperative groups? Should curricular and other activities focus on learning about other categories of people, or should they stress that individuals in other categories are not as different as the students may have supposed? (For contrasting views, see Nieto, 1996; Slavin, 1985; see also Chapter 6.)

Racial Mix and Group Threat

Research on contact theory in educational institutions has allowed us to move toward more refinement in our knowledge of several important details about successful contact situations. One such detail worthy of special attention concerns the optimal "mix" of White and Black students in desegregated schools and classrooms. (The research on other ethnic groups has been too sporadic to allow us to make good estimates.) By examining the question of mix (proportions of each group), we may be able to reconcile two seemingly contradictory social theories: the contact hypothesis and the "power-threat" hypothesis mentioned briefly above. First suggested by Blumer (1958; see also Blalock, 1967, 1982; Smith, 1981a), the power-threat or group-threat hypothesis holds that increases in minority group size, while increasing contact, also stimulate conflict—just the opposite result predicted by contact theory.

Blumer (1958) rejects the idea that race prejudice is a personality trait; instead, he examines it as a product of intergroup relations—those relations, in turn, influence psychological processes. According to Blumer, prejudice arises in or is intensified in a dominant group when its "entitlements" are challenged by a subordinate group. Such threats to privileges lead to prejudice. Thus, "the source of race prejudice lies in the felt challenge" to the dominant group's "sense of group position" (p. 5). In the face of such feelings of threat, whether or not the threat is realistic, contact may have relatively little beneficial effect. Indeed, increased contact may heighten the sense of threat. Blalock (1967) in particular emphasizes the importance of minority group size as an influence on majority group attitudes and behaviors. Quillian (1995) has substantiated and expanded upon the theory in a 12-nation study in which he found that prejudice is indeed greater when the minority group is bigger. Further, and of particular interest for our purposes, he found an interaction of the sense of threat with education. Specifically, "education reduces prejudice more in countries where the perceived threat to the dominant group is greater" (p. 603). In countries where there is less perceived threat, people do not need to be educated to be unprejudiced.

The relation between the density or concentration of the minority group and prejudice and/or discrimination is not universal. For example, in a study of the history of lynchings in the southern United States (1889-1931), Corzine, Creech, and Corzine (1983) found that this most extreme form of discrimination varied by region. Mob murder of Blacks by Whites occurred as the power-threat theory predicted in the Deep South, but not in the Border South. In fact, in the Border South an inverse relation pertained; that is, the higher the percentage of Blacks in the population, the lower the lynching rate. These authors suggest that the difference may be attributable to cultural or ideological differences between the regions, specifically that a "threat-oriented belief system" (p. 790) was very prevalent in the Deep South.

In turning to educational contexts, we find some interesting parallels and differences when we examine the question of group proportions, or mix. In a study of 89 desegregated elementary schools, Longshore (1982) found that the relationship between Whites' attitudes toward desegregation and toward Blacks was influenced by the proportion of Blacks in the school. This relation was curvilinear, not linear, however. This means that Whites' attitudes became increasingly negative as the percentage of Blacks in the school increased, but only up to a point. After Black students became a clear majority, White students' attitudes became more positive. It is also interesting to note that this curvilinear relationship was stronger in schools that were large, were populated by students of low socioeconomic background, and were in the Deep South. But in all cases, negative attitudes of Whites were most prevalent when the proportion of Black students was between 40% and 60% of the total. This led Longshore (1982) to conclude that "threat is most salient in schools where neither group dominates" (p. 78). It would be especially interesting to know whether Blacks had similar reactions to varying proportions of Whites in school, but in this study, as in many others, the question was not investigated. Indeed, the emphasis of Blumer, Blalock, and their followers has almost always been on White (or other majority group) prejudice and discrimination. Only fairly recently have the attitudes of Blacks received systematic treatment.

We do have good comparative data about the preferences of Blacks and Whites in housing, and those data provide an instructive comparison with what we have seen in schools. Massey and Denton (1993) found that most Blacks would prefer living in a neighborhood that is about 50% White and 50% Black, but most Whites would not want to live in a neighborhood with that racial composition. Whereas "blacks strongly prefer a 50-50 mixture . . . whites have little tolerance for racial mixtures beyond 20% black" (p. 93). Historically,

Whites have used quite brutal means to "keep the levels of white-black contact within levels that are tolerable to whites" (p. 111). More recently, methods of maintaining the ghetto have involved simple "White flight." In any case, even were all discrimination in the housing market suddenly to end, these differences in preferences between Blacks and Whites would tend to produce sharply segregated neighborhoods. And segregated neighborhoods produce segregated schools with limited opportunities for intergroup contact.

Preferences for different mixes matter enormously, because, as Schelling (1971) starkly puts it, "if whites want to be at least three-fourths and blacks at least one-third, it won't work" (p. 147). It is logically impossible. Schelling's simple models make clear that demands that add up to more than 100% (such as Whites at 80% and Blacks at 50%) result in extreme segregation. The segregation occurs through the simple exercise of individual choice. Segregation can result from the choices of individuals who are quite willing to see much more integration than currently exists. If Schelling is right, and I think he is, the reasonable preferences of Blacks and Whites can lead to segregation even without economic differences between the two groups, and without redlining and other forms of housing discrimination.

The importance of the subject demands that we briefly examine some implications of Schelling's conclusions. Let's start with something simple: Say that many people in a society with two groups prefer integration, but no one in either group wants to be in a minority in his or her community. In that circumstance, "no mixture will . . . be self-sustaining" (p. 148) except for an exact 50/50 split between the two groups. Extending Schelling's logic, we can see that given the size of the Black minority in the United States at present (say 12.5%), if the maximum number of communities were integrated at the 50/50 mixture, 25% of Whites and all Blacks would live in integrated communities. Thus, 75% of Whites would live in totally segregated communities—there aren't enough Blacks to "go around" to produce any other result. A similar result happens in higher education, and it is intensified because of the presence of historically Black colleges. If something like one-fourth of Black college students attend historically black colleges, that leaves a diminished population of Blacks able to attend other (historically White) colleges. These principles of the arithmetic of segregation directly influence the amount and proportions of possible intergroup contact among students.

In a longitudinal study of 20 elementary classrooms in Northern California (that is, in one of the nation's least residentially segregated areas), Hallinan (1982) examined changes in friendship choices over the course of a year. Her study differed from Longshore's (1982) in key respects: Hallinan looked at the racial composition of classrooms, whereas Longshore recorded the composition of schools; Longshore studied general attitudes of Whites, whereas Hallinan studied the friendship choices of White and Black students. Nonetheless, some of the results their two studies are quite similar. Hallinan found the fewest cross-race friendships in racially balanced classrooms. Ironically, then, the maximum possible desegregation (a classroom with equal numbers of Whites and Blacks) resulted in the maximum student self-segregation in friendship choices. The reason may be that "racially balanced classrooms provide a sufficient number of Black and White students to permit the existence of racially segregated subgroups or cliques" (Hallinan, 1982, p. 70). The least self-segregation happened in majority-White classrooms. The tendency to make cross-race friendships was greater in majority-White classrooms; this was true for both Black and White students. The reason may be that majority-White classrooms are in some sense most "natural." By that I mean, if students were assigned to classrooms in the United States entirely by chance (say, in a big national lottery), most students would end up in majority-White classrooms—for the obvious reason that the majority of students are White. The United States is a majority-White society. Regardless of their race, people will tend to have most experience adjusting to majority-White social settings, such as classrooms. And the less segregated the society, the more this will be true, because the less segregated the society, the more members of a minority group will come into contact with members of the majority group.

Patchen's contributions to this issue of "mix" (the effects of proportions) are perhaps most nuanced because he dealt with a large number of outcome variables as well as a wide range of predictors. His outcomes include students' intergroup attitudes, avoidance behaviors, friendly interactions, and unfriendly interactions. Most relevant for our purposes is that Patchen's subjects, whether Black or White, reported most unfriendly interaction (such as fighting and name-calling) in classes that were 30-50% Black. The match with Hallinan's and Longshore's findings is very close. However, Patchen also found that there were many friendly interactions between members of different races in these balanced classes. In fact, unfriendly interaction was largely independent of friendly contact and largely independent of school situational variables—except mix, or classroom group proportions. Unfriendly interactions, Patchen concludes, were not mainly due to group relations; they depended more on students' personal characteristics, especially whether they were male (boys were more likely to have more friendly *and* unfriendly cross-race contacts) and whether they were aggressive.

Aggressive male students were most likely to fight with students of the other race, but they were just as likely to fight with members of their own race.

In general, then, classes with a substantial (and especially increasing) Black minority are the ones where "the greatest tensions between the races are likely to occur" (Patchen, 1982, p. 338). Although quite a lot of avoidance will occur in such classes, there will also be a fairly large amount of friendly interaction. As Longshore found, the relation is curvilinear. What can be called *status inversion,* where the minority becomes the majority, has positive effects. Patchen's results are the strongest in this regard; he found that "the best social relations between blacks and whites (in all respects) occurred where there was a black majority" (p. 338). The second-best situation was when the Black minority was very small (10% or less). And, in accord with the other studies, the most trouble occurred in racially balanced classrooms.

All of the classroom mix studies (Hallinan's, Longshore's, and Patchen's) date from the early 1980s and are based on data from the 1970s. One may wonder, two decades later, whether the same relations pertain. But these remain among our best studies, and their conclusions strongly indicate some important things. All three studies support the group-threat hypothesis, but the relationship they describe is curvilinear, not linear. The three authors differ on the exact shape of the curve, but they agree that an even balance is the most difficult situation and disagree only on which sort of imbalance (majority White or majority Black) ranks first and which second in the tendency to promote harmony.

Can we reconcile the power-threat hypothesis, which predicts that increased contact will lead to negative attitudes, and contact theory, which proposes that contact can lead to positive attitudes, including tolerance? I think so, along the lines suggested in Figure 5.2. We can accept the general proposition of the power-threat hypothesis, that as the size of an out-group increases (e.g., Blacks in a school), the attitudes of the in-group (e.g., Whites in that school) will become less positive. This is a direct effect indicated by the middle, horizontal arrow in the figure. However, increasing group size also increases opportunities for friendly contact, which in turn increases positive attitudes (the upper pair of arrows). This suppressor variable's effect, on the other hand, will itself be counteracted to some degree, because increasing group size also increases the possibilities of unfriendly contact and thus reduces positive attitudes (the lower set of arrows). What matters in a specific instance for determining the net effect of increased group size and contact is the strength of these relationships, which are indicated in Figure 5.2 only by plus and minus signs. Examining the strength of these relationships in different settings will produce even more nuanced

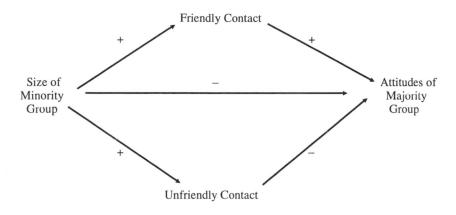

Figure 5.2. Contact and Power Threat

qualifications to the proposition that one of the ways education fosters tolerance is by fostering contact among social groups.

Qualifications such as these are important, because they help us avoid underestimating the difficulty of our task. When the conditions stipulated by contact theorists are not met, and they are stringent conditions, intergroup contact may not help (Sampson, 1986). But the contact hypothesis generally holds up well. In some cases it has even proven robust in the face of violation of its assumptions. The research reviewed above, and much that we have not reviewed, is generally quite supportive of the contact hypothesis. (See Scott & McPartland, 1982, for evidence strongly supporting the effects on attitudes of contact or desegregation drawn from a large, representative national sample.) As Patchen (1982) puts it in a conclusion that nicely captures the findings of many other studies, "Some of the hoped-for social results of biracial schooling—meaningful, nonsuperficial, friendly contacts—did occur at least sometimes for a majority of the students of both races" (p. 79).

What about teachers? They, too, are part of the contact situation. They have not been as well studied, but we can say a few things about them. Patchen found that, as influences on students, contact with other-race peers and the attitudes of same-race peers were more important than contact with or attitudes of teachers. Teachers are probably more important for preventing negative interaction than for promoting positive behaviors and attitudes. This means, in the terms we have been using in this book, that teachers are more important for tolerance than for more lofty goals, such as valuing diversity. Most studies of the issue indicate that the attitudes of teachers and other educators are pretty similar to those of other professionals but somewhat more tolerant than the general population (Lacy & Middleton, 1981; Porter, 1994). One way schooling may foster tolerance, then, is that it brings many children into contact with adults more tolerant than their parents. But this is not likely to be a very strong effect.

Classroom climates as determined by teachers (Bennett, 1979) can be very important in desegregated classrooms. Alexander, Entwisle, and Thompson (1987), like Patchen, found teachers' race to be of little consequence, but they did find that teachers' social class mattered importantly in how they treated low-status and minority group children. High-status teachers, whether Black or White, tended to be particularly hard on such children, had low expectations of them, and had less favorable views of their school's climate when they worked with minority students. Part of the tendency of Blacks, who start out with scores comparable to Whites, to fall behind in the course of schooling may be attributable to such prejudice and discrimination. However, although I can imagine racial screening for teachers in our society, screening teachers by socioeconomic status (SES), although probably more important, is very unlikely to be implemented. We live in a society where people are convinced that race matters. The possibility that SES matters as much or more may seem too "Marxist" for most Americans to consider. Whatever the case, "the environment of the classroom is intensely interpersonal" (Alexander et al., 1987, p. 680), and attitudinal differences can be crucial.[3] When teachers discriminate against first graders in the way that Alexander et al. describe, equal-status contact becomes much more difficult to attain in subsequent grades.

Epstein (1985) has also discovered significant teacher effects. In a study of 886 teachers in 94 elementary schools, she found that teachers who were favorably disposed toward desegregation were more likely to use cooperative and equal-status methods in their instruction, whereas those who had negative attitudes were more likely to use tracking and within-class ability grouping.

Even though we have been treating contact here as a direct and often purposeful mode of fostering tolerance, there are several indirect and unintentional ways it may do so. For example, the education level of non-Jewish Americans is associated with increased social contact with Jews, and that contact, in turn, is associated with reduced levels of anti-Semitism (Martire & Clark, 1982, pp. 46-51). This kind of effect occurs largely after schooling is completed. The mechanism may have something to do with the fact that higher levels of schooling are associated with occupations that increase social contact, at least among some groups.

Returning to the school effects of contact, I suggest that even when schools do not intentionally pursue policies to bring different groups into contact they may do so anyway, just by the nature of the enterprise of organizing schooling. Schools, as segregated as they are, tend to be more racially and culturally diverse than children's nonschool environments, such as their families and neighborhoods. For example, White high school seniors have been found to be more likely to have had contact with Blacks in school than elsewhere—in their neighborhoods, at church, or at work (Dowden & Robinson, 1993). Generally speaking, the higher up the educational ladder students travel, the more likely they are to encounter members of social groups other than their own, and, therefore, the more likely they are to learn to be tolerant of those persons. This rule of thumb is most obvious when we compare elementary schools with high schools, because high schools usually draw from larger and consequently more diverse catchment areas. In institutions of higher education, the results might be more mixed and will certainly vary with institutional type. A steep decline in the social class diversity of students occurs between the early years of secondary education, which include virtually all persons in the relevant age group, and later years of higher education, which include less than one-fourth of the age cohort, a segment in which students of low SES are sharply underrepresented. This decline in social class diversity in higher education might, however, be made up for by increases in other sorts of diversity, such as higher proportions of foreigners, political radicals, social nonconformists, and religious outsiders. There have been few systematic studies on the topic, but it seems reasonable to guess that the average American is more likely to interact with, say, a Muslim, a lesbian, a Marxist, or an atheist in a university than elsewhere in contemporary U.S. society. Finally, the fact that colleges may be less "cliquish" than high schools might mean that the kind of interaction contact theory postulates as necessary to encourage tolerance is more likely to happen in higher education than in secondary education. (However, for caveats, see Cabrera & Nora, 1994; Livingston & Berger, 1994; Sampson, 1986.) Although few studies exist, contact theory suggests that a promising line of research would be to compare, for example, the percentage of high school students who say they have friends of other races with the percentage of college students who report this sort of contact.

We know quite a bit less about students in higher education than one might suppose. Hauser (1993) may exaggerate, but he makes a good point when he says that "once youths leave high school, our statistical system treats them almost as if they had dropped off the face of the earth" (p. 275). We are better informed about elementary and secondary students. We know that progress in interethnic/racial contact in elementary and secondary education has slowed dramatically in the past decade or two. Rivkin's (1994) and Orfield's (1993) reviews of the available data make a few things quite clear: Schools are highly segregated in large part because neighborhoods are highly segregated. Since the end of busing across district lines, children go to school where they live, and they mostly live in segregated districts (and, to a lesser extent, perhaps, neighborhoods are segregated because White parents seek to avoid desegregated schools). States with small school districts, such as New York, tend to be more segregated than states with larger districts, because small districts are more likely to be ethnically homogeneous. In such homogeneous districts there is almost nothing educators can do to foster desegregation, because busing across district lines in order to desegregate is illegal. In general, movement toward school desegregation since the *Brown v. Board of Education* decision in 1954 has historically been greatest in the South. Current (mid-1990s) levels of school segregation are highest in northern cities (especially in Illinois, Michigan, New York, and New Jersey), where desegregation never really occurred in the first place. Up to the 1980s, there had been considerable progress in the southeastern United States. Most progress in residential and school desegregation ended around 1980, and may even have been reversed in the late 1980s during the Bush administration.

Ultimately, school desegregation, and therefore contact, is possible only with residential desegregation, but residential segregation of urban Blacks has been very resistant to change since it became a prominent feature of city life in the 1950s and 1960s. By 1970, according to the most systematic recent study, Blacks in highly segregated cities such as Chicago and Cleveland "were very unlikely to have any contact with whites" (Massey & Denton, 1993, p. 48). When no contact occurs, the criteria for an effective contact situation are, for obvious reasons, no longer pertinent. Looking at the 30 standard metropolitan statistical areas (SMSAs) in which some 60% of Blacks in the United States live, Massey and Denton found very modest declines in recent decades in the "segregation index" (pp. 221-223). Their results are summarized in Table 5.1.

At the rates of change evident in the table, it would take several decades for residential segregation to reach what Massey and Denton call "moderate levels." And high levels of residential segregation are very important in a study of the effects of contact on tolerance, for several reasons. First, and most obvious, the greater the segregation, the less the potential for contact in schools or elsewhere. Second, to the extent that segregation produces a culture of segregation, or an "oppositional culture" of the ghetto, contact between students, even when they go to the same schools, will require more effort. Finally, and most generally, "geographic isolation translates into political isolation, making it difficult for segregated groups to form political coalitions with others" (Massey & Denton,

TABLE 5.1 Segregation Trends in Housing, 1970-1990 (in percentages)

	1970	1980	1990
Northern SMSAs	84.5	80.1	77.8
Southern SMSAs	75.3	68.3	66.5

1993, p. 183). Isolated groups tend to have fewer common political interests (neighborhood schools, fire departments, safe streets). When people are segregated, they have less need or willingness to make deals across ethnic lines, deals that require the tolerance of differences. If the fire station closes down in a segregated neighborhood, for example, it hurts only one group, and only one group can mobilize its political resources to reopen it. If a fire station closes down in a mixed neighborhood, different groups have to learn to tolerate one another if they want to form an alliance to protect their interests.

Measures of residential and school desegregation are not really measures of contact, of course. Attending the same schools is a necessary, but not sufficient, condition for students to have intergroup contact at school. As has often been suggested, school policies such as tracking can lead to resegregation of desegregated schools. Furthermore, students in the same building have a persistent tendency to resegregate themselves socially, school policies notwithstanding (Schofield, 1993). Studies of interracial friendships in high schools are far from encouraging. The number of such friendships in the 1980s was remarkably small. Of more than a million possible friendship pairs studied in the High School and Beyond sample, there were only a few hundred interracial friendships (Hallinan & Williams, 1989). The first reason for the lack of cross-race friendships is that most students attend highly segregated neighborhood schools;[4] therefore, they have few opportunities to make friends with people of different races. (You can hardly have a school friend of another race if no students of that race attend your school.) Controlling for this segregation, which greatly reduces the opportunities to make friends with persons of other races, it is still the case that students are about six times as likely to choose same-race friends as other-race friends. Controlling for a large group of individual variables and school variables (such as parents' education and tracking) reduces that difference by about one-third, to roughly four to one. But four to one and six to one are misleadingly optimistic figures, or figures that are easy to misinterpret. They are arrived at by "controlling for" factors that are almost never "controlled for" in life. What we are saying when we control for certain variables is that if nearly all students didn't go to segregated schools (but they do), and if nearly all schools didn't pursue policies that encourage resegregation (but they do), then students would pick same-race friends four times as often as they pick other-race friends. I think it is much more significant that only about one-tenth of 1% of students' friendships cross the color line. In the world that actually exists, not the controlled world of statistical models, students are about a thousand times (not four or six times) more likely to have same-race friends than to have other-race friends.

On the other hand, a stagnating rate of Blacks and Whites attending school together could mask an increasing rate of the kind of "quality contact" necessary to foster improved interpersonal relations. Contact in a broad social sense is hard to measure, and it is therefore hard to find trends. One indirect measure we have that points in the right direction (and it is a powerful one) is the rising rate of White-Black marriage, as mentioned in Chapter 3. Although the rate is small, it has never ceased to move higher since the official end of American apartheid with the *Love v. Virginia* decision in 1964. Another positive measure comes from the annual surveys of high school seniors called Monitoring the Future. In the 1970s and 1980s, about one-third of White high school seniors claimed to have at least one close personal friend of another race (Dowden & Robinson, 1993).

We have even fewer good measures for intergroup contact in higher education. As with elementary and secondary education, there is evidence that contact changes attitudes, but it is hard to tell how much contact is going on. We can talk about the numbers and rates of attendance for various ethnic groups (Hispanics, African Americans, and so on), and we might expect less racial isolation in colleges than in high schools, but I know of no good college data comparable to what we have for elementary, middle, and high schools. In this kind of situation, we are reduced to anecdotes. Here is one of mine. In my discussions with undergraduates from several universities, one theme has repeatedly emerged: Whites cannot understand Black "separatism." "Why do the Blacks feel like a beleaguered minority?" they ask. "There are lots of them here, aren't there? Actually, I've never seen so many before." The Blacks, on the other hand, often claim that they have never before been adrift in such an endless ocean of Whites. "Why can't they understand that we need to hang together? There are so many of them and so few of us." The irony is that students from both groups are right: Neither Blacks nor Whites have often encountered so many members of the other group in an equal-status situation before. Whether this heightened level of contact leads to anything beneficial is hard to tell. Some good evidence comes from studies conducted by Jomills Braddock (1980, 1985), who found that integration tends to be self-generating: Blacks who attended desegregated elementary and secondary schools were more likely to

TABLE 5.2   Hypothetical Distribution of Individuals to Illustrate How Different
Perceptions of Segregation Can Arise

	A	B	C	D	E	F	G	H	I	J
X	20	20	10	10	10	5	10	5	5	5
Y	0	0	0	10	10	10	15	15	20	20

attend majority-White colleges, and, in turn, were more likely to work in integrated settings as adults.

What is certain is that different groups can experience the same pattern and level of segregation in different ways (Jacobs, 1995). For example, the concentration of people into a limited number of areas limits their opportunities for contact. Table 5.2 provides an illustration. In the table, 100 individuals in each of two social categories (X and Y) are distributed into 10 groups (A through J). The categories could be men and women, Blacks and Whites, sophomores and seniors, or others. The groups A-J could be college majors, individual classes, rooming houses, or any other contained unit.

Say that Table 5.2 depicts an organization with a 50/50 mix, perfect integration. No one is a member of a minority, yet the distribution is experienced very differently by the members of the two groups. In this example, all the Ys have some contact with the Xs, but half of the Xs have no contact whatsoever with the Ys. Such distributions are not uncommon. Say that X and Y represent female and male, respectively, and A through J represent college majors. A and B could be elementary education and nursing, I and J physics and engineering. Many of the women might feel ghettoized, and many of the men might wonder why the women feel that way. The seeds of misunderstanding can be contained in reasonable perceptions of reality.

Some indication of the effects of contact and desegregation in higher education is revealed by a study of the attitudes of students attending the University of Alabama (Muir & McGlamery, 1984). Five surveys conducted over two decades reveal dramatic changes. In 1963, less than 20% of the White students said they would have no objection to eating in the cafeteria at the same table with Blacks; by 1982, around 80% said so. Changes of this magnitude, large though they may be, still reveal 20% of White students who would have an objection to eating with Black students. More interesting, perhaps, is the fact that although Whites strongly supported fundamental economic, political, and social rights for Blacks, and increasingly so over the 20 years, the pattern was different for Whites' perceptions of Blacks' characteristics, such as intelligence and industriousness. Biased attitudes declined sharply from 1963 to 1972, but then leveled off or went back up. In 1982, ironically, Whites were more tolerant of Blacks (supported Blacks' rights) but also more prejudiced about and did more stereotyping of Blacks' traits. Again we see that prejudice and stereotyping can vary independent of tolerance.

To grasp the reality of any contact situation, we have to examine the details of the distributions and the levels of aggregation of the units. Terms we use casually, such as majority and minority, are relative to context. African Americans are in the minority in every state of the United States, but they form a majority in several cities and counties and a very large majority in very many schools and churches. Women are in every state a majority, but in many occupations they are in the minority. What kind of status matters more for contact? These questions need more systematic investigation.

Conclusions on Contact

Contact theory will be a significant part of most explanations for the tolerance-producing effects of education, but it cannot be the whole explanation, for several reasons. First, the standard result of increased contact has not been made very specific by most studies. "Improved intergroup relations" is a phrase commonly used; it includes tolerance, certainly, but also involves much more. When a more specific result is tested for, it is usually something other than or beyond tolerance, such as interracial friendship. Second, some sorts of tolerance, such as support for freedom of the press, are not likely to be learned through contact in elementary and secondary schools. Prior to university, students will seldom come into contact with individuals who might need or demand political tolerance, but the political tolerance-yielding effects of schooling apparently begin, at least modestly, before university-level studies. Third, the school may socialize in ways that encourage tolerance, but that have nothing to do with intergroup contact per se. For example, see the discussion of personality development in Chapter 4.

Patchen et al. (1977) point out the distinctions between attitudes and behaviors that contact may bring about. Most important is that contact "does not have to lead to general attitude change for friendly interaction to occur" (p. 69), nor does attitude change necessarily have to precede friendly contact. What Patchen et al. describe is what Serow (1983) calls "functional tolerance." As discussed in Chapter 4, this involves knowing how to get along with different people, to cooperate with them in a modern social setting. This is true tolerance. And many studies (not only Patchen et al.'s) have shown that changes in specific behaviors are easier to bring about through contact than are changes in general attitudes (see Schofield, 1982).

In sum, we return to the question of whether contact works or not. The answer is clear: It depends—on many things. When conditions are not favorable, contact may make intergroup relations worse rather than better (Ben-Ari & Amir, 1986; Henderson-King & Nisbett, 1996; Miller & Brewer, 1984; Stephan & Brigham, 1985). Examining the conditions or criteria for a successful contact situation involves us in an increasingly complex series of subquestions, each at a higher level of specificity (or lower level of generality). A review of the levels of our research questions, and following one strand of our investigation, helps remind us where we are:

1. We started out asking, Does education foster tolerance? Answering yes led us to the second question.
2. How does education foster tolerance? One possible answer was intergroup contact, which led us to the third question.
3. Does contact increase tolerance? The answer was sometimes, under certain conditions, such as cooperation, which led to the fourth question.
4. Does cooperation across group lines promote tolerance? Answering yes led us to the fifth question.
5. How does cooperation encourage tolerance? One possible answer was that cooperation works by changing individuals' evaluations of members of the out-group. Another was that cooperation works by changing the definition of the boundaries between the in-group and out-group so that the "outs" became part of a larger group of "ins." These possibly opposing answers in turn suggest still further questions.

But we have had to stop at this level of specificity and say that, although we are not exactly sure why or how, we are sure that cooperative contact does have the desired effect. At least we are sure enough to be able to use that conclusion to further our analysis and come to some practical implications.

Take, for example, the issue of academic tracking. Tracking, because it also tends to lead to ethnic and social class "segmentation" (Ringer, 1979; Useem, 1992), certainly tends to reduce the possibilities for equal-status contact. Or does it? Given that each track most often contains both Blacks and Whites, members of the two groups may have more opportunity for meaningful, equal-status contact when sorted by ability than when not (Hallinan & Teixeira, 1987). In short, tracking raises the question, What is most important—equality of group size, equal status of individuals in the group, or equal status between groups?

To the best of my knowledge, there is no way to tell. But we do know that equal proportions tend to produce tension. Also, bonds among friends, such as their influence on one another's aspirations, are stronger in the same track (equal status or similarity of interests) than among friends in different tracks (Hallinan & Williams, 1990).

The two most important outstanding issues pertaining to contact are the generalization problem and the categorical thinking problem. First, *the generalization problem* refers to the fact that although contact may improve relations between the individuals who come into contact, that improvement may not generalize to other individuals or other situations. For example, equal-status contact between Blacks and Whites might not generalize to situations in which status is not equal. Or attitude change might extend to one out-group but not others, such as Hispanics. In short, "attitude change is often limited to the specific situation which produced it" (Hewstone & Brown, 1986, p. 16). If we want the change in attitude to generalize beyond the specific individuals involved in the contact situation, we are confronted with the second problem, *categorical thinking*. The biggest debate in terms of both research and policy focuses on this question. For contact to improve intergroup attitudes, says one side (e.g., Miller & Brewer, 1984), it must destroy category-based thinking and replace it with thinking about individuals as individuals. Quite the contrary, says the other side (e.g., Hewstone & Brown, 1986), broad change will come only with categorical group-focused thinking. The debate is a difficult one. If one stresses individuals as individuals, one runs the risk that the positive effects of contact will not generalize beyond those individuals. But if one stresses individuals as representatives of groups, one runs the risk of promoting stereotypes. This debate has important policy and research implications (see Chapters 6 and 7), but it is unlikely to be resolved any time soon. In addition to problems of research design that make it hard to resolve, I think much of this debate originated in a broader change in social thought away from a focus on individuals to a focus on groups (see the discussion of Jackman, 1994, in Chapter 2). What is really at issue is that debate between the "groupers" and the "individualizers." The specific schooling problem of concern to us here is often just the pretext or occasion for a skirmish in that larger conflict.

Civic, Moral, and Multicultural Education

Thus far, we have looked at the indirect and noncurricular ways institutions of formal education might foster tolerance. Now we turn to how schools have tried to teach tolerance directly as part of the regular course of studies. Direct instruction in tolerance and other values builds upon the distinctive function of schools, that which sets them apart from other socializing agencies. The main business of schooling is curricular and involves transmitting information and ways of organizing it. In the previous chapter we saw that cognitive skills can significantly influence individuals' political, social, and moral values. Here we investigate how knowledge and information can importantly affect individuals' tendencies to be tolerant and nonprejudiced. For example, people who believe that all Blacks are lazy, all Jews are greedy, all Muslims are fanatics, and so on, are poorly educated. They are ignorant of and/or incapable of clear thinking about ethnic and religious groups. Remedying such intellectual deficiencies would seem a task schools are well suited to accomplish. Presuming that those who make and execute curricular policy wish it, formal school curricula could be used to promote social, moral, and political tolerance. Educators have attempted to teach tolerance in a wide variety of ways, which for the sake of convenience I refer to as CMMC (civic, moral, and multicultural) education.

Throughout their history, schools have been expected to teach "good" values and "correct" attitudes and beliefs (Wynne, 1985). Tolerance very often is featured on governments' and educators' lists of the goals they aim to promote in school curricula (e.g., Lickona, 1992). Tolerance has often become one of those empty goals that sound important but commit educators to very little. Seldom has explicit attention been paid to what tolerance in fact is and, therefore, to how one could hope to teach it. Not surprisingly, therefore, studies of the effectiveness of direct attempts to teach tolerance have often been discouraging. There are, in fact, many fewer of such studies than one might suppose.

Tolerance has most often been taught as one value or attitude in a long list of others. When that has been the case, studies of the effectiveness of teaching the list of values have not often focused on tolerance. This means that evidence about CMMC education, particularly about how it relates to tolerance, is quite piecemeal. Most of it is anecdotal. This compares very poorly, for example, with studies of the effects of intergroup contact on values and attitudes, where there is vastly more research on a clear set of questions. Because the research on directly educating for tolerance is scattered and disconnected, it is nearly impossible to keep this discussion of CMMC education from being similarly episodic.

By dealing with civic, moral, and multicultural education under one rubric, I do not mean to suggest that the components of CMMC education are essentially the same. There are many differences among and within types of each. For example, when civic education deals with tolerance, it is mostly focused on political tolerance, whereas moral education is concerned with moral tolerance and multicultural education with social tolerance. To take another example, civic and moral education have usually emphasized conformity to predetermined "universal" norms of good behavior. Multicultural education, by contrast, has from its origins emphasized particularism—sometimes even absurd particularist stereotypes, such as individuals' skin color determining how they think. Despite the great diversity among and within the main types of CMMC education, they have in common the attempt to plan curricula consciously to teach social values and attitudes. Although a huge amount of CMMC teaching is taking place, not much of it has been evaluated in a systematic way. We will review a sample of programs that have been studied well enough that we can come to some reliable conclusions about their effectiveness.

We will look at several clusters of research concerning our topic: (a) civic education and political socialization, (b) moral education as conducted by Kohlberg and others, (c) multicultural education in schools and colleges, and (d) the Minnesota Tolerance Curriculum Project.

Civic Education and Political Socialization

The terms *civic education* and *political socialization* have often been used interchangeably by the political scientists and others who have investigated the topic of how people acquire their political knowledge, attitudes, and values. Regardless of how they have defined and approached the topic, researchers have not found it easy to discover the source or sources of individuals' politics. The two most obvious sources, parents and schools, have been investigated extensively. Despite popular assumptions to the contrary, the link between parents' political views and their children's is not especially strong. Both high school-aged and college-aged youth "agree with their own parents only to a small or moderate degree on most political and politically related values" (Niemi, Ross, & Alexander, 1978, p. 519). Early studies that found stronger relations between children and their parents relied on children's reports of their parents' views, not on the parents' own reports.[5] The main point of interest for our purposes is that, given that parents do not strongly shape their children's political attitudes, it is possible for schools to have an influence.

Measures of the effects of civic education courses in elementary and secondary schools have shown them to be quite inconsequential for the learning of tolerance and other political values. Various studies have judged the effects of civics courses to be nil (Ehman, 1980; Langton & Jennings, 1968), mixed (Remmers, 1963), or slight (Torney, Oppenheim, & Farnen, 1975). Hence, we confront something of a paradox: Although education increases tolerance, courses specifically designed to do so have usually had little measurable effect (Serow, 1983). The best explanation for this puzzling result is probably offered by Zellman (1975; Zellman & Sears, 1971), who says that students are not in fact taught tolerance in any meaningful sense; rather, they are taught slogans or principles, without any understanding of what those principles mean in specific cases.

Schools have little incentive to go beyond sloganeering. Because tolerance involves not repressing "subversive" ideas, "disgusting" practices, and "evil" people, teaching tolerance is usually controversial. Educators are unlikely to enhance their careers by courting controversy and discussing the rights of unpopular minorities, to say nothing of advocating those rights. Prior to university-level studies, public education is usually too vulnerable to popular pressure to handle the conflict of values that can ensue from any serious attempt to deal directly with political tolerance.[6] In sum, although it may be pedagogically possible, it is politically difficult for most schools to teach political tolerance explicitly. This situation is the jumping-off point for and the challenge met by a curriculum experiment described later in this chapter, which provides evidence that teaching tolerance directly is almost surely possible, although doing so may raise difficulties among students' parents and members of the community.

It could be that events in and characteristics of schooling have an influence on political attitudes and values, but we simply do not know how to measure that influence. Niemi (1973) concludes that "the school has an enormous impact, but precisely what affects each student is so variable that it is difficult to measure the overall impact of any one component part" (p. 131). This inability to specify the components of schooling that could affect political attitudes and values may be part of the reason that the stature of political socialization research in the discipline of political science has declined of late (Cook, 1985). The following subsections review our knowledge of civic education and political socialization research by answering three questions: (a) What do we know about the tolerance levels of children at various ages? (b) Why are school effects small? (c) What accounts for school effects, however small?

What Do We Know About Political
Tolerance in Children of Various Ages?

One thing is clear. Children are, on average, less politically tolerant than adults, and the younger they are, the less tolerant. Tolerance in school-aged children increases slowly as a function of age through the high school years (on fifth through ninth graders, see Zellman, 1975; Zellman & Sears, 1971; on older students, see Jones, 1980; on children aged 9, 13, and 17, see Scott & McPartland, 1982). Thus, children learn some tolerance before they get to college, but research has not yet identified where or how. I suspect that the learning of tolerance in the elementary and secondary years is in large part developmental. As students become increasingly cognitively mature, they become more capable of understanding how democracy works and that it entails legal opposition to the government. Although these developmental conclusions have not been reconfirmed recently, the evidence from the 1960s and 1970s is quite conclusive. Democratic attitudes are not yet firmly established among youth as they near high school graduation and voting age, but high school seniors tend to have more commitment to democratic values than do younger students. One final conclusion is pertinent for our purposes: Not only do tolerance levels increase as students age, but the correlates of tolerance change with age. Classroom climate tends to be more important for younger pupils, whereas information is more significant for older students (Jones, 1980). But in all cases, whether attributable to climate or curriculum, school effects have been quite modest.

Why Are School Effects Small?

One reason courses in civic education do not capture students' interest is that they are uninteresting. Rather than exposing students to controversial issues at the heart of democratic government, such courses for the most part present students with platitudes about good government. Civic education courses are usually exercises in political socialization and are generally designed to stress conformity. They tend to be "repetitive, superficial, irrelevant, unrealistic, and boring" (Andrain, 1985, p. 76). Studies of textbooks paint an equally dreary picture. Wirt and Kirst (1992) even suggest that these courses and texts are intentionally made boring so as not to stimulate too much interest, for interest could lead to discussion, questioning, and debate. According to these authors, schools provide "little knowledge of our conflictual pluralistic political world" (p. 68) because their function is to "indoctrinate" students to support the system (p. 86). These claims and most others like them are based on data that are 20 to 30 years old. One wonders whether things have changed. With schools increasingly under pressure from conservative action groups, I doubt it, although there is little systematic evidence available one way or the other (see Gaddy, Hall, & Marzanno, 1996, for a good journalistic account).

A related claim is that even if educators wanted to develop curricula that deal more realistically with the political world, the antidemocratic structure of

schools would lead to a conflict between schools' "learning goals and organizational order" (Merelman, 1980, p. 324). To teach about democracy would be to
invite students to challenge teachers' authority, to invite students to quarrel and
to debate with teachers about the nondemocratic structures that schools routinely
impose on students. In the choice between providing adequate knowledge of
democracy and maintaining order, knowledge takes a backseat: "Schools adapt
by reducing the quality of education" about government (Merelman, 1980,
p. 329). Students naturally lose interest in a subject that adds up to little more
than banal rhetoric. Other subjects can sometimes be challenging without
challenging order, but politics cannot.

What Accounts for the Effects, However Small?

Although school effects are small, they do exist. What have researchers
identified as the elements of instruction that produce more democratic attitudes,
including tolerance? Interestingly, most of the strongest studies (using large
representative samples and controlling for several relevant variables) have been
international efforts conducted in the 1970s. These studies have identified two
main factors accounting for the modest boost schooling gives to the development
of democratic values: classroom climate and knowledge. When students are
taught in a climate in which they feel free to ask questions and actively
participate in the life of their school, they are more likely to have democratic
values and attitudes about nonschool matters. These climate effects are mostly
indirect, and they have been quite small (Nielsen, 1977; Torney et al., 1975). I
mention them here to suggest that there is enough evidence about the indirect
effects of climate as it occurs "in the wild," without any intervention, to suggest
that educators could probably design school climate to be more democratic (see
the section below on Kohlberg's "just community" approach).[7]

Political knowledge has been shown in several studies to predict political
attitudes. The more knowledgeable adults are about the political system, the
more likely they are to support tolerance for nonconformists (Marcus, Sullivan,
Theiss-Morse, & Wood, 1995). The same sort of relationship pertains, although
in a much more modest form, among elementary and secondary students. As
Torney et al. (1975) put it in their study of 10 national education systems,
"Aspects of classroom climate and teacher interaction with students are at least
as important as substantive content in the fostering of democratic values"
(p. 281)—which is to say they are not very important, because substantive
content has a weak impact. On the other hand, the differences among nations
are often huge. The effects of schooling on individual tolerance levels within a

nation are very small by comparison. For example, in one study on attitudes toward freedom of assembly (measured by disapproval of a government law to forbid public demonstrations), tolerance levels ranged from 33% in Austria to 86% in the Netherlands (Muller, Pesonen, & Jukam, 1980, p. 267), with the United States near the high end of that range (73%). The effects of nations' broad patterns of socialization and political cultures must be very powerful to produce differences of this magnitude. Elementary and secondary schools can probably provide little more than minor adjustments to these major tendencies.

Moral Education as Conducted
by Kohlberg and Others

In Chapter 4, I discussed moral education in an account of Durkheim's theories. Here our concern will be mostly with work pertaining to Kohlberg's theories of moral development, because, almost uniquely among studies of moral education, these actually have been evaluated rigorously. Chapter 4 looked at Kohlberg's developmental schema for possible explanations of how education could foster tolerance indirectly by increasing cognitive development. Here we look at assessments of direct Kohlberg-inspired attempts to foster moral development, including movement toward tolerance. Kohlberg's is surely one of the most cognitivist or intellectual approaches in all of the CMMC literature. It builds directly upon his understanding of cognitive stages, which is why I have also discussed it in the cognitive development section of this book.

Tolerance is a central element of Kohlberg's Stages 4 and 5.[8] Kohlberg considers constitutional principles (such as freedom of religion and speech) to be moral principles embedded in a moral document (Power, Higgins, & Kohlberg, 1989). Connections have often been drawn between civic education and Kohlbergian moral education. For example, Patterson (1979) has shown a direct link between children's stages of moral reasoning and their consistent support for free speech. In Patterson's study, fourth- and sixth-grade children's levels of reasoning were as important as their positive or negative feelings about the target group in determining whether they would apply tolerant principles to the group. Given the significance of these cognitive competencies, it is important to discover whether education can foster development, or upward movement through the hierarchy of stages. The question is not whether those who happen to be at a higher stage are more tolerant (this was demonstrated in Chapter 4), but whether educators can promote movement to a higher stage by direct teaching.

Considerable evidence exists in support of the conclusion that moral instruction using Kohlberg's methods can promote moral development (Colby, Kohlberg, Fenton, Speicher-Dubin, & Lieberman, 1977). The basic idea of Kohlbergian moral instruction is to expose children systematically "to moral reasoning one stage above their own"; this will lead them to "be positively attracted to that [higher level of] reasoning" (Power et al., 1989, p. 11). Based on his study of the work of Durkheim, Dewey, and Dreeben (see Chapter 4, this volume), Kohlberg came to believe that the kind of community the school constitutes should also be a powerful influence on the development of moral reasoning. To foster development, Kohlberg concluded, educators need to make the schools "just communities," run according to the moral principles the educators are attempting to convey to the students.

This idea was tested in a small group of quasi-experiments in several high schools and alternative high schools in the 1970s. Although the authors of these studies clearly expected the just community approach to be more effective than the traditional Kohlberg approach of "classroom discussions of hypothetical moral dilemmas," this was not the case. Such discussions were found to be as effective as the restructurings of the two alternative high schools (Power et al., 1989, p. 289).[9] The authors were not willing to abandon the just community approach, however, in large part because they worried about the staying power of the moral discussion curriculum. As they put it, "Moral discussion classes are easy to start but tend to be discontinued, while just communities are very difficult to start but tend to last" (p. 291). When doctoral students working on their dissertations have led moral discussions meant to encourage development as predicted by Kohlberg's theory, they have most often been successful. However, the moral discussions approach "requires an explicit curricular commitment that few [teachers and schools] have been willing to make or sustain" (p. 292) once the doctoral students leave the school.

Much curricular work based on Kohlberg's theories has been conducted in the later elementary grades and in high schools. But there is also an important role for colleges and universities in moral education. The evidence from many studies is very strong that until individuals have developed to the Piagetian stage of "basic formal operations" they cannot attain Stage 4 in Kohlberg's schema. The Piagetian logical stage is a necessary but not sufficient condition for moral development beyond Stage 3. Pure Stage 4 reasoning (not mere adumbrations of Stage 4) is rarely attained by high school students, and Stage 5 is uncommon before early adulthood (Lind, 1996a; Power et al., 1989). There is no question that the brain, particularly the frontal lobes crucial for cognitive operations, continues to develop until around age 18 (Goleman, 1995), and that moral development can extend into adulthood. One of the main determinants of whether moral development is sustained into adulthood is exposure to higher (or postcompulsory) education. Advanced education "is important both for fostering moral-cognitive development *and* for making it self-sustaining" (Lind, 1996a, p. 4). One test of having reached the highest level of development is the ability to "judge oppositional arguments," to be able to tell, for example, that some argument makes a good case for a bad position or is a bad argument for a good position (Lind, 1996a, p. 10). Students who can do that have reached a level at which moral development can be self-sustaining. Capacities such as the ability to judge arguments in favor of one's own views as critically as those that are opposed are importantly developed in higher education. As always, we cannot be certain of the direction of causation, because we confront once again the problem of self-selection effect; that is, do those who are more cognitively developed choose higher education or does higher education enhance their development, or both?[10]

Perhaps the most important criticisms of Kohlbergian approaches to moral education come from adherents of "character education." They usually stress specific values and moral content, not levels of moral reasoning as does Kohlberg. Of course, as we have seen, although Kohlberg's stages are measures of competencies, they entail quite a lot of content, especially as concerns procedural moral values, such as freedom of expression. Thomas Lickona's widely read *Educating for Character* (1992) is probably the best-known work by a member of the character education movement. Lickona does not claim that Kohlberg's theories and the methods based on them are wrong, but he does imply that they are insufficient for two reasons: First, they are concerned with capacities or levels of reasoning, not with the right values; second, they focus on the cognitive side of education to the exclusion of drill, training, and instruction. But Lickona's is a mild critique; he claims that "thinking isn't all there is to morality, but there can be no morality without it" (p. 267).

The main problem with Lickona's book is symptomatic of the main weakness in the work of most authors who write about questions of moral education: His "evidence" is almost exclusively anecdotal. Striking, upbeat examples, although they make for inspirational reading, do not constitute evidence. The same is true of the many commission reports on education. They are rarely more than collections of opinions arrayed so as to support a predetermined and politically charged conclusion (for an example, see American Association of Colleges and Universities, 1995). Such a cavalier approach to the rules of evidence, although very common in educational policy tracts, constitutes dubious research ethics, an ethical transgression that is especially ironic in matters of moral education. A lack of intellectual integrity could even contribute to the very cynicism and relativism that commission reports and character educators so often denounce. The problem, in short, is that "most of the current efforts in values education have not been subjected to a controlled research evaluation" (Lickona, 1992, p. 28). Without such evaluations, it is disingenuous at best to claim to *know* what should be done in moral education.

All that said, Lickona's survey and the sales and influence of his book are indications of the extent of concern about the problem of character or values or moral education. Lickona asserts that tolerance is one of the "foundational values that schools should teach" (p. 46). He has more in mind than the values and beliefs that are the focus of this book, however: "Character consists of *operative values,* values in action. We progress in our character as a value becomes a virtue, a reliable universal disposition to respond to situations in a morally good way" (p. 51).

How is this to be accomplished? Kohlbergian methods of moral reflection are an important tool, but Lickona finds a danger in methods that stress form over content. He and Kohlberg agree that the now largely discredited "values clarification" approach is wholly inadequate, because it merely allows students to discover and express their values—whatever they may be. The problem with values clarification is that it can easily lead to relativism or even nihilism. If students think that moral values are "just my opinion," moral education is impossible. Despite some claims to the contrary, the Kohlberg approach is not relativistic, because the goal of Kohlbergian instruction in moral reasoning is to improve the quality of reasoning about morality and move the child up through the predetermined stages. The discussions of dilemmas do not merely ask students what they *would* do, but also what they *should* and *why* they should do it. The clear implication is that some choices and some reasons are better than others.

Lickona and Kohlberg are agreed on all this. The differences between them are mainly a matter of emphasis. For example, Lickona thinks that schools should teach actual controversial issues troubling contemporary society, even if these are not the best issues for fostering the development of moral reasoning. But both agree that in order to teach controversial issues it is first important to "make the classroom safe for diversity" (Lickona, 1992, p. 276). This amounts to what we have been calling functional tolerance in the classroom. Lickona's ideas are a popularized version of one strand of Kohlberg's later work. Kohlberg, following Durkheim and others, emphasizes restructuring the school. The purpose of so doing is to promote a key element of moral education: Stage 3 conformity to group values through increasing emotional attachment to the classroom as a group. Many advocates of character education would agree with this approach.

Another very promising cluster of methods of teaching skills directly related to tolerance is discussed by Goleman (1995) in his review of work on "emotional intelligence," which he contends "goes hand in hand with education for character, for moral development, and for citizenship" (p. 286). Essentially, emotional intelligence involves cognitive control of emotion. This means subduing emotions such as fear and threat by using conscious thought and suppressing with one part of the brain the "propensity to act" on the emotions arising from another part of the brain (p. 213). Goleman makes a convincing case that cognitive monitoring and control of feelings can be taught. It is not easy to learn cognitive monitoring, in large part because the speed of emotional processing is greater than that of cognitive processing. Emotional perception is faster; it "sacrifices accuracy for speed" (p. 292). We can react to an emotion before we have had a chance to think. Yet, although we may not be able to choose our emotions, we are responsible for how we react to them. The relation of cognitive monitoring of emotions to tolerance is clear, because tolerance arises from thinking before acting on a feeling.

Teaching tolerance through emotional control is also related to topics discussed in the section of Chapter 4 on personality types. Highly aggressive people, for example, who find it very difficult to be tolerant, tend to have a "deep perceptual bias" leading them to "act on the basis of the assumption of hostility or threat" (Goleman, 1995, p. 235), even when there is no basis in reality for that assumption. The importance of this is great. We have several times seen that perceptions of threat from a group are one of the best predictors of intolerance toward it. Although threat is not always associated with intolerance, Marcus et al. (1995) found that nearly all of their subjects "perceived their least-liked group as extremely threatening" (p. 112). Goleman (1995) surveyed many programs that teach violence prevention, including some that concentrate on reducing sense of threat (see pp. 276-279, 301-309). These include programs with names such as Resolving Conflict Creatively and the Social Competence Program. Most of the programs focus on controlling emotional outbursts and helping students deal with their short-term, day-to-day tolerance. Less attention is paid to feelings based on beliefs, or "emotions that flow from thoughts" (Goleman, 1995, p. 293), which are more important for tolerance in the way we have been studying it in this book. But the implications for teaching tolerance are similar whether the "trigger" is long-term hate or short-term anger. In either case, the trick is to teach people to understand their emotions better so as to govern them more effectively.

Discussions of this sort always run the risk of overemphasizing the distinction between feelings and thoughts. In fact, it is rare for one to occur without the other. Emotions may provide the motivation for hard thinking. We can and do think about our emotions, and feelings arise from our thoughts and beliefs. Tolerance occurs when we regulate our negative thoughts and emotions enough so that we do not act in ways that are contrary to the rights of others.

Multicultural Education in Schools and Colleges

Multicultural education is everywhere. No term is more used in the pedagogical literature related to tolerance, except perhaps *diversity*. The diversity and multiplicity of types of multicultural education are so great that it is hard to know what to include in our survey. Many educational activities are routinely listed under the rubric, such as museum exhibits for young children (Walsh, 1996), voluntary workshops in high schools, and required courses for college students. Subjects range broadly and include such topics as Afrocentrism, bilingual education (of which there are several types), sexual orientations, and ethnic differences in learning styles.

One thing that most multicultural education efforts have in common is that the main focus is *social* diversity and the celebration of that diversity. This contrasts with the permitting of differences that political tolerance so often implies. Indeed, multicultural education usually aims at "broadmindedness rather than tolerance" (Pratte, 1985, p. 114), that is, at positive acceptance of differences rather than merely putting up with them. "Respect" for others, rather than tolerance of them, is also a more common and more appropriate goal in multicultural education (Royce, 1982). In ordinary discourse, we often call people who value diversity "tolerant," and when multicultural educators use the term *tolerance* this is often what they mean. For example, Heller and Hawkins (1994) describe the Southern Poverty Law Center's Teaching Tolerance Project, which focuses mostly on racial and ethnic issues and provides free materials to schools. The project publishes a magazine, *Teaching Tolerance,* that tells many heartwarming stories about successful ways tolerance has been promoted in schools, but it reports on almost no systematic studies that one could use as evidence of the effectiveness of various approaches to multicultural education.

Nieto's (1996) categorization of the goals of multicultural education is apt. She sees a progression of goals for multicultural education, a series of steps or stages up from "monocultural education" toward wholehearted support for pluralism. The first step is tolerance. Tolerance is a way one might enter the path leading toward valuing diversity. As students go beyond tolerance, they can attain progressively more advanced goals: acceptance of, then respect for others, and finally affirmation of the importance of other cultures. Hence, for Nieto, tolerance is a jumping-off point at best, the beginning rather than the end of the enterprise.

One of the big issues in multicultural education concerns who or what groups should be included. Some, but not all, racial, ethnic, national origin, and language groups are usually included. But some have argued that other, perhaps equally "ascriptive," groups should be added—such as women, gay men and lesbians, various religions, and social classes. Are there, for example, cultural differences between the sexes that warrant including women's studies in multicultural education?

Even if there is agreement on the list of groups that are the proper subjects of multicultural education, defining membership in these groups can be quite complicated. One reason is that the categories (except for sex) are seldom truly objective. Everyone is a member of more than one group. I have a friend, Ed, whose grandfather, Louis, was from a part of Germany that, as he was emigrating, was becoming part of the new state of Lithuania. Louis emigrated to England, where his son Sam (my friend's father) was born. Sam moved to the United States as a young man, where Ed was born. When approached by a survey researcher and asked to specify his ethnic identity and background, Ed did not know how to reply: German, Lithuanian, East European, English? His father spoke with an English accent, but perhaps the key fact was that his German-Lithuanian-English grandfather was Jewish? His grandmother, however, was Irish Catholic—and this is to say nothing of his mother's side of the family, who were mostly German Lutherans in origin. This level of mixed ancestry and intermarriage is fairly common in the United States and is becoming increasingly widespread (Alba, 1985).

It is no wonder that some 10-20% of people surveyed cannot or will not specify an ethnicity, even when survey researchers, such as those working for the U.S. Census or the General Social Survey, make it clear that they want respondents only to say which group they *identify with* or which group they *feel closest to*. Nor is it surprising that when General Social Survey researchers went back to respondents a month after the first interview and repeated the ethnicity question, one-fourth of the respondents answered the question differently than they had the first time (Smith, 1984b). Ethnicity is an uncertain amalgam of skin color, religion, language, and national origin. Different parts of that mix are important to different people as well as to the same people in different situations. There is a tendency to feel somehow "related" to one's group, but when one remembers that even first cousins have only one-eighth of their genes in common, the actual degree of biological relation among, say, Catholics is no greater than the degree of relation between Catholics and Jews. There are more objective, or behavioral, ways to define a person's ethnicity than how he or she feels about it. One might inquire whether an individual can speak a particular language or attends particular religious services, but when such behavioral criteria are used, *many* fewer people are able to say what their ethnic identities are (Smith, 1984b). It is ironic that multicultural education is based on *group* traits, identities, and cultures, but membership in the groups can be determined only by *individual* subjective choice, sometimes perhaps by whim.

Think of the 25% of the population who, in the space of a month, gave different answers to the same question about their ethnicity. Add to these the 10% to 20% who do not believe they have an ethnicity or do not know what it is. That sums to nearly half the population. One problem multicultural education faces in the United States is the large numbers of people who might feel excluded from an approach that stresses ethnic identity. When one-third to one-half of the population is made up of persons who identify with no particular ethnicity or who change it monthly, and when researchers are, if anything, even more confused about the meaning of ethnicity (Phinney, 1996) and race (Yee, Fairchild, Weizmann, & Wyatt, 1993), it is no wonder that it is sometimes hard to decide what topics multicultural education ought to cover, and that this question is often contested.

The difficulty of defining the "cultural" groups that are the proper subject of multicultural education often generates controversy. Take as an example a situation I encountered when I was writing the first draft of this chapter in the spring of 1996. Some parents in a nearby town were opposing a school district's plan to present a "homosexual tolerance program" in its high school. These parents felt that the district was "trying to reconstruct students' attitudes," and they were surely right. The school claimed that the program was "part of diversity training," no different from programs on Native Americans, to which the community did not object. But the opposed parents said that the program would "prompt homosexuality" and teach students to "tolerate perversion." Using this example to return to our definitional questions: Is being gay "the same" as being Native American? If not, what is the key difference that requires that the rules covering one be inapplicable to the other? Can students be compelled without parental consent to take a course or attend a workshop about both groups, either group, or neither?

The controversies are if anything more intense in higher education, except that, for obvious reasons, they less often involve students' parents. Diversity and multicultural education have also become entangled in the so-called culture wars, battles over the curriculum that pit those who wish to challenge the "White male" curriculum with a more diverse course of studies. All forms of direct teaching of tolerance have the potential for controversy, but multicultural education in higher education seems prone to unusually intense dispute, which receives considerable coverage in the national news media. One well-known suggestion for how to handle debates over the undergraduate curriculum is to make them part of the curriculum. Controversy, says Graff (1992), "is the life and soul of a democratic intellectual institution" (p. 136). By learning about the debates that divide their professors—over whether, for example, the literary canon is biased against women and minorities—students are invited to partici-pate in the curriculum at a high level of intellectual sophistication. Rather than exposing students to a series of mutually contradictory lessons from different professors—which encourages students either to pick a side prematurely or to become cynical relativists, telling their professors what they want to hear—teaching about the controversies "turns the problem into the solution" (p. 56). The problem is not, says Graff, a lack of agreement; rather, it is a lack of "respectful disagreement" (p. 13). By bringing debate into the curriculum, rather than continuing to proliferate antagonistic noncommunicating camps, one re-vives the 12th-century ideal of higher education quoted previously, an ideal that is at the root of intellectual tolerance: "Nothing is perfectly known until it has been masticated in the jaws of debate" (see Chapter 4). As persuasive as I find this line of argument, like so much else pertaining to CMMC education, it is supported only by anecdotal evidence.

We can get a sense of the kinds of metacontroversies that are involved in multicultural education in college by comparing the recommendations of the American Association of Colleges and Universities (1995) with those of a group of faculty and graduate students teaching diversity and pluralism courses at the State University of New York at Albany (Colesante, Smith, & Biggs, 1996a, 1996b). There is ample agreement between the two sets of authors; neither group wishes to ignore diversity or deny its importance. Both agree, for example, that it would be unconscionable for U.S. history courses to ignore the experiences of large sectors of the population (e.g., women and Blacks) or for literature courses to exclude works by members of racial and ethnic minorities. They also agree that learning how to live in a diverse society is one of the key lessons the education system can impart. What they disagree about is how the education system can best help students to learn how to thrive amid heterogeneity. The main point of disagreement concerns whether curricula should stress similarities or differences among individuals and the groups to which they belong.

The AACU report makes recommendations based on a collection of case studies from several colleges and universities. The report's authors do not think that stressing the similarities of racial-ethnic-cultural groups is the best approach; they see this as a denial of diversity. Rather, they recommend "respectful attention" to differences and say that it is important to "prepare students for a world in which unitary agreement does not now exist and is not likely ever to exist" (pp. xx-xxi). I think it is a mistake to think of ethnicity, race, and gender as facts or ideas about which one agrees or disagrees. Doing so is the logical tort known as a category mistake. One agrees or disagrees with ideas, not states of being. It is important to avoid confusing categories such as Hispanic and gay with matters of dispute such as political ideologies and religious doctrines.

Colesante and colleagues (1996a, 1996b) have evolved a better approach. Initially, they taught their diversity requirement courses in ways similar to those suggested in the AACU report, but they found a serious problem: They seemed to be promoting the worst sorts of stereotyping. And they sometimes gave ammunition to student stereotypers by reviewing social science research on group differences. This research usually finds statistically significant, but practically insignificant, differences between groups. Students were using knowledge of the small differences between groups to reinforce their stereotypes about individuals. The instructors were aghast over what they saw happening. Teaching about group differences actually seemed to be making it less likely that students would learn how to tolerate or to respect one another. These observations led them to switch the focus of their courses to answer questions such as, What does it mean to be a good citizen in a pluralistic society? How can social cooperation occur in a diverse community? Colesante et al. (1996a) used a "just community" model drawn from Kohlberg's later works and concentrated their efforts on how to solve the common problems and promote the common good in a diverse society. They did this because they were persuaded that when multiculturalism promotes the "cult of 'us' and 'them' " people cannot learn to solve problems together (p. 11). The professors and graduate students conducting this quasi-experiment in multicultural education are still gathering data. Whatever their final results, their combination of practice and research on practice is a model of what needs to be done to begin to answer the myriad difficult questions about how best to proceed with multicultural education.

In the past, efforts to teach tolerance tended to be less specific and more indirect than those described in this section on multicultural education. One popular approach that began in the 1960s, and one that is still with us today in revised form, is to use subjects in the ordinary curriculum to provide students with facts and concepts that can affect their attitudes about other peoples and cultures in ways that lead them to be more tolerant of human diversity. Examples include world history classes that are expected to broaden students' thinking about other societies and religions, or requirements that each student take a course or two on a non-Western culture. That kind of gentle indirection seems quaint today, though I recall it being quite controversial when it was first widely introduced in the 1960s. In the past, the emphasis was on adding to the menu from which an individual might choose; sometimes today, less gently and indirectly, we hear calls for compulsory training in diversity for White males.

This section about multicultural education has been the most speculative I have offered, because very little of the vast enterprise of multicultural education has been subject to systematic evaluation. Most surveys consist of strings of anecdotes, and most studies are case studies. Perhaps this is the case in part because multicultural educators often want to require students to take courses or attend workshops the educators "know" will be good for the students. Those who have such convictions are not likely to think about, much less advocate, having control groups of students who do not take the courses or participate in the workshops. On the other hand, when such courses or workshops are elective, one has all the problems associated with evaluating programs peopled by volunteer subjects. It would not take much ingenuity to get around these problems, however, especially if, as is usually the case, students take the courses in different semesters or terms.

The main barrier to the gathering of usable knowledge about the effectiveness of multicultural education is a lack of will. Ironically, commitment to the goals of multicultural education, if it leads to impatience with studies, can reduce the probability of finding ways to improve practice.[11] The few studies that I know of have been promising. Pascarella, Edison, Nora, Hagedorn, and Terenzini (1996), for example, found that students who participated in racial or cultural awareness workshops tended to become more open-minded as a result, an effect that was especially strong among White male participants, the very students who most needed improvement—that is, who had scored as the least open-minded on the pretest.

The Tolerance Curriculum Project

Our final case of the direct teaching of tolerance, and the pedagogical program most focused on the issues addressed in this book, was a quasi-experiment conducted in Minnesota in the early 1990s. A 4-week tolerance curriculum was taught to some 300 ninth-grade students (Avery, Bird, Johnstone, Sullivan, & Thalhammer, 1992; Avery et al., 1993). Unlike most of the studies reviewed in this chapter, this one was specifically designed to see whether direct teaching of tolerance would raise the tolerance levels of students significantly above those of control groups of students who were not exposed to the curriculum. The study was also designed to investigate whether the curriculum would be more effective with some students than with others and, if so, why. Because of this study's many strong features, I want to conclude this chapter on the direct teaching of tolerance with a discussion of its methods and findings. Doing so allows me to pull together several themes covered in this and previous chapters.

As we have seen, there is little evidence that taking ordinary civics courses increases students' tolerance. Given that tolerance is rarely taught in such courses, it should come as no surprise that it is seldom learned in them. Building on this insight that the "educational system has failed" to teach tolerance "because it has not tried" to do so (Sullivan, Avery, Thalhammer, Wood, & Bird, 1994, p. 321), the Minnesota researchers designed a curriculum to see whether it is possible to teach tolerance directly, especially political tolerance, in secondary schools. We already know with some certainty that tolerance is learned indirectly in college. Our main evidence for this is the large gap in tolerance measures between the college educated and those who end their formal studies in high school. Interestingly, as the Minnesota researchers point out, were tolerance actually to be taught in secondary schools or earlier, one effect would be to reduce the gap between the more and less educated.

The Minnesota junior high school students in the study sample were first pretested on their tolerance levels. Tolerance was defined using the stringent Sullivan "least-liked group" criterion. As in previous studies, it was found that these adolescents were "more likely to value and apply the principle of majority rule than of minority rights" (Thalhammer, Wood, Bird, Avery, & Sullivan, 1994, p. 330). When comparing students who scored high and low on the pretest tolerance measure, the researchers found that less-tolerant students felt much more threatened by their least-liked groups. Nearly all students found their least-liked groups threatening: "Students frequently expressed their concerns that a rally involving their least-liked group would inevitably end in death and destruction" (p. 342). But this kind of exaggeration was not as strong among the high-tolerance students. It is also interesting that students low in tolerance were more likely to take action in support of their beliefs, whereas students high in tolerance "reported that they would not be as likely to take action either for or against the rights of the groups they dislike" (p. 339; compare Marcus et al., 1995).

The 4-week curriculum (Avery et al., 1993) was implemented as a unit in the civics classes in one urban and two rural schools. Control groups of students who continued to study the regular civics curriculum were drawn from the same schools. The curriculum involved the use of several different methods, but a common theme among them was discussion of political dilemmas so as to develop students' critical thinking about controversial issues. The results can be summarized as answers to two questions: Did students learn the content of the curriculum? Did studying the curriculum influence their attitudes concerning political tolerance? The answer to each is a qualified yes.

Pretest tolerance did not influence how much of the curriculum students learned, but the amount they learned did influence their posttest tolerance scores (Wood et al., 1994, p. 361). Openness to the influence of the curriculum varied by personality type. For example, the scores of students high on an authoritarianism scale changed little as a result of the 4-week unit: "Authoritarian students were highly resistant to the message of the curriculum" (p. 365).

On average, students' scores went up about 2 points on a 30-point tolerance scale. This was the modal effect. Most students' scores went up a modest, but statistically significant, amount. This was also a substantively significant effect, as it involved students' moving "from mild intolerance to mild tolerance" (Avery et al., 1992, p. 401). Especially important to note is that the curriculum brought about changes in tolerance even though it did not affect students' dislike of their least-liked groups or their sense of how threatening those groups are.

Just as interesting as these typical effects were the results for less typical groups of students whose tolerance scores increased or decreased by more than a standard deviation—on average, by 8 to 9 points. There were 85 of these Increasers (25% of the sample) and 22 Decreasers (7% of the sample). Two facts are particularly significant about the Increasers. First, in the pretest they generally did not find their least-liked groups threatening; they simply saw the groups as evil. Second, the curriculum increased their tendency to think of disliked groups in terms of the groups' "rights." Decreasers, by contrast, found their least-liked groups threatening in the pretest, and studying the curriculum heightened their fears (Bird, Sullivan, Avery, Thalhammer, & Wood, 1994). The Decreasers also tended to be low in self-esteem and high in authoritarianism. This suggests that for students who feel threatened, who are high in authoritarianism, and who are low in self-esteem, the direct teaching of tolerance may often backfire. Curriculum designers would do well to keep this in mind.

One especially interesting result of the Minnesota research concerns the question of how quickly tolerance is learned or can be learned. The theorists discussed in Chapter 4 who assume that indirect and unintentional methods are more effective also usually assume that to be truly effective, learning must be slow; it must, as it were, gradually erode students' former attitudes and create new values by sedimentation. These metaphors may accurately describe how attitudes and values are learned in some circumstances, but the Minnesota studies suggest that rapid tolerance learning can take place—in as little time as a few weeks. A similar conclusion can be derived from studies based on Kohlberg's theory. Discussion of moral dilemmas can have effects in a matter of months. Furthermore, such gains in moral reasoning have almost always been shown to be permanent: Once students have attained a higher level of moral reasoning, they rarely slip back.

In general, learning theory has as much room for spurts as for gradual accumulations. There tends to be a presumption in values education in favor of learning that occurs so slowly that the learner does not know what is happening, but "epiphanies," or flashes of insight, may be as possible in the learning of attitudes and beliefs as in the learning of, say, geometry. These suggestive findings from Kohlbergian pedagogy and even more from the Minnesota quasi-experiments are cause for optimism. Comparatively brief units of direct instruction in tolerance can be effective. The evidence from the Minnesota tolerance curriculum should be helpful for countering the debilitating pessimism about teaching democratic values that followed political socialization researchers' early results about the ineffectiveness of civic education courses. If educators actually teach tolerance, students will often learn it.

▨ Conclusion to Chapters 4 and 5:
How Education Increases Tolerance

One does not necessarily have to choose among the theories reviewed in this and the preceding chapter. Cognitive development, personality development, intergroup contact, and CMMC education are not mutually exclusive processes. Rather, it is much more probable that they are mutually reinforcing—or at least additive (see Hall & Rodeghier, 1994). Students can better learn the lessons of civic education, for instance, if they have the cognitive sophistication to appreciate the principles being discussed. Or, to cite another example, direct contact is more likely to work its beneficial effects among individuals who have been indirectly socialized to values such as universalism.

In addition to their being mutually reinforcing, the four educational processes that foster tolerance also overlap to a considerable degree. Even the division between the formal instruction pair versus the socialization pair does not hold completely. All four theories describe processes of learning; they differ mainly in the methods used to achieve the learning outcomes, but those outcomes tend to be quite parallel if not identical. For example, it may be that contact improves intergroup relations because it dispels ignorance (Stephan & Stephan, 1984), in much the same way we might expect courses in multicultural or civic education to do. And it is no serious distortion of the work of individual modernization researchers to say that the personality development they have studied ultimately could be defined as increasing cognitive sophistication.

There are fundamental differences between some of the approaches described in Chapters 4 and 5, of course. Perhaps the most important of these occurs between some goals of multicultural education and those of proponents of personality "modernization." For example, multicultural educators might try to promote ethnic pride to build self-esteem, but this is contrary to the universalism and individualism stressed by Dreeben and Inkeles (see the discussion of personality development in Chapter 4). Personality development in the direction of the "universals" addressed by Dreeben could be seen as homogenizing cultural imperialism by many advocates of multicultural education. Often what is involved in this debate between multiculturalism and personality modernization concerns drawing distinctions between public and private realms of life, distinctions that many feminist theorists, for example, dispute. Dreeben (1968), and others writing in the 1960s at the height of modernization theory, undoubtedly exaggerated the extent to which the public, modern perspective replaces the private, traditional one. Rather, it is an overlay. Or perhaps a better metaphor would be to say that the public world and how to deal with it are elements that the school can add to the child's repertoire or "menu" without reducing the significance of the private realm.

Which of the four theories or processes best explains the correlations between education and tolerance? The answer is undoubtedly "All of the above." Each theory describes an aspect of the relations between various kinds and amounts of education and various types of tolerance. The two socialization theories (personality development and intergroup contact), for example, describe effects that may occur at any education level. These socialization effects may be important for social tolerance at any stage in an education system where the social composition of the student body is sufficiently diverse, but they are more likely to be effective in promoting *moral* and *political* tolerance at the postcompulsory level. The two formal learning hypotheses (cognitive sophistication and CMMC education) describe relations that are probably most salient at higher levels of education, although earlier schooling may be important for laying crucial intellectual foundations. To investigate the accuracy of these and other speculations about the educational roots of tolerance, we will of course need much more research. Specifically, we need to examine more education variables in greater depth in ways guided by theory-based explanations about the potential effects of education on social and political beliefs and attitudes. I present some suggestions for how to do this in Chapter 7.

Although the four explanations for the relation of education to tolerance are overlapping and mutually reinforcing, it is important that we keep them distinct, both to make possible their use as guides to policy making and to facilitate research that can refine them still further. In terms of educational programs and procedures, the socialization group of theories calls for (re)organizing students' social relationships; the formal instruction group requires pedagogical action. The direct pair allows a head-on approach; the indirect pair requires more subtle techniques that may produce significant results that appear only in the long run. Such results are difficult to evaluate except through longitudinal studies such as Braddock's (1985) work on the effects of desegregation. Policy makers with limited resources will need to know which among the four processes is most likely to be effective in a specific context, because what might work in, say, the third grade could be ineffectual or counterproductive in the twelfth, and vice versa. Chapter 6 addresses some of these issues in more detail.

I will conclude here with a few general points about the four theories or categories of explanation discussed above and in Chapter 4. There is not much doubt that intergroup contact can lead to increased tolerance as well as to other positive attitudes and behaviors. But contact has this effect only when the circumstances are "right," and the balance of research on the subject seems to indicate that in schools, the right circumstances occur quite rarely. So, can we use contact to improve intergroup relations? Yes, if we are willing to make the effort, but most often educators have not been willing. Something similar applies to CMMC education. It works, but only in uncommon circumstances. We could foster tolerance using these pedagogical strategies, but we do not often do so. This failure probably has more to do with fear of controversy and lack of political will than with ignorance of pedagogical technique.

Because the "right circumstances" and the political will are and have been so rare, it is probably the case that today contact and civic instruction do not account for much of the current statistical association between tolerance and education. What we are left with, then, as the most likely explanations of the association of education and tolerance, are cognitive sophistication and personality development. We cannot "prove" that cognitive sophistication and personality development are the most important sources of tolerance, particularly given that these indirect effects are so hard to assess. The argument for making that claim ultimately is "residualist." It amounts to saying, As it isn't X or Y, about which we have direct evidence, it must be A or B, about which we have only indirect evidence. In our case, given that it isn't contact or CMMC education, it must be cognitive and personality development. But if this line of thinking is correct, it suggests interesting strategies for teaching tolerance.

Although direct approaches have considerable potential, they are so often blocked by schools and communities that it is hard to rely on them. But we may still be able to make considerable progress using indirect approaches, at least as a fallback position. There are few political and social action committees that admit to trying to repress students' personal and cognitive development. As long as curricula can be maintained that promote this development, tolerance will probably continue to be learned in schools.

CHAPTER **6**

Conclusion

Implications for Policy and Practice

E WILL GET NOWHERE by underestimating the difficulty of the task. As many studies in the research literature show, the job of promoting tolerance and reducing discrimination is indeed formidable. For instance, Tajfel (1978), in repeated studies, has demonstrated the remarkable persistence of group bias and willingness to discriminate against out-groups.[1] From a broader sociological perspective, Blalock (1982) has concluded that "discrimination, aggression, and hatred . . . can increase dramatically at any moment" (p. 118). In comparison to the apparently powerful forces leading to discrimination against out-groups, tolerance and toleration are often inadequate counterweights.

A further set of difficulties for policy and practice arises from the issues of definition discussed in the early chapters of this book. Tolerance is putting up with something you fear, do not like, or otherwise have a negative attitude toward; it involves support for the rights and liberties of *others* and not discriminating against those toward whom you have negative attitudes. We need to remember this so as to be able to distinguish being tolerant from related states, such as being unprejudiced, being indifferent, or valuing diversity. Probably the most common operational definition of tolerance in both social psychology laboratories and survey research (prior to the work of Sullivan, Marcus, Piereson, & Feldman, 1979; Sullivan, Piereson, & Marcus, 1982) has been that it is the opposite of prejudice. Respondents who answer questions about a group or a conduct in a nonprejudiced way are said to be tolerant of it. But this is not a valid definition of being tolerant. In fact, it is quite possible to be prejudiced against and tolerant of someone at the same time. If one supports the equal rights and liberties of persons engaged in conduct of which one disapproves, and if the disapproval is based at least partly on prejudice (as it usually is), then tolerance occurs jointly with prejudice. In fact, tolerance most often occurs thus joined to prejudice. This means that educators may not always need to attempt the formidable job of eradicating prejudice in order to improve intergroup relations. Fostering tolerance, which leads to ending discrimination, may suffice. This is one conclusion that can be drawn from the work of Cabrera and Nora (1994), who show that being the object of discrimination troubles college students (leads to alienation) more than does living in a prejudiced environment (see also Hurtado, 1994; Nora & Cabrera, 1996).

It is also important to remember the distinctions among social, political, and moral tolerance used throughout this volume. Although education level correlates with each kind of tolerance, and in particular cases it may be difficult to distinguish among different sorts of rights and liberties, there is only limited evidence indicating connections among the various kinds of tolerance (see Bryson, 1996, for innovative comparisons of political and musical tolerance). We do not have very good evidence, for instance, about how much individuals who are politically tolerant (who might support civil liberties such as free speech for communists) will also tend to be socially tolerant (and favor, say, the right of persons of the same sex to marry). If tolerance is not (only) a general disposition or personality trait, different kinds of tolerance will probably be learned in different ways and at different times in a person's educational experience. For example, tolerance of social diversity might be acquired rather early on in life through informal processes of socialization; ordinary social interaction among students in racially, ethnically, or religiously diverse schools

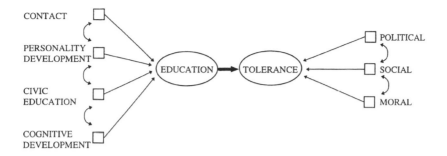

Figure 6.1. Summary of the Model of the Influence of Education on Tolerance

may teach tolerance. Political tolerance, on the other hand, such as freedom of the press for extremist parties, almost certainly cannot be learned in this way and requires appreciation of moderately complex arguments that are probably beyond the cognitive capacities of most preadolescents. In sum, although schooling may foster all three kinds of tolerance (political, social, and moral), it almost certainly does so in different ways at different educational and developmental levels.

The preceding two paragraphs touch on aspects of my model of how education fosters tolerance. Figures 6.1 and 6.2 depict that model in different ways. Figure 6.1 shows that when we say, "Education leads to tolerance," we mean four different processes by *education* and three types of attitude or belief by *tolerance.* That is illustrated here using some of the conventions of a path diagram because I think it is possible (at least conceivable) to gather enough data to test the causal relationships suggested in the figure. In any case, the four educational processes and the three tolerance types are distinct but together add up to what we mean when we say that education promotes tolerance.

Two additional sets of categories are shown in Figure 6.2: *levels* of education and *states* of or outcomes for the tolerant individual. Here the emphasis is less on suggesting possible causal paths and more on showing the full practical range of what is involved when we try to take steps to implement the idea that education can foster tolerance.

There are at least three *levels* of education (elementary, secondary, higher). To these levels of education we need to add the four *processes* discussed in Chapters 4 and 5 (personality development, cognitive development, intergroup contact, and civic, moral, and multicultural education). The components of tolerance are similarly complex. If we consider that the three kinds of tolerance as defined by *objects* of tolerance (political, social, and moral) can be expressed

EDUCATION ──────────────────▶ TOLERANCE

Level	Process	Object	State
1. Primary	1. Contact	1. Political	1. Trait
2. Secondary	2. Personality Development	2. Moral	2. Attitude
3. Higher	3. CMMC Education	3. Social	3. Belief
	4. Cognitive Development		4. Commitment
			5. Action

Figure 6.2. Components of Education and Tolerance

in one of five states of the individual (traits, attitudes, beliefs, commitments, actions), we get 15 kinds of tolerance (3 types of object multiplied by 5 individual states). Multiplying these by our 12 types of education (3 levels × 4 processes), we get 180 possible causal paths. Thus, when we say that education promotes tolerance, we could be saying 180 distinct things. Some of the 180 are so improbable that we can easily eliminate them (e.g., elementary education, leading through contact to political tolerance, ending in political action). Even so, the number is very large. It is possibly larger than 180, given that, as we have seen, some categories span a wide variety of phenomena. For example, political tolerance includes freedom of the press and the right of assembly, but freedom of assembly is distinct from (and less widely supported in the United States than) press freedom.

Despite all of these complications, Sullivan, Avery, Thalhammer, Wood, and Bird (1994) and Avery, Bird, Johnstone, Sullivan, and Thalhammer (1992) have shown that it is possible to teach political tolerance, at a fairly young age, in a relatively brief set of lessons. Of course, their curriculum did not always work with everyone. Some students high in authoritarianism were less tolerant after they experienced the curriculum. Yet the burden of proof has clearly shifted to those who think one cannot teach political tolerance in high schools. Political tolerance might be the easiest kind to teach, at least from the standpoint of avoiding parental and community opposition, because in the last analysis, political tolerance is based on well-established principles of constitutional law. Social and moral tolerance could be more difficult to teach in secondary schools, where peer pressures for conformity are perhaps most extreme. We might expect the curricular approaches to teaching of most forms of tolerance (cognitive development and CMMC education) to be somewhat easier in higher than in secondary education. On the other hand, higher education might be too late in students' personal development to expect strong tolerance outcomes from the socialization approaches (intergroup contact and personality development).

Perhaps Avery, Sullivan, and the rest of the Minnesota team were so successful in part because they worked with clearly delimited levels and processes of education and well-defined objects and states of tolerance. If so, one implication for practice is clear. Educators will likely do better if they focus on one or a small cluster of the causal paths suggested by Figures 6.1 and 6.2. Trying to move ahead on all fronts at once might be appealing because it seems to deal with the whole problem of intergroup relations, but it may not be highly effective. It may be more realistic to hope that lessons learned well through some processes, and aimed at particular objects and states of tolerance, will transfer to others. But, as Hall and Rodeghier (1994) have shown, just because education can foster some sorts of tolerance, it does not automatically follow that it will promote all. In fact, educators would be mistaken to hope (or fear) that their efforts would be likely to encourage tolerance toward political violence. It seems clear that education reduces the likelihood that individuals will tolerate violent political action. Many educators might consider this good news. On the other hand, education also tends to reduce tolerance for blue-collar actions—even orderly, nonviolent actions—which some educators might consider bad news.

Cabrera and Nora (1994) also encourage specificity when they tell us to focus on reducing acts of discrimination in college classrooms rather than on increasing generally tolerant attitudes and campus climate. Given that discrimination in class is the proximate cause of feelings of alienation among students, we should begin there—hoping, perhaps, for long-term improvements in climate. This is, in any case, a more realistic hope than we might have for approaching the problem the other way around (improving climate as a way to influence specific behaviors). Aiming at discriminatory behaviors of faculty also has the big advantage of being the more easily achieved, because it is a more specific goal.

One main general implication for policy and practice might seem paradoxical. Because the relation of education to tolerance is very complex, successful educational efforts are very simple or focused. This is because the relation of education to tolerance is actually many relations. They share a family resemblance, but they are distinct. It is best to work on them one at a time. This can be encouraging news for practitioners. We need not fix everything before we can fix anything. And we can always hope that fixing one thing will have a sort of modeling effect; what students learn through one process about a particular sort of tolerance may provide a pattern of learning for other educational processes and kinds of tolerance. For these reasons, the approach I take below in summarizing the policy implications of this book is disaggregated, broken down by category. There are several ways to discuss specific strategies. As the rubrics developed in Chapters 4 and 5 are by now familiar, I first use those to organize some concluding remarks. These are followed by a checklist of recommendations designed for the use of practitioners.

Personality Development and Cognitive Development

Personality development and cognitive development are broad processes that extend over many years. The evidence reviewed in Chapter 4 suggests that they are very powerful influences on individuals' propensities toward tolerance. However, it is difficult for educators involved in day-to-day teaching, who usually see particular students for 10 months at most, to assess the results of these two long-term processes. Students move on to the next class or grade before gradual, cumulative effects become evident. Because of this, policies to promote tolerance through personality and cognitive development are sometimes more appropriately made at the state and national levels of planning. However, most educators would probably consider personality development and cognitive development worthy goals in their own right. The fact that they can be pursued for the sake of tolerance as well makes them doubly attractive; tolerance becomes a fortunate by-product of the pursuit of students' emotional and intellectual development. Thus, tolerance goals can be tacked on to other educational goals. Teaching tolerance requires at most minor adjustments in what many educators are likely to want to do in any case: to further students' development.

Particularly relevant for tolerance is that set of traits and characteristics that seems to bridge the personality and cognitive spheres of development. I have in mind those aspects of personality development discussed in Chapter 4 that foster the use of and appreciation for the intellect and the rational solving of social problems. Encouraging open-mindedness and discouraging dogmatism are probably the most important steps educators can take to assist in the growth of tolerance. Also important, as we have seen, is the improvement of students' self-confidence, self-esteem, and internal locus of control. All these are useful in helping individuals overcome irrational fears that can lead to discriminatory acts before fears can be checked by tolerant beliefs, attitudes, and values.

Whatever methods educators use to expand students' cognitive development, however, they run the risk of opposition. Reducing dogmatism by, for example, encouraging students to discuss controversial matters often leads to organized resistance from conservative religious groups, some of whom are quite willing to label the promotion of students' intellectual flexibility, cognitive complexity, and higher-level thinking as the work of the devil (Gaddy, Hall, & Marzanno, 1996). As is often the case with courses in civics, so too with educational programs to assist students' personal and intellectual development: Instructors, administrators, and school boards may conclude that it is politically wiser to avoid effective instruction.

Intergroup Contact and
Direct CMMC Instruction

Contact Among Students

Educators' efforts can easily backfire or have unanticipated consequences. This is perhaps most true when educators try to affect attitudes by manipulating the social environment of schooling through intergroup contact. It is here that the "dynamic relationship between individual behavior and collective results" can produce unpleasant surprises, where "small incentives . . . can lead to strikingly polarized results" (Schelling, 1971, pp. 186, 146). For example, if students in a high school or a college have a moderate desire not to be in the minority at a table in the cafeteria, the nearly inevitable result will be total segregation, with all the Whites and all the Blacks sitting only with their own groups (assuming, for the sake of simplifying the argument, that there are only two groups). This does not mean that the students are racist, by most conventional definitions. They may even prefer to sit with members of other groups, as long as this does not put them in a minority of, say, 40% or less. But such preferences produce total segregation every time. A 50/50 split—for example, 6 students from each group at a table—will satisfy everyone's desire not to be in the minority, but a cafeteria represents a fluid situation, with students exiting and entering frequently. Imagine that at our table of 12 students with the 6:6 ratio, 2 students from group X leave. The ratio of X to Y is now 6:4, which is fine for Xs, but beginning to be uncomfortable for Ys. If the next 2 students looking for seats are from group X, and they join the table, it now has an 8:4 ratio. This is still "integrated," of course, but it is just below the comfort threshold of 40%. If one of the Ys finishes quickly so as to exit the slightly uncomfortable situation, that leaves a ratio of 8:3. The empty seat will either remain vacant or be filled by an X, thus moving closer to the complete separation of the two groups. The greater the imbalance in the total population of the two groups, the faster this will happen. The more likely new entrants are to come from one (the bigger) group, the quicker the imbalances at particular tables will occur. (See Schelling, 1971, 1978, for more elaborated models.)

One can vary the percentages, raising or lowering the ratio of Xs to Ys or adjusting the comfort threshold, but the result is always the same—only the speed with which it occurs will vary. (For an empirical verification of these "predictions," see Schofield, 1986.) The main way to eliminate such self-segregation is to assign seats. Although this is easy enough to do in a classroom, it is usually too difficult to be practical in a cafeteria. There is another way out of the dilemma, at least in theory: "Enlarging the area within which a person counts his neighbors . . . attenuates the tendency to segregate" (Schelling, 1971, p. 164). In the cafeteria example, the "area" would be the whole room, not just a particular table. If one can be comfortable because the room contains many "ins," one might be more willing to sit at a table with "outs." But transformations of how students see the world are not easy to effectuate. Failing such changes, self-segregation seems all but inevitable in voluntary settings.

Note that segregation may occur even if the students prefer integration, as long as they have a stronger desire to avoid being in a minority; most students are under enormous peer pressure and have little desire to become pioneers of integrated seating. When I was in school, something similar happened (and perhaps happens still) at junior high school dances, where the boys would gather on one side of the room and the girls on the other. Although many of us were presumably attending because we wanted to dance with members of the opposite sex, it rarely happened—unless a chaperone intervened to "integrate" the groups or a few daredevils broke the ice. Our collective behavior could have badly misled an outside observer (the hypothetical ethologist from another solar system) about our individual motives.

These examples, the dance and the cafeteria, strongly suggest that in matters of intergroup relations, simply letting things take their natural course, or using market models of choice, means that things may not turn out as we would have wished, and that we may often be surprised or puzzled by the results. Neither the students in the cafeteria nor those at the dance have to seek segregation for it to happen. This is why Schofield (1986, 1993) is right to insist that ignoring these problems of group differences and hoping that doing so will make them go away is naive. Effective contact will often not be very subtle. Although scholarship is still divided on how subtle one should be in order to be effective, there is not much doubt that it is less subtle and much more direct than approaches typically used to encourage personality and cognitive development.

As I mentioned briefly in Chapter 5, the controversies among researchers on intergroup contact are mostly versions of a fairly simple question: Should we seek to stress the similarities among individuals across the two groups or to understand the differences between the groups? The design of contact situations such as cooperative work groups hinges importantly on how this question is answered. For many reasons, I do not believe researchers will be able to discover the answer—there probably is no single answer. In general, we are unable to identify the one thing that always works, but we are often able to point to several things that sometimes work. That is acceptable from the standpoint of a decision maker—except when the several things are contradictory and there is no clear guide to choosing the best solution among them. Our decision-making powers here are quite limited.

But what is our best guess? In my opinion, specific sorts of cooperative work groups in desegregated school settings show great promise, so great that it borders on the irresponsible for educators not to use them. As Robert Slavin (1985), one of the creators and strongest advocates of such groups, notes:

The practical implications of the research [on cooperative learning] . . . are unambiguous. There is a strong positive effect of cooperative learning on intergroup relations. Thirty years after Allport laid out the basic principles, we finally have practical, proven methods for implementing contact theory in the desegregated classroom. (p. 60)

The basic steps in cooperative education involve the teacher assigning students to multiethnic, multirace teams of four or five members who work cooperatively on assignments. Students are graded as a team. Each student's contribution to the total grade is his or her improvement over prior performance, which "ensures that no student is automatically a drag on the team score" (Slavin, 1985, p. 56). Three of Allport's conditions surveyed in Chapter 5 are met using these methods: (a) The students cooperate rather than compete; (b) there is equal status among group members—even using the more rigorous definition of *equal* demanded by Cohen (1984); and (c) the teacher indicates, by assignment of students to mixed groups, an unambiguous commitment to cross-ethnic work. The results, in a nutshell, have been that cooperative learning has improved intergroup relations, as measured by cross-ethnic friendships and by general group attitudes. And it has had these positive social effects while also *increasing* students' measured learning beyond that of students in control groups.

I began this chapter by referring again to Tajfel's finding about how quickly in-group solidarity grows. Here we see Slavin (1985, 1990) and Johnson, Johnson, and Maruyama (1984) using in-group solidarity to benefit intergroup relations. But might not cooperative learning groups, by increasing in-group solidarity, lead to out-group hostility, especially when the teams compete with one another? Tajfel found that competing teams did increase out-group bias, even in minimal laboratory groups. Slavin suggests that the increase in ill will came *because* the study was done in minimal laboratory groups. In real settings in field experiments stretching over many weeks, rather than over a few hours, as in Tajfel's experiments, students made cross-ethnic friends outside their teams. In short, there was transfer of what was learned in the contact situation to settings beyond the immediate group interactions (contrast Hewstone & Brown, 1986).[2]

Direct Instruction: CMMC Education

There are many varieties of civic, moral, and multicultural (or CMMC) education. The differences among them depend mainly on two things: (a) the objects of tolerance, or the kinds of tolerance that one envisions teaching directly, and (b) the methods used to do the teaching. Beyond that observation, CMMC education is a realm of activity about which it is quite difficult to generalize. Broad national studies, such as inquiries into whether students have taken courses in civic education, are usually not specific enough about the curriculum followed and the methods used to provide much guidance about the effectiveness of such instruction. On the other hand, specific studies of particular programs, which have the virtue of certainty about what was taught and how, are so varied from one to the next that generalization is difficult at best.

We can be quite certain that knowledge of civics, or information about the political system, is very important. Whereas studies of students who have taken civics *courses* are not encouraging, civics *knowledge* is almost always one of the best predictors of tolerance, especially political tolerance. The seeming riddle is easily solved: Civics courses do not predict tolerance levels because students gain little knowledge about the political system in such courses. It is probably safe to assume, however, that civics knowledge would continue to have tolerance-boosting effects even were it to be gained in schools. I know of no body of knowledge of comparable importance for teaching social and moral tolerance, but we can be fairly certain concerning methods of teaching. The methods used to convey civics knowledge, and presumably other parts of the curriculum, are crucial. Without educational self-direction and a school climate that encourages open discussion and inquiry, attempts to teach (or preach) about democratic values are likely to be of limited effectiveness.

It is probably safe to say that successful approaches for teaching some kinds of tolerance at some levels are not necessarily effective for teaching other kinds at other levels. Routes to teaching political tolerance, in particular, may differ significantly from those likely to lead to social and moral tolerance. One way to examine such differences is to consider the problem of self-interest. This is an issue that often comes up in all varieties of CMMC education, and different varieties seem destined to approach it in different ways.

The Role of Self-Interest

One of the reasons political tolerance may be comparatively easy to teach directly is that in politics self-interested differences are legitimate, ordinary, and expected. Indeed, a main function of politics is to resolve such differences. It is a fairly simple matter to explain to those who value a democratic polity why political tolerance is in everyone's long-term self-interest. It is part of the deal that defines political society in a democracy. One does not need to have nice attitudes toward opponents, one needs only, as Madison (1788/1961) suggested in Federalist Number 10, to normalize competition among self-interested individuals and groups. On the other hand, to say that someone's moral beliefs, such as opposition to abortion, are just self-interest or part of a deal can be inappropriate and insulting. The same might be true of attitudes toward social policies, such as support for affirmative action; thinking of those attitudes as only expressions of self-interest is surely incorrect. Deciding whether attitudes and beliefs are matters of values or prejudices, on the one hand, or matters of self-interest, on the other, will partly determine educational strategies for addressing such attitudes and beliefs.

This whole topic of whether people's attitudes reflect their self-interest is quite complex. One recent study helps to set the stage. Bobo and Kluegel (1993) compared Whites' and Blacks' attitudes toward policies meant to enhance social equality. The researchers categorize the policies in two ways: (a) whether the policies focus on opportunities or outcomes and (b) whether they are aimed at income equality or at racial equality. The four resulting categories are summarized in Figure 6.3. Whites are most supportive of policies that fit into Category 1, that is, policies that aim to increase opportunities to improve incomes. They are least supportive of Category 4, that is, policies that try to equalize outcomes

	Increase Opportunities	Equalize Outcomes
Income Targeted	1	2
Race Targeted	3	4

Figure 6.3. Categories of Goals for Social Policy

for racial groups. By contrast, Blacks support the two categories (1 and 4) about equally.

Bobo and Kluegel looked into why Whites oppose race targeting. The explanations they tested were as follows: (a) self-interest, whether the individual type (good for me) or the group type (good for us); (b) prejudice or racism, whether old (simple bigotry) or new (symbolic racism); and (c) stratification ideology, such as beliefs about what is fair or right given values about equality, individualism, and so on. Neither individual self-interest, nor prejudice and racism, nor stratification beliefs and values explained Whites' opposition to race targeting. Not only did Whites' attitudes about policy not originate in racism and prejudice, "our results cast serious doubt on the validity of" taking "attitudes toward policy as a measure of racism or prejudice" (p. 460). Of the explanations tested, only group self-interest accounted for Whites' views: "The strongest aspect of group self-interest seems to be a straightforward calculation by whites that members of their own group will not benefit" from a policy (p. 459). Assuming the correctness of these conclusions, a pedagogy focused on reducing racism, for example, would be quite unlikely to influence attitudes toward social policy. What we do not know at this point is how far Bobo and Kluegel's conclusions can be generalized. Must teaching tolerance focus on group self-interest, or might it build upon *enlightened* individual self-interest? Until we have a better grasp of the origins of attitudes, we will not know how to design pedagogies to influence them. Advanced though it is, Bobo and Kluegel's research deals only with some aspects of the problem.

A self-interested explanation can be quite complex and more difficult to separate from a prejudiced explanation than might at first be evident. If someone has a negative attitude toward group X because he believes it is a real threat to his self-interest, the origins of the negative attitude seem clear. But what if the belief is clearly wrong, paranoid even? The government and the Jews are out to get me, for example (Ezekiel, 1995). Then the threat to self-interest is just a prejudice (an erroneous negative belief), and a good educational strategy would focus on eliminating prejudice. If the threat to self-interest is realistic, on the other hand, the pedagogical strategy for discussing tolerance should reflect this difference. Lessons should turn to consideration of the idea that some real challenges to one's self-interest have to be endured, whereas others do not. Distinguishing among them would be direct, practical instruction in tolerance. (See the discussion of rights in Chapter 1.)

There may also be another type of group self-interest, broader than what Bobo and Kluegel describe. This can be especially important for tolerance of moral and cultural differences. Often this group self-interest expresses itself as what appears (especially to those on the receiving end of the intolerance) to be mean-spirited opposition to other people having fun (with sex, drugs, entertainment, or whatever). Any systematic count of legislative acts through history would yield a considerable percentage of this sort of morals legislation. Opposition to the sexual practices or orientations of others is perhaps the most telling example. For instance, a person who is not gay and who does not expect ever to be bothered by gays might still believe that it is wrong to ensure equal rights for gays. That belief would be hard to explain as a threat to the person's individual self-interest—or to his group self-interest, in the sense of Bobo and Kluegel's "straightforward calculation" of his group's benefit. Rather, tolerating gays might be seen by such an individual as a threat to a broader national culture or to a way of life that defines his or his group's self-concept. We might call this *cultural* self-interest.

Cultural self-interest could be, for example, what is behind some opposition to bilingualism in the United States (Huddy & Sears, 1995). A person motivated by simple self-interest might be expected to say: "What's it to me? What do I care if they want to speak Spanish?" An educator might wish to build upon or foster such attitudes, and they could lead to mere tolerance rather than, say, appreciation of diversity or multicultural understanding. But I suspect that cultural self-interest will be strong enough in many instances to defeat a strategy founded upon simple self-interest.

Self-interest can be an important determinant of attitudes toward policies and groups, but it is rarely the only one. Values and beliefs often intervene to shape conceptions of self-interest, sometimes even to override them: Consider White males who favor affirmative action, for example. Even when people wish to act on their self-interest they may not do so effectively, because their biases (values) lead them to misperceive their interests. Our values influence how we perceive, so when it comes to interests and values as determinants of policy preferences, the influences can come from either, neither, or both. In one especially well designed study, Tedin (1994) discovered that "self-interest and symbolic values make about equal contributions to explaining the variance in support for the equalization of public school finances" (p. 640). A final point on the relation of self-interest to values is that, as Tedin points out, when people are not certain of their facts (and thus of their self-interest) they can always fall back on their values—and they routinely do so.

A sound educational strategy for the direct teaching of tolerance will have to include some way of discovering the origins of the negative attitudes that are to be restrained by tolerance. But it is no easy matter to identify the origins of negative affect. Negative feelings do not always emerge simply out of prejudice, ignorance, crude self-interest, complex group or cultural self-interest, or feelings of inadequacy. Negative affect can arise from any and all of these. The educator has to ask: Is the negative feeling a prejudice that ought to be eradicated (thus eliminating the need for tolerance), or is the negative feeling legitimate or reasonable in some way? The latter suggests tolerance as an alternative. The former does not.

Assimilationist Versus Pluralist Strategies

A big policy issue in direct teaching for social tolerance (and moral tolerance, on the rarer occasions when this is addressed) concerns the basic curricular strategy. Should the course of studies stress to students how we are all fundamentally alike and are gradually becoming more so, or is a more viable approach to accentuate differences in cultures, attitudes, and perspectives of different groups? Most emphasis today among educators (at least those who write extensively about what they think) seems to be on the multicultural approach. Stressing similarity is thought to mean that the minority has to assimilate and acculturate. Thus, de-emphasizing differences has often been thought to be insensitive and oppressive. On the other hand, multiculturalism can form the ideological basis for resegregation, which is one of the forces that most subverts the benefits of the contact approach. Furthermore, stressing differences among groups can lead to category-based thinking about social continua. This is one of the main ways cognitive sophistication in social thought is undermined.

It is interesting to note that a similar disagreement divides scholars who study and make recommendations about intergroup contact. In Chapter 5, we saw that some believe that group differences should be highlighted, whereas others believe that they should be de-emphasized, especially in comparison to individual similarities that cut across group lines. The scholarship on the matter is by no means definitive. My reading of the evidence suggests that we should stress individual similarities when social, particularly racial, tolerance is the goal. Focusing on differences is more appropriate for matters of political tolerance.

▨ Bounded Rationality and Flexible Policies

Educators and managers (and perforce educational managers) are often accused of seizing upon cure-alls with snappy names—total quality management, authentic assessment, and the like. Mere methods, useful if limited, are transformed into "movements." Sadly for sales, but happily for their ultimate effectiveness, the conclusions in this book will not spawn a movement. So, I have been asked, what does this book offer the practitioner? That depends on one's view of expert practice. Mine is heavily influenced by the work of Herbert Simon (1983, 1993). The first point Simon might make is that this book contains more information than a person can pay attention to at one time. Paths from education to tolerance number in the dozens if not hundreds (180 by the count in Figure 6.2). The trick, Simon would say, is *not* to optimize, or examine each path carefully and pick the best method to apply in all cases. The paths vary by circumstances that are themselves more complex than any person can entirely master. On the other hand, no one is likely to become the "tolerance czar" responsible for all aspects of education and tolerance in U.S. society. Most of us will paint on a smaller canvas, whether that be, for example, engaging in practices that help grade-schoolers to get along better with others, thinking about a program to eliminate violence toward gays in a high school, deciding how to handle the invitation of an inflammatory speaker on the Arab-Israeli conflict at a college, or advising the graduate admissions committee on the likely effects on students' attitudes of a proposed change in the affirmative action plan.

When dealing with one of the wide variety of problems that fit under the rubric of tolerance and education, one can use this book to look for ideas, to get a sense of the range of strategies. But no one of those strategies will always be effective. In short, according to Simon, one needs to "satisfice," not optimize, to find an approach to problem solving that will probably be satisfactory, rather than delude oneself into believing that there is a one best solution, a magic bullet. There really is no rational alternative to satisficing. There are various irrational alternatives, of course—these range from relentlessly sticking with traditional ways to tirelessly chasing the latest fads.

An expert dealing with problems of tolerance and education will, like all experts, be most effective when specific problems are recognizable. Experts (according to Simon) are people with large bodies of knowledge organized or indexed into "chunks." They use cues from the world to recognize or decide which chunks are most applicable in specific cases. I have tried to write this book in such a way that it can help readers develop an organized array of such chunks.

Decision making is done at several levels, and there are several kinds. First, there is deciding which problems are important enough to focus on, which are worthy of using up some of our "very small budget of attention" (Simon, 1993, p. 394). I have argued that tolerance is one such problem, crucial to a modern society that values diversity, equality, and peace. The second form or level of decision making has to do with finding possible solutions to the problems identified in the first step. If we want to teach tolerance, we need to find effective ways by looking at the correlates of tolerance. The review of the main correlates (Chapter 3) led us to the four general solutions of personality development, cognitive development, CMMC education, and intergroup contact (Chapters 4 and 5). The third step is choosing among the solutions defined in the second step: What will work (if not best, well enough) for this particular situation? A final step is deciding about implementation. We have just reviewed suggestions for policies and how to implement them, but there is always a more detailed level of implementation. I have generally stopped well short of what teachers and other educators might do on a day-to-day basis, realizing that at the most detailed levels of implementation, considerable latitude and discretion have to be left to the teacher or administrator actually putting a plan into action.

For example, say that one is convinced that the best solution to problems identified in a school is cooperative learning among mixed groups of elementary students. That decision leaves many implementation decisions still unmade. For example, How should one form the groups? Should the groups compete with one another? Might competing groups be an ineffective strategy at one grade level (e.g., first grade) but quite productive at another (e.g., sixth grade)? I pick cooperative learning to illustrate because our knowledge of the details of a successful implementation is more advanced here than for any of the other processes we have discussed. But it is not advanced enough or routinized enough, and it probably never will be, to yield decision trees or algorithms we can use to make all our choices. We can talk about the bigger branches of the decision tree, but the smaller branches and, perforce, the leaves will be left to expert decision makers on the spot, most often teachers in their classrooms. In other terms, we can talk about principles of implementation, but not rules; strategies are within our competence, but not tactics.

Despite all of these cautions, suggested by Simon's principles of decision making as well as by the tentative conclusions of much of the research reviewed in this book, it is possible to make some recommendations for practice. What follows is a practitioner's checklist, with supporting commentary and reflections. It is vaguer than a decision tree, but more specific than some of the strictly research-based generalizations reviewed above. It is a series of rules of thumb for practice that flows quite directly from the preceding analyses. An additional advantage of putting the book's practical conclusions in this format is that it enables us to notice a few nuances about the relationships among some of the more general conclusions discussed so far. For that reason, I think this summary list might be of interest to researchers as well as to practitioners.

Recommendations for Practitioners

Recommendation 1: Focus on a clearly defined type of tolerance.

1a. To begin, select one category of tolerance (political, social, or moral). It is probably even better to start with one aspect of one of those categories, such as free speech or religious liberties.

1b. Avoid letting colleagues define tolerance as reducing prejudice or eliminating stereotyping.

1c. When evaluating your work, remember what you set out to do. Do not court disappointment by using methods that, for example, promote tolerance while evaluating different outcomes, such as increasing respect for other cultures or reducing prejudice. It is easy to become distracted, for several reasons. One is simply that prejudice and stereotyping are easier to measure than tolerance. Also, because of the widespread confusion about the relation between tolerance and prejudice, there will be much pressure on programs to measure increases in tolerance by gauging reductions of prejudice. Finally, you may be tempted to evaluate your success at goals you did not set out to achieve because many colleagues and community members value tolerance less highly than other goals.

Recommendation 2: Begin by trying to increase tolerance (and thus to reduce discrimination). Then, if resources permit, turn to other important intergroup outcomes, such as increasing mutual respect, valuing diversity, eliminating prejudice, and so on. There is a clear relation between beliefs and behaviors, between attitudes and actions, but it is less clear which is more likely to influence the other. Although the evidence is not perfectly solid on this point, it is solid enough to suggest that beginning with the behavioral side (increasing tolerance and reducing discrimination) is the better bet. Attitudes and beliefs (e.g., prejudices and stereotypes) can follow behaviors. For example, in the 1950s and

1960s, school desegregation in the South ran well ahead of attitudes favoring it. Ironically, today, of course, support for integration is very widespread, whereas the actual practice of integration in schools is stable or declining.

2a. Prohibit discrimination and insist upon functional tolerance among students. This is the minimum necessary for social peace and is prerequisite to all further progress. Students may dislike one another because of their stereotyped beliefs, but one can require them to be minimally tolerant regardless of their beliefs and attitudes. In other words, one doesn't need to change people's values to get them to be more tolerant. We can have civility without uniformly good thoughts.

2b. In other words, the order in which tolerance arises is not necessarily the order in which it should be taught. Toward the end of Chapter 4, we looked schematically at the way tolerance arises (Figure 4.3). First one has a negative feeling or belief (such as a fear or a prejudice), then action on that feeling is checked by the interposition of thoughts (or possibly by other feelings). If successful, that check leads to tolerance, or not discriminating. Figure 6.4 depicts those relationships. Because the order in which tolerance occurs, as described in Figure 6.4, is fairly certain, many educators think this is the order in which it should be promoted. I believe, however, that the weight of the evidence indicates that the most productive approach is just the opposite. One should start at the right of the figure and work left. The most important thing is to put an immediate halt to discrimination. There is little hope of attacking prejudice, to say nothing of promoting respect for diversity, or understanding why one might need to check one's negative feelings until tolerance is first in place.

Recommendation 3: Combine educational methods or processes—such as cooperative learning and direct instruction in constitutional principles. This is easier than and almost surely more effective than combining goals. Combining methods can be useful as long as it does not stretch the program's or teachers' resources. It is particularly important to combine processes when engaging in direct CMMC instruction. As the sad case of civic education in the 1950s and 1960s makes clear, most often direct instruction will be ineffective unless it is supplemented by methods that encourage cognitive and personality development. Reciting slogans may pass for training, but it is not education. Similarly, multicultural education that does not bring students from different cultures into meaningful contact is likely to degenerate into preaching—to the converted or at the recalcitrant.

Negative Feeling or Belief	$\rightarrow$	Cognitive or Emotional Restraint	$\rightarrow$	Tolerance or Not Discriminating

Figure 6.4. The Sequence of Tolerance

Recommendation 4: Pursue educational practices that promote cognitive and personality development, even though you will rarely see the results of these pedagogical strategies in short-term, measurable tolerance outcomes. Self-esteem, lack of dogmatism, probabilistic thinking, and logical problem solving are intrinsically worthwhile goals even if the tolerance "by-product" may be years off.

Recommendation 5: When in doubt, political tolerance may be the best place to start, especially for older students (see Recommendation 7).

5a. Because political tolerance is encapsulated in the First Amendment to the Constitution, it can be taught by building on values that nearly everyone at least claims to support.

5b. Appreciation of political tolerance can be built upon the crudest values, such as self-interest. Democratic politics assumes that differences in self-interest are legitimate; a goal of democratic politics is to resolve conflicts stemming from self-interest. In Kohlberg's terms, political tolerance can be taught, at least in a rudimentary fashion, at Stage 2 of a child's development.

5c. Appreciation of political tolerance can take advantage of students' interest in and growing appreciation for rules as rules (Stage 3 in Kohlberg's scheme).

5d. Using political tolerance as a starting point, it is comparatively easy to make links to other kinds of tolerance—by discussing the political rights of nonpolitical, social and moral, groups. Also, religious liberties are guaranteed in the First Amendment, which provides another avenue to consideration of other varieties of tolerance.

Recommendation 6: Retain the complexity of the social, political, and moral worlds. Simplifying and making tolerance a goody-goody platitude will teach nothing. Tolerance involves difficult decisions.

6a. Remember that teaching tolerance should also involve teaching limits on tolerance, things that cannot or should not be tolerated.

6b. Teaching complexity involves teaching the often difficult specific applications of general principles (Corbett, 1982). Saying that free speech is good is easy; deciding whether a particular speech constitutes a "clear and present danger" is hard. Announcing that freedom of religion is good is easy; deciding whether this applies to the polygamy of Mormons is more complicated.

Recommendation 7: Vary methods according to the students' ages. The direct teaching of tolerance through CMMC curricula is not likely to be effective until students are at least 12 or 13 years old. Younger students have seldom attained a level of cognitive development that will allow them to benefit from direct CMMC education.

7a. Direct teaching can be effective for younger children when using methods of intergroup contact.

7b. Indirect approaches, such as those encouraging self-esteem, may also be effective with preadolescents.

7c. Fostering tolerance indirectly through increasing students' cognitive sophistication is also unlikely to be effective for preteen students, for the same developmental reasons that direct CMMC instruction yields few positive results prior to adolescence.

7d. Researchers are divided about the most effective age for fostering moral development with Kohlberg-inspired discussions of moral dilemmas. Depending on how moral development is defined and measured, the optimum age is either 11-16 years old or age 23 and above. Although there can be controversy concerning at which age the gain scores are the greatest, average scores increase for participants of all ages; the method is effective for all ages beyond 11 years (Lind, 1996b).

Recommendation 8: Remember that Kohlbergian Stage 3 (which involves interpersonal conformity) will be central for most school-aged children. Younger ones will be moving from the narrow individualism of Stage 2 to the more peer-aware Stage 3 in adolescence. Later adolescents may begin to see a broader social world (beyond small group conformity) as they near Stage 4, which occurs about the time most people exit the school system. Trying to teach principled reasoning (Stage 5 and above) to children too young to grasp it reduces moral education to little more than pontificating about platitudes.

Recommendation 9: When teaching about group differences, especially in multicultural education, avoid the great danger of reinforcing stereotypes. Students need to be made aware of the distinction between statistically significant but small differences and substantively important differences among groups. In ANOVA language, the differences within a group on almost any individual trait are usually greater than are the differences between group averages.

9a. More advanced students can have this ANOVA-based concept explained to them and, in doing projects, can come to understand it.

9b. For younger students, teaching about group differences easily degenerates into stereotyping. For older students, the danger is stereotyping that appears to be buttressed by the social sciences. It is probably better, especially for younger students, to focus on the common interests shared by different members of the same class or school. Of course, it would be folly to ignore or deny differences in customs, traditions, and so on, but these need not be the central focus in CMMC education.

Recommendation 10: CMMC courses should devote some time to research methods and the logic of inference in the social sciences; this is one way to introduce the good thinking that is a component of tolerance. One of the biggest problems teachers in CMMC education face is figuring out how to make useful generalizations without making invidious distinctions, without harmful stereotyping. As a teacher of a CMMC course, especially a multicultural course, one should strive to *tolerate no generalizations from oneself or students except probability generalizations.* For example, instead of "Boys shout out answers; girls don't," one might say, "Boys are more likely than girls to shout out answers." This may seem like a trivial distinction, but it is the difference between an honest generalization and a stereotype. Indeed, otherwise excellent popularizations of educational research are sometimes guilty of stereotyping when they take probabilistic findings and turn them into categorical generalizations. There is hardly a more irresponsible way for a social or behavioral scientist to undermine tolerance than by using such "scientific" stereotyping.

Recommendation 11: Remember that active intervention is usually required to make intergroup contact work. Putting children in the same vicinity and hoping that they will "naturally" interact is a very uncertain approach at best. By tightly packing segregated groups into a smaller space, one actually runs the risk of increasing conflict, not tolerance.

Recommendation 12: Remember that voluntary self-segregation is not intolerance, nor is it invariably a sign of prejudice. Voluntary self-segregation is not necessarily a cause for concern or an indication that a program has failed—as long as students from different groups can and do work together in some contexts.

12a. Working in groups that cut across ethnic or racial group lines must be learned at some point. Intervention to bring this about is most appropriate during formal instruction.

Recommendation 13: Avoid tracking. Although there is little direct evidence that tracking by ability or achievement undermines tolerance, there is enough indirect evidence about its pernicious effects on intergroup relations to render the practice suspect. At least, given that it is hard to demonstrate that tracking improves students' performance (Slavin, 1990), the burden of proof should rest on those who wish to maintain tracking.

Recommendation 14: Remember that cooperative learning using work groups that cut across ethnic lines (or religious or other boundaries) is the method of best-demonstrated success. This method should be used whenever possible—and it is possible much more often than current practice suggests.

14a. At minimum, it is safe to say that the demonstrated benefits of cooperative learning are great enough that the need to make an argument to justify practice rests on those who do not use cooperative learning.

Recommendation 15: Support curricular reforms that strengthen the place of the social sciences and humanities in education. Conversely, resist efforts to vocationalize the curriculum. Evidence (reviewed in Chapter 4) is quite strong that education in professional and vocational fields is not likely to increase tolerance, whereas liberal arts studies are more likely to do so.

Recommendation 16: Offer incentives for students to attend multicultural workshops and similar programs, which seem to have positive effects for college students. They are particularly effective, and needed, for White members of fraternities (Pascarella, Edison, Nora, Hagedorn, & Terenzini, 1996). Weigh carefully the benefits and drawbacks of making such workshops compulsory. Imposing this kind of education may backfire by creating resentment, and making programs wholly voluntary may reduce numbers of participants below acceptable levels. The best compromise is probably to encourage participation and to offer incentives so as to increase the number who choose to attend.

Recommendation 17: Support educational methods that emphasize open discussion, cooperative work, and educational self-direction. Details and labels may vary, but the general point is clear. This kind of education encourages personal and cognitive development and can thus teach tolerance indirectly; it also fosters prosocial attitudes more directly. This broad kind of education has been shown to be more effective in study after study, both for teaching the traditional curriculum and for developing tolerance and other prosocial attitudes. All of the authors reviewed here, using widely different approaches and samples, converge on this point (e.g., Slavin, Nieto, Kohlberg, Nielsen, Kohn).

Recommendation 18: If direct teaching of tolerance is too controversial to bring into your educational setting, a good fallback position is to teach critical thinking about social and political issues. If opposition to critical thinking emerges, one can retreat to teaching research methods in the social sciences. Indeed, just about any way of introducing rationality and serious methods of investigation into teaching about political and social life will tend to promote tolerance, at least as a by-product.

Recommendation 19: College students should confront the full array of uncertainties discussed in this book. Graff's idea of "teaching the conflicts" is surely beneficial for college students. A curriculum for college students is indirectly sketched in Chapter 7. In that chapter, by pointing out the most promising lines for future research, I outline what we do not know but have some chance of finding out. Chapter 7 amounts to an inventory of what constructive study in higher education should encourage students to try to understand. Thus, as we conclude with implications for research, we will indirectly be reviewing implications for college curricula designed to nourish tolerant beliefs, attitudes, and values.

7

Conclusion

Implications for Research

ife is complex. Research designs, by comparison, are simple, sometimes even simplistic. The inevitable mismatch between the world and our ability to study it is what is behind, for example, the often confusing and apparently conflicting findings in medical research about the benefits and risks of various foods or exercise regimes. We have a similar problem of similar origins when we try to untangle the research about the relations between education and attitudes and beliefs such as tolerance. We saw in our policy conclusions in Chapter 6 that educational planners are often befuddled by the fact that a claim about the links between schooling and tolerance can be any one of 180 claims—depending upon the levels and aspects of schooling on the one hand and the kinds of tolerance to which we refer on the other. And even the typology of 180 different relationships is a simplification. But most policy makers have an easier time of it than these

222

complexities would suggest, because they rarely have to make policy for a whole system. Rather, they are more likely to be responsible for a very limited element in a system, such as setting up a dispute resolution clinic in a high school, drawing up an admissions plan for a magnet elementary school, or implementing a multicultural curriculum in a college.

The same simpler tasks of more modest level of difficulty characterize the work of most researchers. They usually follow only one or a small number of threads that constitute the whole fabric of the topic. This leads to fairly clear if limited conclusions. It is when researchers try to talk more broadly about the influence of education as a whole on attitudes and beliefs as a whole that the complexities become almost impossibly intricate. Ultimately, however, we must try to talk broadly about the whole complex of relations in which we are interested. But when we do so, we will never escape the plight of our fellow researchers in medicine, who find one year that Americans will live longer if they eat less animal fat and discover the next year that animal fat from salmon increases longevity. Despite the apparent contradiction, the second finding constitutes progress; it specifies the effects of different kinds of animal fat. Such specifications often require contradictions or partial refutations of previous findings. Although this can be confusing, especially to practitioners attempting to apply the most up-to-date knowledge, it is how one moves ahead on complex problems with many variables, such as the relation of education to attitudes and values.

One way to begin the process of thinking about implications for further research is to compare the approach in this book to the approaches used in two recent studies, each of which illustrates ways we could expand the scope of research on tolerance and education. The first is an investigation of attitudes toward the homeless conducted by Phelan, Link, Stueve, and Moore (1995). The second is a study of education's varying effects on attitudes toward political protest conducted by Hall and Rodeghier (1994).

Phelan et al. (1995) examined the effects of education level on support for the civil liberties of the homeless, support for economic programs to help the homeless, and general attitudes toward the homeless. The authors call the last of these their "tolerance scale," but, following the usage of this book, it is not a tolerance scale but rather something more like a "sympathy scale." Like many students of the question, Phelan et al. conclude that the empirical finding of a statistical association between education and attitudes is less in doubt than are the explanations for this finding. They offer three general explanations: (1) developmental (a combination of what I have presented as cognitive development and personality development); (2) socialization (more or less what I have called CMMC education); and (3) Jackman's "ideological refinement," which basically means that people know how to claim to be liberal or tolerant when it is in their self-interest to do so (see Chapters 2 and 3 for discussion of Jackman's theories). I would have included contact with the homeless as a variable, but there are otherwise no major differences between Phelan et al.'s work and this book in the kinds of explanations examined.

There is one key methodological difference, however. Phelan et al. used a strategy of trying to find the one best explanation. By contrast, I have argued that it is more fruitful to discover several lines of understanding in a network of multivariate relations. In fact, Phelan et al. employed measurement techniques and provided data that help one sketch in a few of those lines. Rather than using one big liberalism or tolerance scale, or one composite scale of attitudes toward the homeless, Phelan et al. disaggregated attitudes and beliefs. Further, they made an uncommon but important distinction in their education scale by adding a dummy variable for graduate education. Their results are most interesting. First, level of education was strongly related, more strongly than any other variable, to what Phelan et al. call tolerance—what I would call general positive attitudes or sympathy toward the homeless (measured by answers to questions such as, "Does laziness contribute to homelessness?"). This link with education holds up even after the researchers controlled for other variables, such as gender, ethnicity, and age. Second, the relation between education level and support for the civil liberties of the homeless (what I would call political tolerance) was very weak, and only the highest (postbaccalaureate) levels of education had any effect. Indeed, almost nothing explained variance in attitudes toward the civil liberties of the homeless (as assessed by answers to questions such as, "Should the homeless have the right to sleep in public parks?"). The only significant variable besides education was age, with younger people being more politically tolerant; but a mere 2% of the variance was explained by all variables together.

Finally, and perhaps most interesting, is Phelan et al.'s measure of support for economic aid for the homeless. This was defined by agreement or disagreement with statements such as, "The federal government should spend more on affordable housing" and "More low-income housing would reduce homelessness."[1] There was a general *negative* relationship between education level and belief in the effectiveness of economic aid, with more highly-educated people saying that the federal government should not spend more for shelters. However, the relationship for people with post-baccalaureate education was positive; they were more likely to believe that the government should spend more. So, in two of the three scales in this study, the relation of attitudes to education was curvilinear, not linear; what mattered most for positive attitudes toward the homeless was whether the respondent had a graduate education. *Graduate* education was associated with positive attitudes on all three measures, but only graduate education was.

What is distinctive about graduate education that would produce this kind of result? And would graduate education have similar effects on other forms of tolerance? The answers to these questions are potentially important enough that I would strongly recommend future researchers distinguish more among the higher levels of education, particularly now that a growing proportion of the population earns postbaccalaureate degrees. Doing so would require very large samples or, better, a target population in which all subjects have at least a bachelor's degree. But if we wish to study adequately the effects of level of education, we need to examine all the levels.

The second study I want to look at here, by Hall and Rodeghier (1994), shows how the education-tolerance link can be better understood if researchers specify more precisely some of the things they mean by *tolerance*. Researchers have often noted how frequently statistical associations are found between attitudes (just about any attitudes) and education, even education measured in the crudest way possible as years of schooling. Nonetheless, when they begin to specify the attitudes they are investigating, they begin to uncover more complex relations. Sometimes education has little effect; for example, it is not a good predictor of attitudes about capital punishment. People with more years of education are about as likely to favor capital punishment as are those with fewer (Hyman & Wright, 1979). And, as we have seen in the example concerning policies to help the homeless, as well as at other points in this book, sometimes increased education (at least up to the bachelor's level) can reduce liberalism— especially when liberalism is broadly conceived to include attitudes toward income redistribution and programs to help the economically disadvantaged. What this means, in brief, is that if we want to improve our studies of the relations between education and tolerance, we need not only better ways to study the independent or predictor variable (education), but also a more elaborated conception of the dependent or outcome variable (tolerance).

Hall and Rodeghier (1994) show us one way to do this and indicate other potentially useful lines of research. They state that "it is misleading to treat tolerance as an enduring personal trait that applies in all cases" (p. 298). Hall and Rodeghier's dependent variable is support for freedom of assembly (or the right to protest). By seeing how individuals differ in their support for different groups' rights and for different protest actions of those groups, Hall and

Rodeghier work "backward" to postulate educational processes that could account for those differences. Then, of course, if these processes are valid, they can be used to work forward to predict the size of the relation between education level and tolerance in various situations—depending upon the nature of the group and its means of protest.

Education influences political tolerance—specifically, attitudes toward protest—in four ways, according to Hall and Rodeghier. First, the more educated individuals are, the more likely they are to understand and support civil liberties in general. Second, increased education is associated with increased commitment to peace and order—and increased opposition to violence, whether by protesters or authorities. Third, education increases knowledge of the reasons that particular groups are likely to protest, as well as sympathy for those reasons—if they conform to values of justice and fairness roughly equivalent to those at Kohlberg's Stages 4 and 5. Fourth, and most complicating, education increases the tendency to identify with high-status values and the values of the educated; it decreases the tendency to support causes associated with the working class or the poor or the poorly educated.

The best research strategy is not to choose among these four forces. They are all likely to be present for any issue pertaining to a political protest. They are additive, but because they can have positive or negative signs, they can sometimes cancel one another out. Thus, support for civil liberties and a belief in the fairness of a cause can be counterbalanced if the members of the protest group are lower-class and they threaten violence. For instance, support for a disorderly protest by welfare recipients of cuts in the food stamp program is not likely to be positively associated with level of education. On the other hand, an orderly demonstration by college professors demanding an end to censorship on the Internet is very likely to win the support of highly educated persons, and support is likely to increase as a function of their education level. We see, then, that education contributes to "several (possibly conflicting) attitudes toward various features the group is believed to possess" (Hall & Rodeghier, 1994, p. 303). By itself, any one of these attitudes toward protest and protesters is not likely to tell the whole story of whether education is associated with support for a particular protest. The four attitudes must be taken together, for together they influence individuals' choices about whether to support specific political protests.

Both of the studies just reviewed, on attitudes toward the homeless and toward political protest, lead to the same conclusion about productive paths for future research. Progress on the topic of tolerance and education is most likely to be made through investigations that more precisely specify the variables and that disaggregate their possible effects on one another; then researchers can examine the "additive contributions to an overall effect" (Hall & Rodeghier, 1994, p. 306).

At all points in the causal chain, from background, through education, to attitudes and values, we need to disassemble the components so as to analyze them in preparation for better syntheses. In the pages that follow, I will suggest additional ways to accomplish some of these research goals. There are two broad areas in which I believe further research would be most helpful: (a) tolerance and toleration in modern societies and (b) more detailed consideration of the correlates of tolerance. Each is considered in turn below.

Tolerance and Toleration in Modern Societies

This section addresses some of the more promising lines of inquiry that build on the findings reviewed in Chapters 1 and 2. It is also parallel to Simon's problem-selecting stage or level. The main theme is the broad societal and institutional (or macro-level) foundations of micro-level phenomena. The basic question is, How do characteristics of societies promote or hinder tolerance in individuals?

Macro-Level Historical and Comparative Work

Macro-level contexts provide critical background shaping the effectiveness of the individual-level or micro-level forces that are the focus of this book. Changes in individuals can be quite rare and inconsequential in the face of large historical antagonisms, fundamental conflicts of interest, or institutional barriers to intergroup harmony. For example, a program providing opportunities for friendly contacts between some Arab and Jewish students in order to influence their attitudes will not accomplish a great deal if the political leaders of the Arabs and Jews are unable to keep the two peoples from war (Ben-Ari & Amir, 1986).

In the last analysis, the ability to sustain micro-level tolerance depends on general social conditions conducive to macro-level "toleration." By *toleration,* I mean governmental and other institutional policies and principles that limit discrimination and ban some restraints on individuals' liberties. Toleration, then, involves legal and institutional prohibitions of discrimination, whether that be done by broad constitutional principles limiting government action (such as the First Amendment's guarantee of a free press) or by more narrowly gauged legislation (such as open housing laws). Toleration also has an intellectual component; it involves not only laws and organizations, but also societal and governmental principles of justice and fairness. Investigations of the sociohistorical conditions that promote toleration are not well advanced. In a paper titled *Social Origins of Toleration* (Vogt, 1990), I have suggested that six social conditions foster the appearance and continuance of toleration: social diversity, a market economy, democratic political institutions, epistemological uncertainty, the predominance of rational calculation over tradition, and a critical mass of knowledge occupations. A review of these will help to clarify the several parallels between the micro and macro levels of analysis in matters of social, political, and moral liberty. The social origins of toleration are, by extension, indirect social origins of, or facilitating conditions for, tolerance.[2]

Social Diversity

Toleration is fostered by a large, socially diverse society with a unitary state and good communications, so that different sorts of people are likely to interact with one another. In a small, homogeneous society—or a society in which social groups are isolated from one another by poor communications—the issues of tolerance and toleration may never come up. The reader will recall that in Chapter 1, I made a similar point about how diversity can promote tolerance among individuals. Whether we approach the question from a micro or macro level of analysis, it is clear that only in societies in which diverse individuals are likely to come into contact will governments, or other social institutions, have any need to promulgate rules of tolerant contact and interaction.

The importance of diversity is hardly a new idea. It was insisted upon in the 18th century by some of the most formidable advocates of toleration. Voltaire (1734/1980) put it epigrammatically: "If there were only one religion in England there would be danger of despotism, if there were two they would slit each other's throats, but there are thirty and they live in peace and happiness" (p. 41; see also Voltaire, 1764/1985, p. 390). James Madison (1788/1961) made the same argument that toleration and rights depend on pluralism:

> In a free government, the security for civil rights must be the same as for religious rights. It consists in the one case in the multiplicity of interests, and in the other in the multiplicity of sects. The degree of security in both cases will depend on the number of interests and sects; and this may be presumed to depend upon the extent of the country and the number of people comprehended under the same government. (pp. 351-352)

The ideas of these two political philosophers could not have been further removed from the worldview of medieval Europe. Thinkers in the Middle Ages had an outlook that did not differentiate moral, social, religious, and political principles. The point of view was rather one of "undifferentiated Christian wholeness" (Ullman, 1975, p. 12). Toleration and the celebration of diversity were literally inconceivable in medieval times. But since the emergence of modern societies, characterized as they are by social differentiation, it has become increasingly difficult not to see healthy social arrangements as dependent upon toleration.

Of course, not all types of diversity are equally conducive to toleration. Indeed, social diversity based mainly on ascriptive differences among groups (race, ethnicity) often leads to the most vicious sorts of intolerance. Most effective in promoting tolerance and toleration is diversity that cuts across ascriptive lines, that keeps social categories from having convergent boundaries. Social arrangements that result in multiple cleavages and "cross-cutting socioeconomic linkages" (Horowitz, 1985, p. 102) are great stimulants to toleration and, by extension, to tolerance. Such crosscutting divisions mean that it is possible that today's opponent (for example, in a political dispute) will be tomorrow's ally (in an economic contest, perhaps). Under those conditions the intensity of conflict is likely to be moderated, and toleration can become a guiding principle.

On the other hand, there may exist what we could call a *paradox of diversity*. Diversity seems at the same time to aid in the development of tolerance and of conflict. Indeed, without conflict, there is no real occasion for tolerance. Gibson (1988, 1989) has suggested that tolerance can carry the seeds of its own destruction: When it makes dissent and disruption more common, tolerance can trigger repression and thus reduce tolerance. Similarly, Hodson, Sekulic, and Massey (1994), in a study of the war of all against all in the former Yugoslavia, say that "factors associated with modernism [including diversity] produce greater tolerance, but increase the possibility of ethnic conflict" (p. 1534). Further work on the contradictory consequences of diversity is among our more important research tasks. A fruitful direction for research could involve weighing the relative importance of the power-threat hypothesis and the contact hypothesis along the lines suggested in Chapter 5 (see Figure 5.2).

A Market Economy

A market economy requires *peaceful* economic competition. Such limited competition, in turn, requires the establishment of rules for settling disputes.

When economic markets become salient in social life and mercantile classes gain influence in setting social and political policy, toleration is encouraged, in two ways. First, the market provides a paradigm that can be transferred from economic relations to social, religious, and political interaction. Second, toleration is good for business. The benefits to business were seen as an especially compelling argument as early as the 17th century. British and Dutch writers in particular stressed that intolerance in religion undermined commerce, reduced markets, prevented the free circulation of manufacturing techniques, and thus weakened the nation (for examples, see Kamen, 1967, pp. 224-227).

Markets produce their toleration-encouraging effects not through any inherent virtue, but mostly by multiplying the number of crosscutting social ties. To avoid slipping into any right-wing sentimentality about the morality of capitalist markets, one need only remember also that "capitalism provided the principal motives and the ideological underpinnings of British Atlantic slavery" (Drescher, 1986, p. 20). It is surely one of the great ironies, tragedies, and/or paradoxes of our subject that those nations so far in advance of others in the 17th century in promoting individual liberty and toleration (England and the Netherlands) were also the two most important slave-trading nations.

Democracy

Although toleration can emerge out of a nondemocratic political context (consider the Edict of Nantes of 1598 or Joseph II's Patent of Toleration of 1781), there is no question that democracy cannot survive without political toleration. Hence, any social conditions that foster or perpetuate democracy will likewise promote (at least some kinds of) toleration. It is best here to think of democracy as a continuous variable; societies can be more or less democratically organized, and the more democratic they are the more likely toleration is to be a central political value and practice.

Democracy *entails* the right to oppose the current holders of political power and their policies. If peaceful opposition to the government and its policies is illegal, democracy does not exist. Seditious libel (the idea that the government may be criminally harmed by the expression of an opinion) is a contradiction in terms in a democracy. Because it is possible in a democracy to change the holders of political power without revolution, the regime can tolerate criticism of its power holders—because they are distinct from the regime. In nondemocratic regimes in which power is vested in persons more than in institutions, criticism of the head of state (e.g., Louis XVI or Nicolae Ceausescu) actually is subversive, seditious, and can lead to revolution. It is also subversive to criticize institutions when they are constitutive of a regime—such as apartheid in South Africa or the Communist Party in the Soviet Union.

It certainly is no accident that the main democratic revolutions culminated in the promulgation of documents featuring the kind of negative liberties that add up to toleration: "Congress shall make no law . . . abridging the freedom of speech, or of the press" (U.S. Constitution, Amendment 1, 1791). "The right of demonstrating one's thoughts and opinions, whether by means of the press or in any other manner . . . , cannot be prohibited" (Declaration of the Rights of Man and of the Citizen, Article 7, 1793).

It would, of course, be ridiculous to conclude from the above that power holders in a democratic state are always tolerant; nor can we infer that the population is. The protected rights of the French Revolution lasted not much longer than it took the ink to dry on the Declaration. The Sedition Act of the Federalists (1798) nearly put an end to the First Amendment and legal criticism of the government. Even in democratic states, it has not been all that hard to muster popular enthusiasm for intolerance of "aliens," "subversives," "immoral threats to our way of life," and so on. But, in the not so long run, if the holders of power and the populace are not tolerant, democracy cannot survive. As Robert Dahl (1989) puts it, "Not only as an ideal but in actual practice, the democratic process is surrounded by a penumbra of personal freedom" (p. 89). The negative freedoms of toleration are a key element of the democratic process. When the process is well established, so is toleration. And toleration provides a context in which tolerance is more likely to thrive.

The main exception to this rule about the link between democracy and toleration was ancient Greek democracy, which had little room for the individual's right to dissent. The Greek polis, because it was small, and because democracy was restricted to a limited number of its residents, could ostracize or execute dissidents and thus maintain a limited "democratic" consensus. Democracy is more likely to foster toleration when it is coupled with diversity. In larger, diverse societies, where democratic institutions must be representative, the intimate community of the polis is no longer possible. "As diversity and political cleavages grow, and adversarial political conflict becomes a normal and accepted aspect of political life," Dahl (1989) concludes, "*individual rights may be seen as a substitute for political consensus*" (p. 220; emphasis added).

Epistemological Uncertainty

The theories of toleration that so often accompany governmental acts of toleration cannot emerge in just any "intellectual field" (Bourdieu, 1985). The field must contain theories (and theorists) of knowledge that assume some uncertainty or some degrees of probability in moral, religious, and political truths. And, indeed, two philosophies of knowledge appeared in Europe more or less simultaneously with the literature of toleration: skepticism and probability theory. Europeans of the 17th century who were unwilling to accept Richard Hooker's advice to "remember ye are men; deem it not impossible for ye to err" were unlikely to find the reasons for toleration very compelling. Belief in absolute truths, or in infallibility of religious leaders, leads directly to doctrines such as Pius IX's blunt assertion, "Error has no rights."

Skepticism, or the position that the grounds for any knowledge claim are at best uncertain, was not invariably linked with religious unbelief or even tolerance in the 16th and 17th centuries. Probably most thinkers who used skeptical arguments did so in order to undermine their opponents' reasoning; when that was done, the way was left clear for belief based purely on faith. Nonetheless, the rise of toleration was made possible by the fact that "the intellectual crisis brought on by the Reformation coincided in time with the rediscovery and revival of the arguments of the ancient Greek sceptics" (Popkin, 1964, p. xii). It is hard to think of any theory of toleration, from Castellio's *Concerning Heretics* (1554/1931) to Mill's *On Liberty* (1859/1979), that has not rested importantly on one, basically skeptical, idea: Because it is hard to be certain of the "true" path, we ought to limit the means we are willing to use to compel others to follow it. Probability theorists such as Pascal and Huygens, by mathematicizing skepticism, turned it into the positive doctrine of statistical inference. Probability, thus understood, was invented in the 17th century and was "probably" a completely new phenomenon in intellectual history (Hacking, 1984). Combined with more ordinary varieties of uncertainty, it provided an intellectual context in which theories of toleration could emerge.

The similarities between these broad intellectual currents giving rise to toleration at the macro level and the variables we have studied at the micro or individual level of analysis are many. Intellectual flexibility, personal acceptance of ambiguity, and open-mindedness are the individual personality parallels of skepticism and probability theory in intellectual history. Dogmatism and authoritarianism in persons are the enemies of individual tolerance. Doctrinaire governments and social institutions, by repressing diversity, provide a social context in which individuals who fear diversity are able to thrive. In the study of tolerance and toleration, bridging the gap between the macro and the micro levels of analysis is perhaps easiest in these cognitive areas.

Predominance of Reason Over Tradition and Faith

Like tolerance in individuals, toleration in societies is largely an intellectual virtue. Toleration requires rational calculation of means and ends, because it is the price one pays for valuing something more highly than the enforcement of conformity. Other virtues, such as kindness, are their own reward; they are based on character or on feelings, and they self-destruct if one introduces balance-sheet thinking. The idea of toleration, in contrast, arises mostly through cost-benefit analysis. The main argument for toleration has always been something like this: In the long run, we are better off if society and government check their impulses to repress things that appear threatening, because unless they do so they run an even greater risk, such as the loss of liberty or democracy. Until the Age of Reason and the secularism that accompanied it, governments seemed most often unable to think this way, particularly about religious and moral issues. And unless governments and their advisers are able to think and legislate in this way, toleration is impossible.

Otherwise put, the "elite settlements" that have established the conditions for some tolerant, democratic political regimes have required self-interested, but farsighted, conscious deliberations—not emotionally based reactions in defense of traditional values. Only through the abandonment of traditional allegiances could "compromises among previously warring elite factions" be reached (Burton & Higley, 1987, p. 295). Rules of toleration are often a significant component of elite settlements. These settlements, by establishing political stability and norms of "restrained partisanship" or peaceful competition, are part of that consensual unity among elites that is a "necessary precondition for stable representative regimes which tend to evolve along democratic lines" (Burton & Higley, 1987, pp. 296, 304).

A Critical Mass of Knowledge Occupations

Given that tolerance is an intellectual or cognitive virtue, it should not be surprising that it is also an intellectuals' virtue. When intellectuals (in the broadest sense of that term) begin to constitute important and influential groups in a society, the likelihood of toleration, and therefore tolerance, increases considerably. *Workers in knowledge occupations* might be a better description than *intellectuals*. Even that may be too exclusive for what we might call CICKOs for short: culture, information, communication, and knowledge occupations. Examples include theologians, professors, lawyers, printers, publishers, journalists, artists, writers, librarians, archivists, advertisers, publicists, teachers, bureaucrats, judges, and government officials. The emergence of printing made a dense population of these occupations possible; it is probably no mere coincidence that the time of the first major impact of printing was shortly followed by first edicts of and treatises advocating toleration.

The knowledge occupations, singly and especially together, have a vested interest in toleration, as they cannot flourish without it. In some cases their interest is clear and direct: Journalists have a vested interest in freedom of the press, artists in freedom of expression, professors in academic freedom, and so on. Any one of these professions, however, by itself and aligned with the state, might well oppose the toleration of unorthodoxy; it is the multiplicity of competing CICKOs that facilitates toleration in society and government and thereby provides a context in which tolerance among individuals is encouraged.

One might be tempted to believe that certain sorts of information professionals should not be included among those whose presence constitutes a stimulus to toleration. In this category we could put those who work in occupations in which the work is strictly technical and is not involved directly in social, political, economic, religious, or moral issues—such as accountants, engineers, natural scientists, and statisticians. In fact, however, historically speaking, from Galileo to Oppenheimer, those who specialize in scientific or technical knowledge have had a need for the protection of the formal rules of toleration—often enough, at any rate, that they, too, have a vested interest in toleration. When on the "right" side, the more technical of the CICKOs have been powerful allies of the others—increasingly so as their economic and military importance has grown.

Whereas professional intellectuals (or members of the CICKOs) are most likely to make the argument for toleration, they are also, as society's professional arguers, most likely to make the argument against it. In some respects, what matters most is that social rules are loose enough that there can be an argument. Once the issue of where and how to "draw the line" gets on the agenda and becomes a matter of public debate, the battle for toleration is half won. Extensive public debates, as much as the content of the arguments themselves, have often provided the context out of which governmental acts of toleration have emerged. Much in the way that Alan Kors (1990) has argued that orthodox theologians created atheism for heuristic purposes, I would contend that ideologues can be driven—by their social status as professional controversialists—to promote intellectual toleration. If these speculations are accurate, one way that education fosters tolerance is by stimulating the development of a knowledge society

(Stehr, 1994). This increases the need for CICKOs and raises their social status, all of which makes their values more widely appreciated.

Even in societies in which anti-intellectualism is extensive, such as the United States, appreciation of technical expertise can be widespread. Technical experts have sometimes been the entering wedge of toleration in repressive regimes, such as in the former Soviet Union. To compete with other nations, such regimes need computer programmers, theoretical physicists, medical researchers, and the like. These can sometimes constitute a critical mass of CICKOs sufficient to change the regime, to introduce the toleration that makes CICKOs comfortable in their work, and to provide the political context in which interpersonal tolerance is encouraged. In short, a society that values its intellectuals is more likely to promote toleration. And, as we have seen in previous chapters, individuals who value ideas are more likely to advocate tolerance. The individual and societal values are mutually supportive, and each can be better understood when studied in the context of the other.[3]

Theoretical Work in Social Psychology

Social psychology is a theoretically rich discipline, and its theories have often guided important empirical research. Social psychologists have frequently examined the phenomena of prejudice and stereotyping, but they have devoted much less effort to tolerance as defined in this book. Here I will make a few suggestions about what seem to be some promising lines of theoretical work. One interesting area of theoretical investigation for understanding tolerance involves elaboration of the tradition running from Simmel to Tajfel on the web of group affiliations, role salience, and diversity arising from overlapping social circles and how these are related to social and moral tolerance. Tolerance is a distinct form of social relationship particularly relevant to explaining patterns of interactions in small groups. As such, it requires a higher level of theoretical attention than it has typically received.

A related intellectual tradition that can add to our understanding of tolerance is the "niche elaboration" theory of social evolution (for a discussion, see Simon, 1983, chap. 2). The basic idea goes back to Durkheim (1893/1964) and ultimately to Darwin. Rather than all species competing for the same niche, ecosystems, and modern societies, have a very large number of different kinds of niches to which various species can adapt. Other species in the social or biological system can themselves be part of, or components of, the niches. In the human social world, where differentiation is more rapid than in biological evolution, niches are indefinitely numerous. Society conceived of in this fashion is not the tooth-and-claw world of the survival of the fittest; rather, it is a world in which fitness is measured by ability to adapt to diversity and change. Tolerance is a key social value in such a world.

We often think of tolerance as quite rare in modern society, yet people sometimes display amazing amounts of tolerance and put up with situations to which, in other contexts, they would react very negatively. An example of what I have in mind is the subway at rush hour. This is an experience that involves lots of pushing and nudging from people one has no reason to like; it often takes place in an otherwise distasteful environment. Rat-running psychologists of the 1960s repeatedly demonstrated that crowding increases aggression, yet there is remarkably little overt conflict in the subway at rush hour, even in violent societies such as the United States. Why? Perhaps because the subway is an extremely impersonal environment. It is precisely because one has no ties to others in the subway, because one's relation to them is entirely functional and temporary, that it is relatively easy to tolerate the crowding, physical discomfort, loud voices, body odor, and the rest.

Ever since Tonnies, it has been common in social theory to contrast two types of social organization: the "community" (*Gemeinschaft*), bound together by ties of tradition and affection, and the "association" (*Gesellschaft*) that exists to meet functional or practical ends. Most social theorists have claimed that modern societies have become increasingly dominated by associations, and have seen a concomitant decline in the importance of communities. This change has generally been considered a major social problem in the modern world. I would argue, however, that the distinction between community and association has been greatly overdrawn. Community and association are likely to exist together within most groups. Friendships and loyalties to the organization are common in economic institutions, and communities invariably have a functional side. Even couples bound together by love are almost inevitably also an economic, functional unit.

Rare as they are, *purely* functional associations may have something to teach us, especially about tolerance. Perhaps the subway can be thought of as a social psychology experiment, the results of which would repay careful study. Similar natural experiments might include rush hour in automobiles rather than on trains. My guess is that being in one's car lessens the amount of frustration one is willing to abide. Are subway commuters more tolerant than automobile commuters? To find out, we would have to do extensive interviewing to ask members of the two groups to reconstruct their reactions to various situations.

If there is a difference in the two commuting situations, and if we could pinpoint its origins, that could have interesting implications for understanding how tolerance arises in various social settings. These speculations are meant only to raise questions that suggest some promising lines of theoretical research. Although social psychology has contributed crucially to our understanding of phenomena related to tolerance, such as stereotyping and prejudice, the theoretical work on tolerance itself in social psychology is so underdeveloped that almost any systematic investigation is likely to be productive.

Social Philosophy and Jurisprudential Work

My conclusion in Chapter 2—that tolerance is a key social value that we ought to teach—cannot ultimately be justified. I say this because I am convinced by the old philosophical argument that one cannot use evidence about what is to come to draw conclusions about what ought to be. In short, trying to proceed from what is to what ought to be is a fallacious form of reasoning. However, if a particular value (such as tolerance) is seen as a means to other, more final, values (such as equality or diversity), then this means-value (such as tolerance) can be objectively or rationally studied. As soon as it becomes a means to other values rather than an end in itself, we can use evidence to decide how to foster it.

Scholarship pursuing lines of inquiry related to the task of analyzing tolerance as a means to promote other values can be found in many fields, chiefly philosophy, social and political theory, and jurisprudence. Ronald Dworkin's work has been very influential on questions similar to those discussed in this book. His conclusions point to ways of merging some of the types of tolerance treated separately in these pages, such as political and moral tolerance. In a recent article, Dworkin (1996) argues that the U.S. Constitution mostly contains broad general principles that must be interpreted if they are to be applied. The interpretations are inevitably influenced by the prevailing moral values of society and of the interpreters, such as lawyers and judges. This means that, like it or not, jurisprudential thought will always imply philosophical, especially moral, theory. This conclusion reinforces the view that tolerance may be a legal principle, but it is also a moral value.

Sociologists such as Durkheim have made similar arguments when they have claimed that laws are, in essence, institutionalized morality. Consensus on moral values often leads to laws to impose that consensus. But the relations between law and moral consensus are more complicated than is often thought (Rossi & Berk, 1985; Vogt, 1993). Take a society in which consensus on a general principle is very high, such as the value of freedom of speech. There can nonetheless be considerable disagreement about exactly what constitutes free speech and what constitutes unprotected speech, such as slander or incitement to illegal action. Following the assassination of Prime Minister Rabin in 1995, for example, Israelis engaged in intense debate about the freedoms of press and speech. The big issue in those debates was how to define "inciteful speech," speech that should be prohibited because it is the proximate cause of an illegal action.

Even assuming agreement on the definition of a crime, such as inciteful speech, which also means agreement on the limits of tolerance, there is still considerable room for disagreement about how severely transgressions of those limits should be punished. And consensus on particular values leaves room for disagreement about how to rank various of those values when they come into conflict. For example, in the United States attempts to prohibit racist speech or Nazi marches or KKK rallies have pitted social egalitarianism and social tolerance on one side against political tolerance and civil liberties on the other. There is no objective way to rank the importance of, for example, social tolerance and political tolerance. Discussions of such rankings will always be philosophical or theoretical in some sense. This means that to advance work on tolerance and education, we will need to seek insights from a broader range of theoretical disciplines than is commonly done in social research.[4]

In any complex society, there is always a range of moral opinion. Even when the range is very narrow on principles, specific cases can be hard to fit to the principles and will thus divide a society. The relation of education to such divisions is fairly complicated. People with more advanced education often value conformity less than do those with lower levels of education. This leads them to be more tolerant of diversity. However, people with higher education also are more likely to have values close to the national average views (Rossi & Berk, 1985). In a society characterized by national norms of toleration, these two tendencies among highly educated people can coexist. People with advanced levels of education in such societies may be more likely to conform to national values, such as those stated in the First Amendment. They can be both more conformist and more tolerant of diversity. Considerations such as these are another reason that advances in the study of the association between tolerance and education will more likely be fruitful if broad social and political phenomena are studied for their relevance to the microindividual facts of tolerance among individuals.

▓ Research on the Correlates of Tolerance

In addition to the broad macro-level societal influences on tolerance examined in the previous section, much research needs to be conducted at the individual or micro level of analysis. A review of Chapters 3 through 5 suggests seven main areas in which further research investigations would be most productive:

1. other correlates of tolerance besides education;
2. quasi-experiments on various educational treatments;
3. natural experiments on students currently in schools who are experiencing different types of education;
4. studies of adults who have different educational backgrounds;
5. studies of children and adults who vary in knowledge and/or mental processes;
6. psychometric research on how to measure tolerance and better models of its relationships to other variables; and
7. event history reconstructions of how individuals came to have their current attitudes.

Other Correlates of Tolerance

How could we study correlates of tolerance other than education better so as to control for their influence, find where they interact with education, and discover any mediating effects? The best strategy is disaggregation. Religious affiliation can serve to illustrate. For example, one often finds that Jewish individuals are among the most tolerant of survey respondents. But Jews are a highly diverse group that includes atheists and agnostics as well as religious persons; among the religious-minded are many categories, including Reform, Conservative, Orthodox, and Hasidic groups. Equally large differences exist among most broad denominational groups, such as Islam and Protestantism. It makes little sense to treat broad denominational groups as undifferentiated lumps. Although there are differences in between-group average levels of tolerance of Jews and Protestants in the United States, one suspects that a more fine-grained analysis (distinguishing among degrees of fundamentalism, for example) might find more differences on some attitudes within groups than between them. Some religious orientations (ecumenicism, for example) might increase individuals' propensity to seek advanced education—or might be promoted by advanced education.

Quasi-Experiments

Quasi-experiments comparing different curricula, such as the one by the Minnesota group discussed in Chapter 5, have a great deal of promise for the study of tolerance and education. Many fewer of these controlled, systematic studies have been conducted than might be supposed. They are crucial to furthering our ability to specify what aspects of schooling can be used to influence attitudes and values. Despite some methodological problems with quasi-experiments, they are most often preferable to true experiments on our topic, because quasi-experiments are conducted in real educational settings, not in artificially isolated (experimental) contexts. Quasi-experiments can extend over weeks or months and test ideas *in situ* with students in actual classrooms rather than laboratory simulations. In the study of the effectiveness of school programs and curricula, these advantages outweigh the advantages of the more certain, but synthetic, controls of laboratory studies.

Natural Experiments

Natural experiments have been widely used to test contact theory and to assess desegregation efforts. They continue to be very important for the study of tolerance and education because, for the most part, researchers will not be able to manipulate environments to determine the effects of different degrees of contact. Researchers cannot, for example, assign students to schools in ways designed to test whether different proportions of ethnic group memberships influence tolerance levels. Student assignments are determined by residential patterns, or sometimes by government policies. It is important for researchers to remain alert; changes in government policies or programs (such as the creation of new magnet schools) can provide opportunities to study the effects of variations in educational settings. Often the chances of gathering important information are enhanced if one is ready to gather data before a new policy or program is actually in place.

Perhaps the most neglected opportunity for natural experimentation in education is summer vacation. In most areas of the United States, school effects begin in September, stop in May or June, and recommence in September. This provides the natural experiment equivalent of an interrupted time-series design. The "treatment" starts and stops at regular intervals, and this provides an ideal opportunity to test its effects. Although the regular intervals of schooling have been used almost exclusively to test the influence of formal education on academic achievement, they could be used to examine attitudes as well (Alexander, Entwisle, & Bedinger, 1994).

Adults With Different Educational Backgrounds

Studying adults with different educational backgrounds is a powerful method because it can easily be used to generate a great many data. Indeed, this method has provided a very large proportion of the evidence reviewed in this book. Studying adults is especially important because it enables us to determine whether the effects of particular kinds of education wear off or grow with the passage of time, or, perhaps, whether there are sleeper effects that show up only years after the educational experience.

One easy way to gain many relevant data would be to ask respondents to social and political tolerance surveys more questions about their educational backgrounds than are now usually asked. Of greatest importance would be questions about higher education, because this level appears to matter most for differences in tolerance and because respondents' memories are likely to be more reliable about their college educations than about their primary and secondary schooling. It would be possible to learn much about a great number of variables by adding a few questions to standard surveys such as the General Social Survey. Three questions about respondents' higher education could yield very large amounts of information: (a) Which institution(s) did you attend? (b) When? (c) For how long? Coders could then, without relying on respondents' judgments and using publicly available information, classify educational backgrounds by such variables as size of institution attended, type of institution attended (public or private, single-sex or coed, 2-year, 4-year, or university), racial composition of institution, location of institution (rural or urban, Northeast, West, or South), and selectivity and/or prestige of institution. Educational background data such as these might tell us a good deal about respondents with different levels of social and political tolerance and would enable us to investigate various hypotheses about which aspects of the higher-education experience most strongly correlate with tolerance levels (compare Hall & Rodeghier, 1994).

Variations in Knowledge and Mental Processes

Differences in individuals' knowledge and in the ways they think about social and political problems has been found in several studies to be important determinants of their tolerance (see Bobo & Licari, 1989; Marcus, Sullivan,

Theiss-Morse, & Wood, 1995; McClosky & Brill, 1983). The relation between political knowledge and political tolerance is a frequently obtained result. But that finding has not led to subsequent investigations pursuing the initial insight. For example, what kinds of political knowledge are associated with differences in attitudes and values? Is the relation linear, with increasing amounts of political information leading to increasing political tolerance? Would social knowledge lead to social tolerance in the same way that being politically informed seems to lead to being politically tolerance? These questions would be comparatively easy to investigate, and the answers could lead directly to curricular policy.

In addition to refining our understanding of any links between knowledge and tolerance, we should also focus on ties between cognitive characteristics and tolerance. Previous studies have been very suggestive. Both Kohn (1969) and Bobo and Licari (1989) estimate that about one-third of the effect of years of schooling is due to the tendency of education to foster cognitive sophistication. The other two-thirds is much more difficult to specify (see Figure 7.1). Kohn's and Bobo and Licari's estimates are based on very limited (almost antiquated) measures of cognitive ability. Using some of the more refined and nuanced ways of conceiving cognitive capacity now available (suggested, for example, by Perkins, 1995, 1996) could greatly enhance our understanding of this path from years of education to social, political, and moral attitudes and beliefs.

Psychometric Research

Because tolerance has often been casually defined, there is considerable fuzziness in the overall picture presented by the extant research. It is hard to make progress when little agreement exists about how to define and operationalize the dependent variable. Sullivan and his colleagues have done much to correct this problem in the area of political tolerance. There are still some questions to be answered about the Sullivan "least-liked group" operationalization of political tolerance (see Chapters 4 and 5), but the main areas in which further clarifications are needed are social and moral tolerance.

Another continuing set of issues worthy of persistent psychometric vigilance is formed by the related problems of social desirability bias, misreporting on the part of survey respondents, and variations due to question wording ambiguities (see Chapter 3). For example, in mid-November 1990 one would have gotten a very different picture of Americans' support for the Gulf War depending upon which question was asked by survey researchers: 38% of the population was willing to "go to war," 46% would "engage in combat," and 65%

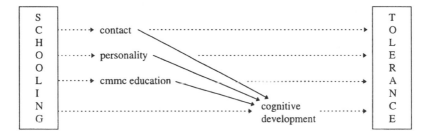

Figure 7.1. Schooling Related to Tolerance, With Educational Processes as Mediating Variables

would "use military force" (Mueller, 1994, p. 30). Was one-third or two-thirds of the population ready for battle? There is no way to tell. That uncertainty reinforces the importance of tending to issues of question wording; apparently minor differences in how researchers phrase questions can sometimes lead to dramatic differences in the answers they get. At a more macro level of analysis, Timur Kuran, in his *Private Truths, Public Lies* (1995), makes a convincing case that at least under extreme circumstances there can be dramatic differences between the population's opinion as expressed publicly and what people actually believe. Kuran's illustrations are often persuasive. Prime examples include the rapid speed with which regimes that seemed solid have crumbled when challenged, because they were not really supported by the public—for instance, in Eastern Europe in 1989 and France in 1789.

Gough and Bradley (1993) point out that most work on intolerance is based on "self-definition or (to put it more strongly) self-incrimination" (p. 66). To improve the level of accuracy of reports of individuals' attitudes, Gough and Bradley studied couples. Each partner rated him- or herself on the F(ascism) scale and rated the other on an Intolerance Index drawn from the Adjective Checklist, a widely used personality trait measure. The ratings on the two intolerance measures were not close; that is, a partner's self-rating on intolerance and that of his or her spouse did not yield the same profile. Which was the more accurate? It is impossible to say. But the fact of the difference led Sniderman, Tetlock, and Carmines (1993b) to conclude that Jackman's position claiming the essential duplicity of subjects "has received a new lease on life and deserves to be considered a scientifically plausible possibility" (p. 9). Sniderman et al.'s claim has added force because Sniderman has long been one of Jackman's opponents. But Sniderman has jumped the gun. The differences Gough and Bradley found between spouses' reports were mostly dissimilarities in an odd congeries of personality trait measures; the measures did not involve the kinds of attitudes and beliefs we have studied in this book or that Jackman (1994) has examined in hers.

But the core idea behind the method holds considerable promise: Comparing self-reports with others' reports *of the same thing* (a carefully conceptualized tolerance scale)[5] might well be very helpful in broadening our knowledge of people's attitudes and beliefs. Deciding which others' reports to compare with self-reports is no simple choice, however. I especially like Gough and Bradley's idea of comparing college students' self-descriptions to those of their fraternity or sorority mates. There may be too much potential bias with couples; however, this possible disadvantage may be counterbalanced by the fact that couples presumably know one another better than do college acquaintances. In general, obtaining perspectives about values and attitudes from several people participating in the same social context is a largely unused method that could generate new kinds of data. It would not be more "objective" than self-reports, but it would at least be more "intersubjective"; that is, it would allow researchers to juxtapose different perspectives on the same phenomenon.

In addition to new measurement techniques, we will also need more complicated models of how education fosters tolerance. Figure 7.1 gives a small example. It suggests a few likely paths of influence that lead from years of schooling to tolerant social and political attitudes. The figure depicts the explanations discussed in Chapters 4 and 5, and adds one new wrinkle. In the figure, schooling and tolerance are linked by the four processes of contact, personality development, CMMC education, and cognitive development. The new wrinkle takes the form of indirect effects. All of the processes lead to tolerance in themselves, but three of them also stimulate cognitive development, which further increases the likelihood of tolerance. When looking for indirect effects and interactions among the four processes, the next most promising line of inquiry, I believe, would involve focusing on cognitive development. But I use the figure here more as an example of the kind of models needed than as a substantive statement about cognitive development. Other potential interactions and indirect effects are not depicted. For example, cognitive sophistication could foster a desire for more schooling and/or more intergroup contact. Also, it is likely that cognitive and personality maturity often occur together. More complicated explanations such as the one advanced in Figure 7.1 are necessary, because neither schooling nor tolerance is a simple variable. Both are multiplex, as are the relations among their elements. All evidence indicates that we are not dealing with a Gordian knot to be sliced through with one new theoretical effort or a single crucial experiment. Rather, we must pick our way delicately through the tangled skein of multiplex relationships.

Event History Reconstruction

Event history reconstruction is a method not widely used in the study of attitudes, but it is one that has considerable potential for gaining access to more nuanced accounts of the origins of individuals' thoughts and emotions. Rather than merely asking people what their beliefs, attitudes, and values are, researchers could also ask them to ponder how they came to hold those beliefs, attitudes, and values. Subjects could be used as "expert witnesses" and asked to reflect on what aspects of their educational experiences influenced their intergroup attitudes. This might be an especially useful approach for investigating the propositions of contact theory. Intergroup contact is a good example because research on it using more traditional methods is highly advanced.

If we want subjects to reconstruct how they acquired their attitudes and beliefs, in-depth interviews would probably be the best method. If we work with college students, initial interview questions designed to gain insight into the contact hypothesis might be as follows: What was the racial/ethnic mix of your high school? How did that compare with what you had experienced in elementary school and in your neighborhood? How similar or different was it from what you have experienced here (in college)? What was your first reaction to the changes (from elementary to secondary and/or from secondary to higher education)? How would you describe your thoughts and feelings about the members of the other racial/ethnic groups? Did those thoughts and feelings change over time? If so, what led to the changes?

We have made considerable progress using correlational analysis of variables constructed on the basis of forced-choice, short-answer survey questions. And there is more progress to be made through the collection and analysis of such data. But on some topics, particularly contact theory, the number of potential correlates is so high that generalization is becoming exceedingly difficult. More in-depth research using qualitative methods could help us to find new ways to investigate our topic.[6] One study indicating the benefits of research along these lines was conducted by Chong (1993), who probed interview subjects regarding political tolerance. Chong asked respondents to reflect on their political beliefs and attitudes. I am suggesting that we should also ask them to reflect on how they came to have those beliefs and attitudes, and especially on whether their educational experiences had any influence in that process.

Of the four ways in which tolerance is taught and learned in schools, intergroup contact is the one that has been most thoroughly studied. Despite the huge literature on the subject and its many refinements, most of what has been produced stands as mere footnotes to Gordon Allport's great work *The Nature of Prejudice* (1954). For example, Allport's list of the kinds of contact and the variables in a contact situation (some 30 in all) is exhaustive and still directs most research (pp. 262-263). The problem is that there have been no compelling theoretical advances over Allport's original formulations. We still cannot come up with an answer better than "It depends." And it depends on so many things that we hardly know where to go from here. That is why I recommend adding a different approach. Adding the expert-witness approach to our repertoire of research methods has much promise. Asking people to reflect on why they think what they think and how they came to think that way is certainly worth a try.

How did people come to change their attitudes and beliefs about other ethnic groups, especially in school settings? Was it through the process Miller and Brewer (1984) call "decategorization"? Or were they influenced by a multicultural approach to learning about, and coming to appreciate, other cultures? Did cooperative work groups have anything to do with the process? In sum, we can use our current theories to formulate questions to pose to subjects to prompt them to consider the educational origins of their (in)tolerance.

Conclusion

Educational experiences influence students' tolerance in several ways. Education not only gives students new information, it can change how they think, alter their personalities, and provide them with new social experiences. These are sweeping claims, but they are supported by extensive research. Educational institutions affect students' beliefs, attitudes, and values whether or not educators control the ways in which they do so. We have seen that some powerful education effects can be unintentional and indirect. Others may arise from purposive action of educational planners. Education is not the only institutional sector to socialize and educate people so that they develop the capacity to tolerate diversity. Similar instruction can occur in the family, in religious groups, and among peers. But schools are uniquely positioned among modern institutions to teach lessons that make it possible for individuals to develop tolerance. The study of how educational experiences foster tolerance provides the only reliable information we have about how they could be constructed to do so more effectively in the future.

Notes

Chapter 1. What Is Tolerance?

1. The effect of education on these beliefs is significant. Between 1972 and 1980, the NORC in several of its General Social Surveys asked 7,167 Whites whether they thought there should be laws against intermarriage between Blacks and Whites. Among those whose educations ended with high school graduation, the percentage of respondents opposed to miscegenation laws averaged 11 points lower than the percentage of those with a year or more of college; respondents with 0-11 years of schooling were 34 percentage points lower than the college group (Davis, 1982, p. 581). In the 1990s, comparatively few Whites thought that the law "should forbid" intermarriage (19%) or believed that there should be "laws against" it (14%). However, 32% did not think the law "should allow" intermarriage (NORC, 1994). See the discussion of the forbid-allow problem in Chapter 3. Lastly, it should be noted that all of these responses were made after 1967, when the U.S. Supreme Court ruled antimiscegenation laws to be unconstitutional.

2. To illustrate how incoherent the concepts "race" and "ethnicity" are, even in the works of very careful scholars, I will examine two recent articles in the *American Psychologist* meant to tackle the problems of definition. The argument of Yee, Fairchild, Weizmann, and Wyatt (1993) on race can be summarized as follows: (a) Biological races do not exist; (b) hence, there can be no scientific definition of race; (c) therefore, researchers studying race use "lay stereotypes" or subjects' "self-identification" to define race (pp. 1133-1134); (d) therefore, we need a "blue ribbon interdisciplinary commission" (p. 1138) to establish a definition of race. Although the fourth point flows logically from the third, it flatly contradicts the first two steps in the argument.

Phinney's (1996) recommendations for the study of ethnicity have similar problems. She points out that because there is more within-group than between-group variation in ethnic groups, ethnicity "cannot predict behaviors or attitudes in any psychologically meaningful way" (p. 919). She says that many of the problems with using ethnicity as a variable would be reduced if we would consider ethnic groups as continuous rather than as categorical variables. But it is far from clear how we could do so. Ethnic groups and cultures, Phinney rightly argues, are not "unified structures to which one belongs" (p. 922), and individuals "cannot simply be categorized by group membership." However, she concludes that one could study ethnicity by holding it constant; that is, one could "study processes within groups rather than make comparisons across groups" (pp. 924-925). But how can one study ethnicity, within or across groups, if there is no reliable way to assign individuals to the groups?

It is much easier to point out the problems in articles such as those of Yee et al. (1993) and Phinney (1996) than to solve them. Indeed, they are insoluble. I mention them only to say once more to the reader of the following pages, *Caveat lector.* For a history of sociologists' equally vain efforts to define race, see McKee (1993).

Chapter 2. Should We Teach Tolerance?

1. Wolff's essay also appears in his collection *The Poverty of Liberalism* (1968), where it is put into the context of a more elaborate and general political philosophy.

2. Although I have drawn on several of Jackman's critics and her responses to them in the writing of the next paragraphs, for the sake of simplicity I will focus mainly on where my interpretation differs importantly from Jackman's. (The interested reader may want to consult Jackman, 1978, 1981a, 1981b; Kuklinski & Parent, 1981a, 1981b; Margolis & Haque, 1981; Sniderman, Brody, & Kuklinski, 1984.)

3. One partial measure of the influence of an article is how frequently it is cited. A quick review of the *Social Sciences Citation Index* reveals that from 1990 through 1994, Jackman and Muha's 1984 article was cited 31 times. By comparison, other articles in the same or a similar journal, written by well-known scholars, and used in this book have been cited less frequently in the same years: Davis's 1982 article, 12 citations; Weil's 1985 article, 12 citations; Bobo and Licari's 1989 article, 17 citations; and Slavin's 1985 article, 19 citations.

4. As Ezekiel (1995) puts it, most—perhaps all—Whites have some racially prejudiced and stereotyped attitudes and beliefs. What set the racists he studied apart from ordinary Whites was that his exemplars of the "racist mind" had no other attitudes and beliefs to counteract their racism.

Chapter 3. Does Education
Really Foster Tolerance?

1. Full knowledge is not necessary for an individual to have a meaningful opinion about an issue; for example, one might favor or oppose raising the minimum wage on general principles, without knowing exactly what the current minimum wage is.

2. For example, in the 1920s and 1930s, somewhat less than 3% of the age group in Germany attended university-level institutions. The figure was about the same in

France, perhaps somewhat smaller in England, and rather larger in the United States (Ringer, 1979, pp. 62, 148, 229, 252).

3. Extensive information from the membership rolls of the National Socialist Party is available and could perhaps be used to clarify this question.

4. This decline in anti-Semitism is not the same thing as an increase in tolerance. It may be more closely related to increasing indifference or universalism. See Figure 1.1.

5. It could be seen as a measure of anti-White racism were it not for the fact that most Blacks opposed to busing favor school integration.

6. For example, on most surveys only about one-fifth of Whites have favored busing, whereas nearly all support the principle of school integration. The gap for Whites is usually about 60-70%, but the gap for Blacks is generally in the 40-50% range.

7. There is a tendency for education to promote socially liberal explanations of inequality more among Blacks and women than among White males, but it is not a large difference, especially on issues of income equality (Kluegel & Smith, 1986, pp. 133, 297-298; see also Lipset, 1981). And, looking at the relation from another angle, increased income is more often than not negatively correlated with favoring racial equality (Steeh & Schuman, 1992), especially after education is controlled for.

8. This is a clear example of how an issue can be both one of moral tolerance, because of the "target group," and a matter of political tolerance, because the rights being denied to the morally defined group are political.

9. One interesting example of this concerns the influence of acculturation and social assimilation of Catholic European Americans. Alba (1978) has shown that those Catholic "ethnics" who married outside their own group and/or those who were of mixed ancestry were more politically tolerant (measured by support for freedom of the press for communists) and less authoritarian (in child-rearing attitudes) than those who married within their own group. Among the background variables other than ethnicity that Alba studied, education was the most important predictor of tolerance, but education's effect was the smallest among those who had inmarried.

10. See Sniderman et al. (1989) for a critique of McCutcheon's methodology. Corbett (1982), using 11 tolerance questions from the General Social Survey, found that only 9% of the population gave the tolerant response on all questions, and only 3% gave it on none of the 11 items; the connection of education level and tolerance level was very clear, and it was stronger when items were combined into scales (pp. 120-125).

11. Sullivan and his coauthors have already responded to many of these points (see Marcus et al., 1995; Mueller, 1988; Sullivan & Marcus, 1988). I merely summarize the criticisms here without their responses because my purpose is less a fair literature review than as concise a substantive review of the meaning of political tolerance as possible.

12. This is not a direct challenge to Sullivan et al., because they say that to be tolerant, not intolerant, of something, one must first dislike it.

13. On a personal note, I might add that findings of this sort have never surprised me. As I remember civics instruction in that era, it was mostly patriotic bombast, not thoughtful study likely to instill an appreciation for the finer points of the Bill of Rights.

14. These relationships are drawn from Jackman and Muha (1984, p. 757, Table 2), in which controls are introduced for several variables such as age, region, and family

income. All of the counts I report are more dramatic without the controls. For example, for Whites' attitudes about Blacks without controls (p. 756, Table 1) the count is 36 positive, 9 nonsignificant, 0 negative.

Chapter 4. How Does Education
Promote Tolerance Indirectly?

1. For example, if a college graduate had been 35 years old when surveyed in 1985, he or she would have graduated around 1973—some years before AIDS was identified.

2. Because traits are general, they probably have even less influence on specific behaviors than do attitudes (see Chapter 3). The weak effect of traits on specific behaviors would especially be the case if the influence of traits on behaviors were, as I believe likely, mainly indirect, through attitudes and beliefs. The path of influence would be as follows: traits → attitudes → behavior. One might also conceptualize traits as strong attitudes. In that case we could simplify our model and say that strong attitudes predict action better than weak ones. But measuring attitude strength is no easy matter. It amounts to studying attitudes about attitudes: How strongly do you feel about how you feel? For an excellent review and possible solution, see Bassili (1996).

3. See Young-Bruehl (1996) for a recent analysis of the authoritarian personality in which great skepticism about the effects of education on prejudices is expressed.

4. It is important to remember that this lack of direct effect is demonstrated only for political tolerance defined in reference to subjects' "least-liked" groups. Education could be directly associated with other forms of tolerance and/or for tolerance of other groups, such as moral tolerance of people an individual finds only mildly objectionable.

5. It is difficult to use McClosky and Brill's findings to study the effects of education. Because they did not use multivariate methods that would enable us to weigh the relative importance of the many predictors of tolerance they studied, we have to accept their conclusions with caution.

6. Of course, not all intellectuals or academics are equally committed to pluralistic debate. I mean only to suggest that they *tend* to be more so committed and have more of a vested interest in open debate than do people in other social roles.

7. In one quite old study, scores on the F scale varied considerably for students majoring in various fields at one midwestern university. The highest scores on the "fascistic" tendencies scale were earned by students majoring in administration, pharmacy, physical education, military science, and agriculture. The least "fascistic" students majored in physics, speech, English and art, and psychology and sociology. The differences were substantial, with the highest fields having scores three to four times as large as the lowest (Remmers, 1963). See also Feldman and Newcomb (1969).

8. *Liberal* and *tolerant* are not the same thing, of course, but subjects identifying themselves as liberal on surveys are much more likely than those identifying themselves as conservative to score high on tolerance scales.

9. Kuklinski, Riggle, Ottati, Schwarz, and Wyer (1991) come to apparently opposed conclusions. These researchers found that asking subjects to "think about the consequences" of tolerating a group such as the KKK reduced the subjects' initial tolerance. Of course, asking people to think about the consequences after they respond

is not the same as asking them to think before they respond, as Marcus et al. did. Also, in this case, opposition to tolerating the KKK is not necessarily an antidemocratic attitude. One could reasonably be judged more democratic because one is less tolerant of such a group.

10. Festinger's (1957) classic work on "cognitive dissonance" indicates that contradictory beliefs are more troublesome for people with more education, who are, therefore, more motivated to remove such contradictions than are people with less education. See also Westie (1965) and Bishop (1976).

11. For a longitudinal study linking good grades in college with advancing to higher stages of moral reasoning, see Biggs and Barnett (1981).

12. This "openness index" has interesting parallels with the earlier "simplism index" of Selznick and Steinberg (1969). Simplism, measured by agreement with statements such as "I don't like to hear a lot of arguments I disagree with," was a strong predictor of anti-Semitic prejudice. Responses to the openness index were gathered from some 3,000 students studying at 18 4-year colleges and universities in 15 states. The study was longitudinal; the students were surveyed in the fall of 1992 when they entered college and again some 8 or 9 months later, in the spring of 1993.

Chapter 5. Can We Teach Tolerance Directly?

1. In some contexts, as Hamilton, Carpenter, and Bishop (1984) have shown in their study of neighborhood desegregation, even minimal and superficial contact can reduce ignorance, assuage fears, and foster tolerance.

2. Social policy that leads to more contact (voluntary or nonvoluntary) can influence attitudes, but social policy does not always lead to more contact, and it has sometimes been designed to do just the opposite. For example, in Bavaria, Germany's largest state, in the 1980s, foreign children were educated in separate classes (Wagner & Machleit, 1986).

3. Brian McKenna and I are currently conducting a series of focused interviews with groups of teachers to investigate the dimensionality of their tolerance. This work has not led us to be especially optimistic about teacher attitudes.

4. Perhaps this focus on neighborhoods will someday become obsolete as local boundaries are crossed more and more frequently via the Internet, teleconferencing, distance learning, and the like. Such contact would certainly be less threatening than face-to-face contact and could reduce some of the inherent limitations to intergroup contact suggested by Schelling. I owe this insight to Dan Levy.

5. Because individual children and their parents often disagree, it does not follow that young and old people taken as groups disagree. Indeed, the generation gap is bigger between individual parents and their children than between the averages for generations as a whole.

6. Schools recently have had more incentives (both political pressures and financial resources) to address issues of social and moral tolerance, mostly through multicultural education, diversity workshops, and the like.

7. In a recent study of the effects of climate and students' sense of the extent to which their schools are communities, Battistich, Kim, Watson, and Schaps (1995) found that sense of community had important effects on students' (in grades 3-6) attitudes and

values, such as concern for others and self-efficacy, but it had no significant effects on democratic values.

8. Kohlberg revised his theory several times, and different researchers have based their work on different versions or stages of Kohlberg's theory. Although these differences are quite important for the development of the theory, they are usually not especially relevant for our purposes here, as we are considering only the broad outlines of the theory as they relate to teaching tolerance.

9. In a specific test of Gilligan's (1982) thesis, Power et al. (1989, p. 288) also found no significant gender differences in how students deal with the moral dilemmas. See also Umberson, Chen, House, Hopkins, and Slaten (1996) for an especially nuanced examination of male/female differences in interpersonal relations.

10. See Pascarella and Terenzini (1991) for some good evidence that higher education fosters cognitive and Kohlbergian moral development, even when self-selection effects are controlled for.

11. To the extent that multiculturalism is associated with one version or another of "postmodernism," the lack of research may also be based on a more principled opposition to any empirical investigations. See Searle (1994) for a discussion.

Chapter 6. Conclusion:
Implications for Policy and Practice

1. Tajfel's laboratory experiments revealed that even groups based on ephemeral criteria, such as a toss of a coin, can quickly begin discriminating against other groups. The "heads" versus the "tails" showed in-group favoritism as strong as that shown by members of real groups such the Protestants versus the Catholics. And this tendency to favor the members of one's own group endured even when it was in the subjects' self-interest not to discriminate against other groups. For recent work on the tendency to stereotype and discriminate, even in "very fleeting encounters," see Henderson-King and Nisbett (1996, p. 662).

2. I should add one caution about the usefulness of this research for purposes of this discussion, however. Because the dependent variable in these studies was not tolerance, strictly speaking, these conclusions have to be quite tentative, even on this otherwise indubitable point about the value of cooperative learning.

Chapter 7. Conclusion:
Implications for Research

1. On their face, these statements may actually refer to beliefs about the effectiveness of government programs, not to whether one supports them. Notions about the effectiveness of programs can have little to do with tolerance and may even have no link to liberalism. For example, one might believe that such programs will not do much to reduce homelessness (which is what the question literally asks), but may be committed to doing what one can in the short run to help particular individuals who are freezing in the streets—even if doing so will not solve the broader social problem.

2. A methodological note: The six social conditions constitute predisposing rather than precipitating causes. They make toleration more likely; they do not trigger it. None

of them is a sufficient cause. These six conditions form a cluster; they are mutually reinforcing and all push in the same direction. Their presence makes toleration very likely; their absence makes it very unlikely.

One major explanatory pitfall in the paths of researchers who do this kind of work is teleological functionalism in which social "needs" generate their own means of fulfillment. This is not an easy trap to escape. One can fall into it by thinking in terms of an evolution that naturally culminates in "like us" as the predetermined high point. The paradigm of social systems obstructs another path to clear understanding. If social systems, like all other systems, are made up of relations among parts, then toleration can be seen as a set of relations among the parts of a particular kind of social system, specifically the kind of social system that has the six characteristics I am about to list. Although I think this is true, saying it comes perilously close to uttering the tautology, A tolerant social system is a tolerant social system.

3. My work on the social origins of toleration represents a yet-unfinished general theory of toleration and education, especially education conceived of as the cognitive development of societies or populations. The current book, by contrast, is a special theory of education and tolerance at the micro or individual level.

4. Philosophical work on tolerance and toleration since the Second World War has been fairly extensive, but also somewhat sporadic (e.g., Cranston, 1967; Crick, 1971; King, 1976). The philosophical field of tolerance studies has never really "taken off" in the way that inquiries into rights or justice have. Perhaps more recent efforts indicate a sustainable revival of interest on the part of social and political philosophers (see, e.g., Fotion & Elfstrom, 1992; Heyd, 1996; Mendus, 1989).

5. Perhaps I am not as persuaded as I ought to be because of my skepticism about the value of psychological inventories that jumble together personality traits in a manner suggestive of the astrology page of a newspaper: "Alphas can be dictatorial and invasive"; "Deltas can be torn apart by their inner battles" (Gough & Bradley, 1993, p. 76).

6. Brian McKenna and I are finding focus groups to be particularly helpful in the study of teachers' tolerance. Because tolerance is an interpersonal variable, an interpersonal method of investigating it holds great promise.

References

Abramson, P. R. (1983). *Political attitudes in America: Formation and change.* San Francisco: W.H. Freeman.

Abramson, P. R., & Inglehart, R. (1994). Education, security and postmaterialism: A comment on Duch and Taylor's "Postmaterialism and the economic condition." *American Journal of Political Science, 38,* 797-814.

Adamek, R. J. (1994). Public opinion and *Roe v. Wade*: Measurement difficulties. *Public Opinion Quarterly, 58,* 409-418.

Adelman, C. (1994). *Lessons of a generation: Education and work in the lives of the high school class of 1972.* San Francisco: Jossey-Bass.

Adelson, J., & O'Neil, R. P. (1966). Growth of political ideas in adolescence. *Journal of Personality and Social Psychology, 4,* 295-306.

Adorno, T. W., Frenkel-Brunswick, E., Levinson, D. J., & Sanford, R. N. (1950). *The authoritarian personality.* New York: Harper.

Ajzen, I., & Fishbein, M. (1977). Attitude-behavior relations: A theoretical analysis and review of empirical research. *Psychological Bulletin, 84,* 888-918.

Alba, R. D. (1978). Ethnic networks and tolerant attitudes. *Public Opinion Quarterly, 42,* 1-16.

Alba, R. D. (1985). *Italian Americans: Into the twilight of ethnicity.* Englewood Cliffs, NJ: Prentice Hall.

Alexander, K. L., Entwisle, D. R., & Bedinger, S. D. (1994). When expectations work: Race and socioeconomic differences in school performance. *Social Psychology Quarterly, 57,* 283-299.

Alexander, K. L., Entwisle, D. R., & Thompson, M. S. (1987). School performance, status relations, and the structure of sentiment: Bringing the teacher back in. *American Sociological Review, 52,* 665-682.

Allport, F. H. (1953). The effects of segregation and the consequences of desegregation: A social science statement. *Minnesota Law Review, 37,* 429-440.

255

Allport, G. W. (1954). *The nature of prejudice.* Reading, MA: Addison-Wesley.

American Association of Colleges and Universities. (1995). *American pluralism and the college curriculum: Higher education in a diverse democracy.* Washington, DC: Author.

Amir, Y. (1969). Contact hypothesis in ethnic relations. *Psychological Bulletin, 71,* 319-342.

Andrain, C. F. (1985). *Social policies in Western industrial societies.* Berkeley, CA: Institute of International Studies.

Apostle, R. A., Glock, C. Y., Piazza, T., & Suelzle, M. (1983). *The anatomy of racial attitudes.* Berkeley: University of California Press.

Aquinas, T. (1988). *On law, morality, and politics* (W. Baumgarth & R. Regan, Eds.). Indianapolis: Hackett.

Armer, M. (1976). Review of Inkeles and Smith 1974. *Social Forces, 55,* 552-553.

Astin, A. (1993). *What matters in college.* San Francisco: Jossey-Bass.

Avery, P., Bird, K., Johnstone, S., Sullivan, J. L., & Thalhammer, K. (1992). Exploring political tolerance with adolescents. *Theory and Research in Social Education, 20,* 386-420.

Avery, P., Hoffman, D., Sullivan, J. L., Theiss-Morse, E., Fried, A., Bird, K., Johnstone, S., & Thalhammer, K. (1993). *Tolerance for diversity of beliefs: A secondary curriculum unit.* Boulder, CO: Social Science Education Consortium.

Bagozzi, R. P., & Yi, Y. (1989). The degree of intention formation as a moderator of the attitude-behavior relationship. *Social Psychology Quarterly, 52,* 266-279.

Bar-Tal, D., & Saxe, L. (1990). Acquisition of political knowledge: A social-psychological analysis. In O. Ichilov (Ed.), *Political socialization, citizenship education, and democracy* (pp. 116-133). New York: Teachers College Press.

Bassili, J. N. (1996). Meta-judgmental versus operative indexes of psychological attributes: The case of measures of attitude strength. *Journal of Personality and Social Psychology, 71,* 637-653.

Battistich, V. S., Kim, D., Watson, M., & Schaps, E. (1995). Schools as communities, poverty levels of student populations, and students' attitudes, motives, and performance: A multi-level analysis. *American Educational Research Journal, 32,* 627-658.

Beatty, K. M., & Walter, O. (1984). Religious preference and practice: Reevaluating their impact on political tolerance. *Public Opinion Quarterly, 48,* 318-329.

Bellas, M. L. (1994). Comparable worth in academia: The effects on faculty salaries of the sex composition and labor-market conditions of academic disciplines. *American Sociological Review, 59,* 807-821.

Ben-Ari, R., & Amir, Y. (1986). Contact between Arab and Jewish youth in Israel: Reality and potential. In M. Hewstone & R. Brown (Eds.), *Contact and conflict in intergroup encounters* (pp. 45-58). London: Basil Blackwell.

Beniger, J. R. (1984). Mass media, contraceptive behavior, and attitudes on abortion. In C. F. Turner & E. Martin (Eds.), *Surveying subjective phenomena* (Vol. 2, pp. 475-500). New York: Russell Sage Foundation.

Bennett, C. (1979, May). Interracial acceptance in desegregated schools. *Phi Delta Kappan,* pp. 683-684.

Berlin, I. (1969). *Four essays on liberty.* Oxford: Oxford University Press.

Bernstein, B. (1975). *Class, codes, and control: Theoretical studies towards a sociology of language.* New York: Schocken.

Biggs, D. A., & Barnett, R. (1981). Moral judgment development of college students. *Research in Higher Education, 14,* 91-102.

Bird, K., Sullivan, J. L., Avery, P., Thalhammer, K., & Wood, S. L. (1994). Not just lip-synching anymore: Education and tolerance revisited. *Review of Education, Pedagogy, and Cultural Studies, 16,* 373-386.

Bishop, G. F. (1976). The effect of education on ideological consistency. *Public Opinion Quarterly, 40,* 337-348.

Blalock, H. M. (1967). *Toward a theory of minority-group relations.* New York: John Wiley.

Blalock, H. M. (1982). *Race and ethnic relations.* Englewood Cliffs, NJ: Prentice Hall.

Blumer, H. (1958). Race prejudice as a sense of group position. *Pacific Sociological Review, 1,* 3-7.

Bobo, L., & Kluegel, J. R. (1993). Opposition to race-targeting: Self-interest, stratification ideology, or racial attitudes? *American Sociological Review, 58,* 443-464.

Bobo, L., & Licari, F. C. (1989). Education and political tolerance: Testing the effects of cognitive sophistication and target group effect. *Public Opinion Quarterly, 53,* 285-308.

Bourdieu, P. (1985). The genesis of the concepts of habitus and field. *Sociocentricism, 2,* 11-24.

Braddock, J. H. (1980). The perpetuation of segregation across levels of education: A behavioral assessment of the contact hypothesis. *Sociology of Education, 53,* 178-186.

Braddock, J. H. (1985). School desegregation and Black assimilation. *Journal of Social Issues, 41*(3), 9-22.

Breslin, A. (1982). Tolerance and moral reasoning among adolescents in Ireland. *Journal of Moral Education, 11,* 112-127.

Britton, D. M. (1990). Homophobia and homosociality: An analysis of boundary maintenance. *Sociological Quarterly, 31,* 423-439.

Bryson, B. (1996). "Anything but heavy metal": Symbolic exclusion and musical dislikes. *American Sociological Review, 61,* 884-899.

Bullock, C. S. (1978). Contact theory and racial tolerance among high school students. *School Review, 86,* 187-216.

Burton, M. G., & Higley, J. (1987). Elite settlements. *American Sociological Review, 52,* 295-307.

Byrne, R., & Whiten, A. (1988). *Machiavellian intelligence: Social expertise and the evolution of intellect in monkeys, apes, and humans.* Oxford: Clarendon.

Cabrera, A., & Nora, A. (1994). College students' perceptions of prejudice and discrimination and their feelings of alienation: A construct validation approach. *Review of Education, Pedagogy, and Cultural Studies, 16,* 387-409.

Cacioppo, J. T., & Petty, R. W. (1982). The need for cognition. *Journal of Personality and Social Psychology, 42,* 116-131.

Castellio, S. (1931). *Concerning heretics.* New York: Columbia University Press. (Original work published 1554)

Chong, D. (1993). How people think, reason, and feel about rights and liberties. *American Journal of Political Science, 37,* 867-899.

Cohen, E. G. (1984). The segregated school: Problems in status power and interethnic climate. In N. Miller & M. B. Brewer (Eds.), *Groups in contact: The psychology of desegregation* (pp. 77-96). New York: Academic Press.

Cohen, E. G., & Lotan, R. A. (1995). Producing equal-status interaction in the heterogeneous classroom. *American Educational Research Journal, 32,* 99-120.

Colby, A., Kohlberg, L., Fenton, E., Speicher-Dubin, E., & Lieberman, M. (1977). Secondary school moral discussion programmes. *Journal of Moral Education, 6,* 90-111.

Colesante, R., Smith, J., & Biggs, D. A. (1996a). *Citizenship education for urban youth.* Paper presented at the International Conference on Problems of Russian and Foreign Education at the End of the 20th Century, Kursk, Russia.

Colesante, R., Smith, J., & Biggs, D. A. (1996b). *Whatever happened to good citizens?* Paper presented at the International Conference on Problems of Russian and Foreign Education at the End of the 20th Century, Kursk, Russia.

Collins, R. (1975). *Conflict sociology.* New York: Academic Press.

Condran, J. G. (1979). Changes in White attitudes toward Blacks: 1963-1977. *Public Opinion Quarterly, 43,* 463-476.

Converse, P. E. (1964). The nature of belief systems in mass publics. In D. E. Apter (Ed.), *Ideology and discontent* (pp. 206-261). New York: Free Press.

Cook, T. E. (1985). The bear market in political socialization and the costs of misunderstood psychological theories. *American Political Science Review, 79,* 1079-1093.

Corbett, M. (1982). *Political tolerance in America: Freedom and equality in public attitudes.* New York: Longman.

Corbett, M. (1991). *American public opinion.* New York: Longman.

Corzine, J., Creech, J., & Corzine, L. (1983). Black concentration and lynchings in the South: Testing Blalock's power-threat hypothesis. *Social Forces, 61,* 774-796.

Coser, L. A. (1956). *The functions of social conflict.* New York: Free Press.

Cranston, M. (1967). Toleration. In P. Edwards (Ed.), *The encyclopedia of philosophy* (Vol. 8, pp. 143-146). New York: Macmillan.

Crenshaw, E. M. (1995). Democracy and demographic inheritance: The influence of modernity and proto-modernity on political and civil rights, 1965 to 1980. *American Sociological Review, 60,* 702-718.

Crick, B. (1971). Toleration and tolerance in theory and practice. *Government and Opposition, 6,* 144-171.

Cunningham, I. (1973). The relationship between modernity of students in a Puerto Rican high school and their academic performance, peers, and parents. *International Journal of Comparative Sociology, 14,* 203-220.

Cutler, S. J., & Kaufman, R. L. (1975). Cohort changes in political attitudes: Tolerance of ideological nonconformity. *Public Opinion Quarterly, 39,* 69-81.

Dahl, R. (1989). *Democracy and its critics.* New Haven, CT: Yale University Press.

Dasgupta, P. (1993). *An inquiry into well-being and destitution.* Oxford: Oxford University Press.

Dasgupta, P. (1995). Population, poverty and the local environment. *Scientific American, 272*(2), 40-45.

Davis, J. A. (1975). Communism, conformity, cohorts, and categories: American tolerance in 1954 and 1972-73. *American Journal of Sociology, 81,* 491-513.

Davis, J. A. (1982). Achievement variables and class cultures: Family, schooling, job, and forty-nine dependent variables in the cumulative GSS. *American Sociological Review, 47,* 569-586.

Davis, J. A. (1985). *The logic of causal order.* Beverly Hills, CA: Sage.

Davis, J. A. (1992). Changeable weather in a cooling climate atop the liberal plateau: Conversion and replacement in forty-two General Social Survey items, 1972-1989. *Public Opinion Quarterly, 56,* 261-307.

DeMaio, T. J. (1984). Social desirability and survey measurement: A review. In C. F. Turner & E. Martin (Eds.), *Surveying subjective phenomena* (Vol. 2, pp. 257-282). New York: Russell Sage Foundation.

Deutscher, I. (1966). Words and deeds: Social science and social policy. *Social Problems, 13,* 235-254.

Deutscher, I. (1969). Looking backward: Case studies on the progress of methodology in sociological research. *American Sociologist, 4,* 35-41.

Devine, P. G. (1989). Stereotypes and prejudice: Their automatic and controlled components. *Journal of Personality and Social Psychology, 56,* 5-18.

Devlin, P. (1965). *The enforcement of morals.* Oxford: Oxford University Press.

de Waal, F. (1996). *Good natured: The origins of right and wrong in humans and other animals.* Cambridge, MA: Harvard University Press.

Dey, E., Astin, A., & Korn, W. (1991). *The American freshman: Twenty-five year trends.* Los Angeles: American Council on Education.

Dillon, M. (1993). Argumentative complexity of abortion discourse. *Public Opinion Quarterly, 57,* 305-314.

Dinnerstein, L. (1994). *Antisemitism in America.* New York: Oxford University Press.

Dowden, S., & Robinson, J. P. (1993). Age and cohort differences in American racial attitudes: The generational replacement hypothesis revisited. In P. M. Sniderman, P. E. Tetlock, & E. G. Carmines (Eds.), *Prejudice, politics, and the American dilemma* (pp. 86-103). Stanford, CA: Stanford University Press.

Dreeben, R. (1968). *On what is learned in school.* Reading, MA: Addison-Wesley.

Drescher, S. (1986). *Capitalism and antislavery.* London: Macmillan.

Dubey, S. N. (1979). Positive discrimination policy and ethnocentric attitudes among the scheduled castes. *Public Opinion Quarterly, 43,* 60-67.

Duch, R. M., & Taylor, M. A. (1993). Postmaterialism and the economic condition. *American Journal of Political Science, 37,* 747-779.

Duch, R. M., & Taylor, M. A. (1994). A reply to Abramson and Inglehart's "Education, security, and postmaterialism." *American Journal of Political Science, 38,* 815-824.

Dugger, K. (1991). Race differences in the determinants of support for legalized abortions. *Social Science Quarterly, 72,* 570-587.

Durkheim, E. (1961). *Moral education.* New York: Free Press.

Durkheim, E. (1964). *The division of labor in society.* New York: Free Press. (Original work published 1893)

Durkheim, E. (1969). *L'Evolution pedagogique en France.* Paris: Presses Universitaires de France.

Dworkin, R. (1996). The moral reading of the Constitution. *New York Review of Books, 43*(5), 46-51.

Ehman, L. H. (1980). The American school in the political socialization process. *Review of Educational Research, 50,* 99-119.

Epstein, J. L. (1985). After the bus arrives: Resegregation in desegregated schools. *Journal of Social Issues, 41*(3), 23-43.

Ezekiel, R. S. (1995). *The racist mind: Portraits of American neo-Nazis and Klansmen.* New York: Viking.

Fairweather, J. S. (1995). Myths and realities of academic labor markets. *Economics of Education Review, 14,* 179-192.

Fazio, R. H. (1986). How do attitudes guide behavior? In R. M. Sorrentino & E. T. Higgins (Eds.), *Handbook of motivation and cognition* (pp. 204-243). New York: Guilford.

Fazio, R. H., Jackson, J. R., Dunton, B. C., & Williams, C. J. (1995). Variability in automatic activation as an unobtrusive measure of racial attitudes: A bona fide pipeline? *Journal of Personality and Social Psychology, 69,* 1013-1027.

Feldman, K. A., & Newcomb, T. M. (1969). *The impact of college on students.* San Francisco: Jossey-Bass.

Festinger, L. (1957). *A theory of cognitive dissonance.* Evanston, IL: Row, Peterson.

Firebaugh, G., & Davis, K. E. (1988). Trends in antiblack prejudice, 1972-1984: Region and cohort effects. *American Journal of Sociology, 94,* 251-272.

Fishbein, M., & Ajzen, I. (1975). *Belief, attitude, intention, and behavior: An introduction to theory and research.* Reading, MA: Addison-Wesley.

Fotion, N., & Elfstrom, G. (1992). *Toleration.* Tuscaloosa: University of Alabama Press.

Funk, R. B., & Willits, F. K. (1987). College attendance and attitude change: A panel study, 1970-1981. *Sociology of Education, 60,* 224-231.

Gabennesch, H. (1972). Authoritarianism as a world view. *American Journal of Sociology, 77,* 857-875.

Gaddy, B. B., Hall, T. W., & Marzanno, R. J. (1996). *School wars: Resolving our conflicts over religion and values.* San Francisco: Jossey-Bass.

Gallatin, J., & Adelson, J. (1971). Legal guarantees of individual freedom: A cross-national study of the development of political thought. *Journal of Social Issues, 27*(2), 93-108.

Gans, H. J. (1995). *The war against the poor: The underclass and antipoverty policy.* New York: Basic Books.

Gibson, J. L. (1988). Political intolerance and political repression during the McCarthy red scare. *American Political Science Review, 82,* 511-529.

Gibson, J. L. (1989). The policy consequences of political intolerance: Political repression during the Vietnam War era. *Journal of Politics, 51,* 13-35.

Gibson, J. L. (1992a). Alternative measures of political tolerance: Must tolerance be "least-liked"? *American Journal of Political Science, 36,* 560-577.

Gibson, J. L. (1992b). The political consequences of intolerance: Cultural conformity and political freedom. *American Political Science Review, 86,* 338-356.

Gibson, J. L., & Tedin, K. L. (1988). The etiology of intolerance of homosexual politics. *Social Science Quarterly, 69,* 587-604.

Gilligan, C. (1982). *In a different voice: Psychological theory and women's development.* Cambridge, MA: Harvard University Press.

Goleman, D. (1995). *Emotional intelligence.* New York: Bantam.

Goodrich, H. L. (1996, April). *Intellectual character and intellectual standards.* Paper presented at the annual meeting of the American Educational Research Association, New York.

Goody, J. (1986). *The logic of writing and the organization of society.* New York: Cambridge University Press.

Gough, H. G., & Bradley, P. (1993). Personal attributes of people described by others as intolerant. In P. M. Sniderman, P. E. Tetlock, & E. G. Carmines (Eds.), *Prejudice, politics, and the American dilemma* (pp. 60-85). Stanford, CA: Stanford University Press.

Grabb, E. G. (1979). Working-class authoritarianism and tolerance of outgroups. *Public Opinion Quarterly, 43,* 36-47.

Graff, G. (1992). *Beyond the culture wars.* New York: W. W. Norton.

Granberg, D. (1991). Conformity to religious norms regarding abortion. *Sociological Quarterly, 32,* 267-275.

Greeley, A. M. (1974). *Ethnicity in the United States.* New York: John Wiley.

Greeley, A. M., & Sheatsley, P. B. (1971). Attitudes toward racial integration. *Scientific American, 225*(6), 13-19.

Green, D. P., & Waxman, L. M. (1987). Direct threat and political tolerance: An experimental analysis of the tolerance of Blacks toward racists. *Public Opinion Quarterly, 51,* 149-165.

Guimond, S. (1989). Education and causal attributions: The development of "person-blame" and "system-blame" ideology. *Social Psychology Quarterly, 52,* 126-140.

Hacking, I. (1984). *The emergence of probability.* Cambridge: Cambridge University Press.

Hall, R., & Rodeghier, M. (1994). More is sometimes less: Education's effects on tolerance. *Review of Education, Pedagogy, and Cultural Studies, 16,* 297-314.

Hallinan, M. T. (1982). Classroom racial composition and children's friendships. *Social Forces, 61,* 56-72.

Hallinan, M. T., & Teixeira, R. A. (1987). Students' interracial friendships: Individual characteristics, structural effects, and racial differences. *American Journal of Education, 95,* 563-583.

Hallinan, M. T., & Williams, R. A. (1989). Interracial friendship choices in secondary schools. *American Sociological Review, 54,* 67-78.

Hallinan, M. T., & Williams, R. A. (1990). Students' characteristics and the peer influence process. *Sociology of Education, 63,* 122-132.

Hamilton, D. L., Carpenter, S., & Bishop, G. D. (1984). Desegregation of suburban neighborhoods. In N. Miller & M. B. Brewer (Eds.), *Groups in contact: The psychology of desegregation* (pp. 97-121). New York: Academic Press.

Hamilton, R. F., & Hargens, L. L. (1993). The politics of the professors: Self-identifications, 1969-1984. *Social Forces, 71,* 603-627.

Hart, H. L. A. (1982). *Law, liberty, and morality.* Oxford: Oxford University Press. (Original work published 1963)

Hartley, E. L. (1946). *Problems in prejudice.* New York: King's Crown.

Hauser, R. M. (1993). The decline in college entry among African Americans: Findings in search of explanations. In P. M. Sniderman, P. E. Tetlock, & E. G. Carmines (Eds.), *Prejudice, politics, and the American dilemma* (pp. 271-306). Stanford, CA: Stanford University Press.

Heller, C., & Hawkins, J. A. (1994). Teaching tolerance: Notes from the front line. *Teachers College Record, 95,* 337-368.

Henderson-King, E., & Nisbett, R. E. (1996). Anti-Black prejudice as a function of exposure to the negative behavior of a single Black person. *Journal of Personality and Social Psychology, 71,* 654-664.

Hewstone, M., & Brown, R. (1986). Contact is not enough: An intergroup perspective on the "contact hypothesis." In M. Hewstone & R. Brown (Eds.), *Contact and conflict in intergroup encounters* (pp. 1-44). London: Basil Blackwell.

Heyd, D. (Ed.). (1996). *Toleration: An elusive virtue.* Princeton, NJ: Princeton University Press.

Hippler, H.-J., & Schwarz, N. (1986). Not forbidding isn't allowing: The cognitive basis of the forbid-allow asymmetry. *Public Opinion Quarterly, 50,* 87-96.

Hochschild, J. L. (1984). *The new American dilemma: Democracy and school desegregation.* New Haven, CT: Yale University Press.

Hodgkinson, H. L. (1995). What should we call people: Race, class and the census for 2000. *Phi Delta Kappan, 77,* 173-179.

Hodson, R., Sekulic, D., & Massey, G. (1994). National tolerance in the former Yugoslavia. *American Journal of Sociology, 99,* 1534-1558.

Hoge, D. R., & Hoge, J. L. (1984). Period effects and specific age effects influencing values of alumni in the decade after college. *Social Forces, 62,* 941-962.

Holsinger, D. B. (1973). The elementary school as modernizer: A Brazilian study. *International Journal of Comparative Sociology, 14,* 180-202.

Holsinger, D. B., & Theisen, G. L. (1977). Education, individual modernity, and national development: A critical appraisal. *Journal of Developing Areas, 11,* 315-334.

Horowitz, D. L. (1985). *Ethnic groups in conflict.* Berkeley: University of California Press.

Huddy, L., & Sears, D. O. (1995). Opposition to bilingual education: Prejudice or defense of realistic interests? *Social Psychology Quarterly, 58,* 133-143.

Hurn, C. J. (1993). *The limits and possibilities of schooling* (3rd ed.). Boston: Allyn & Bacon.

Hurtado, S. (1994). Graduate school racial climates and academic self-concept among minority graduate students in the 1970s. *American Journal of Education, 102,* 330-350.

Hyman, H. H., & Sheatsley, P. B. (1956). Attitudes toward desegregation. *Scientific American, 195*(6), 35-39.

Hyman, H. H., & Sheatsley, P. B. (1964). Attitudes toward desegregation. *Scientific American, 211*(1), 16-23.

Hyman, H. H., & Wright, C. R. (1979). *Education's lasting influence on values.* Chicago: University of Chicago Press.

Inglehart, R. (1990). *Culture shift in advanced industrial society.* Princeton, NJ: Princeton University Press.

Inkeles, A. (1973). The school as a context for modernization. *International Journal of Comparative Sociology, 14,* 163-179.

Inkeles, A., & Holsinger, D. B. (1973). Introduction to special number on education and individual modernity. *International Journal of Comparative Sociology, 14*, 157-162.

Inkeles, A., & Smith, D. H. (1974). *Becoming modern: Individual change in six developing countries.* Cambridge, MA: Harvard University Press.

Isaac, L., Mutran, E., & Stryker, S. (1980). Political protest orientations among Black and White adults. *American Sociological Review, 45*, 191-213.

Jackman, M. R. (1973). Education and prejudice or education and response-set? *American Sociological Review, 38*, 327-339.

Jackman, M. R. (1976). The relation between verbal attitude and overt behavior: A public opinion application. *Social Forces, 54*, 646-668.

Jackman, M. R. (1977). Prejudice, tolerance, and attitudes toward ethnic groups. *Social Science Research, 6*, 145-169.

Jackman, M. R. (1978). General and applied tolerance: Does education increase commitment to racial integration? *American Journal of Political Science, 22*, 302-324.

Jackman, M. R. (1981a). Education and policy commitment to racial integration. *American Journal of Political Science, 25*, 256-269.

Jackman, M. R. (1981b). Issues in the measurement of commitment to racial integration. *Political Methodology, 8*, 160-172.

Jackman, M. R. (1994). *The velvet glove: Paternalism and conflict in gender, class, and race relations.* Berkeley: University of California Press.

Jackman, M. R., & Muha, M. J. (1984). Education and intergroup attitudes: Moral enlightenment, superficial democratic commitment, or ideological refinement? *American Sociological Review, 49*, 751-769.

Jackson, P. W., Boostrom, R. E., & Hansen, D. T. (1993). *The moral life of schools.* San Francisco: Jossey-Bass.

Jacobs, J. A. (1995). Gender and academic specialties: Trends among recipients of college degrees in the 1980s. *Sociology of Education, 68*, 81-98.

Jelen, T. G., & Wilcox, C. (1992). Symbolic and instrumental values as predictors of AIDS policy attitudes. *Social Science Quarterly, 73*, 737-749.

Johnson, D. W., Johnson, R., & Maruyama, G. (1984). Goal interdependence and interpersonal attraction in heterogeneous classrooms: A meta-analysis. In N. Miller & M. B. Brewer (Eds.), *Groups in contact: The psychology of desegregation* (pp. 187-212). New York: Academic Press.

Jones, R. S. (1980). Democratic values and preadult virtues: Tolerance, knowledge, and participation. *Youth & Society, 12*, 189-220.

Kamen, H. (1967). *The rise of toleration.* London: Weidenfeld & Nicolson.

Karabel, J., & Halsey, A. H. (Eds.). (1977). *Power and ideology in education.* New York: Oxford University Press.

Keinan, G. (1994). Effects of stress and tolerance of ambiguity on magical thinking. *Journal of Personality and Social Psychology, 67*, 48-55.

Kekes, J. (1993). *The morality of pluralism.* Princeton, NJ: Princeton University Press.

Kelman, H. C. (1974). Attitudes are alive and well and gainfully employed in the sphere of action. *American Psychologist, 29*, 310-324.

Kenny, C. B. (1993). Social influence and opinion on abortion. *Social Science Quarterly, 74*, 560-574.

Khushf, G. (1994). Intolerant tolerance. *Journal of Medicine and Philosophy, 19*, 161-181.

King, P. (1976). *Toleration.* London: Allen & Unwin.

Klineberg, S. (1973). Parents, schools and modernity: An exploratory investigation of sex differences in the attitudinal development of Tunisian adolescents. *International Journal of Comparative Sociology, 14*, 221-244.

Kluegel, J. R., & Bobo, L. (1993). Dimensions of Whites' beliefs about the Black-White socioeconomic gap. In P. M. Sniderman, P. E. Tetlock, & E. G. Carmines (Eds.), *Prejudice, politics, and the American dilemma* (pp. 127-147). Stanford, CA: Stanford University Press.

Kluegel, J. R., & Smith, E. (1986). *Beliefs about inequality: Americans' views of what is and what ought to be.* New York: Aldine de Gruyter.

Knox, W., Lindsay, P., & Kolb, M. (1993). *Does college make a difference?* Westport, CT: Greenwood.

Knutson, J. N. (1973). Personality in the study of politics. In J. N. Knutson (Ed.), *Handbook of political psychology* (pp. 28-56). San Francisco: Jossey-Bass.

Kohlberg, L. (1982). *Essays in moral development.* New York: Harper & Row.

Kohlberg, L. (1984). *The psychology of moral development.* New York: Harper & Row.

Kohn, M. L. (1969). *Class and conformity: A study in values.* Homewood, IL: Dorsey.

Kohn, M. L. (1971). Bureaucratic man: A portrait and an interpretation. *American Sociological Review, 36,* 461-474.

Korman, A. K. (1975). Work experience, socialization, and civil liberties. *Journal of Social Issues, 31*(2), 137-151.

Kors, A. C. (1990). *Atheism in France, 1650-1729.* Princeton, NJ: Princeton University Press.

Kuklinski, J. H., & Parent, W. (1981a). Race and big government: Contamination in measuring racial attitudes. *Political Methodology, 7,* 131-159.

Kuklinski, J. H., & Parent, W. (1981b). Rejoinder to Professor Jackman. *Political Methodology, 7,* 173-179.

Kuklinski, J. H., Riggle, E., Ottati, V., Schwarz, N., & Wyer, R. S., Jr. (1991). The cognitive and affective bases of political tolerance judgments. *American Journal of Political Science, 35,* 1-27.

Kuran, T. (1995). *Private truths, public lies: The social consequences of preference falsification.* Cambridge, MA: Harvard University Press.

Labrousse, E. (1973). Religious toleration. In P. P. Wiener (Ed.), *Dictionary of the history of ideas* (Vol. 4, pp. 112-121). New York: Scribner's.

Lacy, W. B., & Middleton, E. (1981). Are educators racially prejudiced? A cross-occupational comparison of attitudes. *Sociological Focus, 14,* 87-95.

Langton, K. P., & Jennings, M. K. (1968). Political socialization in the high school civics curriculum in the United States. *American Political Science Review, 62,* 852-867.

LaPiere, R. T. (1934). Attitudes vs. actions. *Social Forces, 13,* 230-237.

LaPiere, R. T. (1969). Comment on Irwin Deutscher's "Looking backward." *American Sociologist, 4,* 41-42.

Lau, R. R., & Sears, D. O. (Eds.). (1986). *Political cognition: The 19th Annual Carnegie Mellon Symposium on Cognition.* Hillsdale, NJ: Lawrence Erlbaum.

Lawrence, D. G. (1976). Procedural norms and tolerance: A reassessment. *American Political Science Review, 70,* 80-100.

Legge, J. S. (1983). The determinants of attitudes toward abortion in the American electorate. *Western Political Quarterly, 33,* 479-490.

Levy, L. (1985). *Emergence of a free press.* New York: Oxford University Press.

Leyens, J.-P., Yzerbyt, V., & Shadron, G. (1994). *Stereotypes and social cognition.* Thousand Oaks, CA: Sage.

Lickona, T. (1992). *Educating for character: How our schools can teach respect and responsibility.* New York: Bantam.

Lillydahl, J. H., & Singell, L. D. (1993). Job satisfaction, salaries, and unions: The determination of university faculty compensation. *Economics of Education Review, 12,* 233-243.

Lind, G. (1996a, April). *Educational environments which promote self-sustaining moral development.* Paper presented at the annual meeting of the American Educational Research Association, New York.

Lind, G. (1996b, April). *The optimal age of moral education: A review of intervention studies and an experimental test.* Paper presented at the annual meeting of the American Educational Research Association, New York.

Lindbloom, C. E., & Woodhouse, E. J. (1993). *The policy-making process* (3rd ed.). Englewood Cliffs, NJ: Prentice Hall.

Lipset, S. M. (1981). *Political man* (expanded ed.). Baltimore: Johns Hopkins University Press.

Livingston, M., & Berger, M. (1994). Developing a coalition and principles for a just community. *Review of Education, Pedagogy, and Cultural Studies, 16,* 427-433.

Locke, J. (1968). *A letter on toleration* (R. Klibansky & J. Gough, Eds.). Oxford: Oxford University Press. (Original work published 1689)

Longshore, D. (1982). Race composition and White hostility: A research note on the problem of control in desegregated schools. *Social Forces, 61,* 73-78.

Lynxwiler, J., & Gay, D. (1994). Reconsidering race differences in abortion attitudes. *Social Science Quarterly, 75,* 67-84.

Madison, J. (1961). *The federalist* (J. E. Cooke, Ed.). Middletown, CT: Wesleyan University Press. (Original work published 1788)

Marcus, G. E., Sullivan, J. L., Theiss-Morse, E., & Wood, S. L. (1995). *With malice toward some: How people make civil liberties judgments.* Cambridge: Cambridge University Press.

Marcuse, H. (1969). Repressive tolerance. In R. P. Wolff, B. Moore, Jr., & H. Marcuse, *A critique of pure tolerance* (pp. 81-123). Boston: Beacon.

Margolis, M., & Haque, K. E. (1981). Applied tolerance or fear of government: An alternative interpretation of Jackman's findings. *American Journal of Political Science, 25,* 241-255.

Martire, G., & Clark, R. (1982). *Anti-Semitism in the United States: A study of prejudice in the 1980s.* New York: Praeger.

Maslow, A. H. (1954). *Motivation and personality.* New York: Harper & Row.

Massey, D. S., & Denton, N. A. (1993). *American apartheid: Segregation and the making of the underclass.* Cambridge, MA: Harvard University Press.

McClosky, H. (1964). Consensus and ideology in American politics. *American Political Science Review, 58,* 361-382.

McClosky, H., & Brill, A. (1983). *Dimensions of tolerance: What Americans believe about civil liberties.* New York: Russell Sage Foundation.

McCutcheon, A. L. (1985). A latent class analysis of tolerance for nonconformity in the American public. *Public Opinion Quarterly, 49,* 474-488.

McIntosh, M. E., MacIver, M. A., Abele, D. G., & Nolle, D. B. (1995). Minority rights and majority rule: Ethnic tolerance in Romania and Bulgaria. *Social Forces, 73,* 939-968.

McKee, J. B. (1993). *Sociology and the race problem: The failure of a perspective.* Chicago: University of Illinois Press.

Mendus, S. (1989). *Toleration and the limits of liberalism.* London: Macmillan.

Merelman, R. M. (1980). Democratic politics and the culture of American education. *American Political Science Review, 74,* 319-332.

Merrick, J. W. (1990). *The desacralization of the French monarchy in the 18th century.* Baton Rouge: Louisiana State University Press.

Merton, R. K. (1976). Discrimination and the American creed. In R. K. Merton, *Sociological ambivalence and other essays* (pp. 189-216). New York: Free Press.

Meyer, J. (1977). The effects of education as an institution. *American Journal of Sociology, 83,* 55-77.

Mill, J. S. (1979). *On liberty.* Indianapolis: Hackett. (Original work published 1859)

Miller, A. S. (1994). Dynamic indicators of self-perceived conservatism. *Sociological Quarterly, 35,* 175-182.

Miller, J., Slomczynski, K. M., & Kohn, M. L. (1985). Continuity of learning generalization: The effect of job on men's intellective process in the United States and Poland. *American Journal of Sociology, 91,* 593-615.

Miller, K. A., Kohn, M. L., & Schooler, C. (1986). Educational self-direction and personality. *American Sociological Review, 51,* 372-390.

Miller, N., & Brewer, M. B. (Eds.). (1984). *Groups in contact: The psychology of desegregation.* New York: Academic Press.

Miller, S. D., & Sears, D. O. (1986). Stability and change in social tolerance: A test of the persistence hypothesis. *American Journal of Political Science, 30,* 214-236.

Miller, S. M., & Riessman, F. (1961). Working-class authoritarianism: A critique of Lipset. *British Journal of Sociology, 12,* 263-276.

Moore, B., Jr. (1969). Tolerance and the scientific outlook. In R. P. Wolff, B. Moore, Jr., & H. Marcuse, *A critique of pure tolerance* (pp. 53-79). Boston: Beacon.

Mueller, J. (1988). Trends in political tolerance. *Public Opinion Quarterly, 52,* 1-25.

Mueller, J. (1994). *Policy and opinion in the Gulf War.* Chicago: University of Chicago Press.

Muir, D. E., & McGlamery, C. D. (1984). Trends in integration attitudes on a Deep-South campus during the first two decades of desegregation. *Social Forces, 62,* 963-972.

Muller, E. N., Pesonen, P., & Jukam, T. O. (1980). Support for freedom of assembly in Western democracies. *European Journal of Political Research, 8,* 265-288.

Myrdal, G., with Sterner, R., & Rose, A. (1944). *An American dilemma: The Negro problem and modern democracy.* New York: Harper & Row.

National Opinion Research Center (NORC). (1986). *General Social Surveys, 1972-1986: Cumulative codebook.* Chicago: Author.

National Opinion Research Center (NORC). (1994). *General Social Surveys, 1972-1994: Cumulative codebook.* Chicago: Author.

Netanyahu, B. (1995). *The origins of the Inquisition in fifteenth-century Spain.* New York: Random House.

Nielsen, H. D. (1977). *Tolerating political dissent: The impact of high school social climates in the Unites States and West Germany.* Stockholm: Almqvist & Wiksell.

Niemi, R. G. (1973). Political socialization. In J. N. Knutson (Ed.), *Handbook of political psychology* (pp. 117-138). San Francisco: Jossey-Bass.

Niemi, R. G., Ross, R. D., & Alexander, J. (1978). The similarity of political values of parents and college-age youths. *Public Opinion Quarterly, 42,* 503-520.

Nieto, S. (1996). *Affirming diversity: The sociopolitical context of multicultural education* (2nd ed.). White Plains, NY: Longman.

Nora, A., & Cabrera, A. F. (1996). The role of perceptions of prejudice and discrimination on the adjustment of minority students to college. *Journal of Higher Education, 67,* 119-148.

Nunn, C. Z. (1973). Support for civil liberties among college students. *Social Problems, 20,* 300-310.

Nunn, C. Z., Crockett, H. J., & Williams, J. A. (1978). *Tolerance for nonconformity: A national survey of Americans' changing commitment to civil liberties.* San Francisco: Jossey-Bass.

Oakes, J. (1985). *Keeping track: How schools structure inequality.* New Haven, CT: Yale University Press.

O'Donnell, J. P. (1993). Predicting tolerance of new religious movements: A multivariate analysis. *Journal for the Scientific Study of Religion, 32,* 356-365.

O'Gorman, H. J. (1979). White and Black perceptions of racial values. *Public Opinion Quarterly, 43,* 48-59.

Orfield, G. (1993). *The growth of segregation in American schools: Changing patterns of separation and poverty since 1968.* Alexandria, VA: National School Boards Association.

Owen, D., & Dennis, J. (1987). Preadult development of political tolerance. *Political Psychology,* *8,* 547-561.

Pascarella, E. T., Edison, M., Nora, A., Hagedorn, L., & Terenzini, P. (1996). Influences on students' openness to diversity and challenge in the first year of college. *Journal of Higher Education, 67,* 174-195.

Pascarella, E. T., & Terenzini, P. (1991). *How college affects students.* San Francisco: Jossey-Bass.

Patchen, M. (1982). *Black-White contact in schools: Its social and academic effects.* West Lafayette, IN: Purdue University Press.

Patchen, M., Hofmann, G., & Brown, W. R. (1977). Determinants of students' interracial behavior and opinion change. *Sociology of Education, 50,* 55-75.

Patterson, J. W. (1979). Moral development and political thinking: The case of freedom of speech. *Western Political Quarterly, 32,* 169-185.

Perkins, D. N. (1995). *Outsmarting IQ: The emerging science of learnable intelligence.* New York: Free Press.

Perkins, D. N. (1996, April). *Culture, gender, and intellectual character.* Paper presented at the annual meeting of the American Educational Research Association, New York.

Perry, W. G. (1970). *Forms of intellectual and ethical development in the college years.* New York: Holt.

Phelan, J., Link, B., Stueve, A., & Moore, R. (1995). Education, social liberalism, and economic conservatism: Attitudes toward homeless people. *American Sociological Review, 60,* 126-140.

Phinney, J. S. (1996). When we talk about American ethnic groups, what do we mean? *American Psychologist, 51,* 918-927.

Piereson, J., Sullivan, J. L., & Marcus, G. E. (1980). Political tolerance: An overview and some new findings. In J. Pierce & J. L. Sullivan (Eds.), *The electorate reconsidered* (pp. 157-178). Beverly Hills, CA: Sage.

Plotnick, R. D. (1992). The effects of attitudes on teenage premarital pregnancy and its resolution. *American Sociological Review, 57,* 800-811.

Popkin, R. (1964). *The history of scepticism.* New York: Harper Torchbooks.

Porter, G. (1994). White educators' tolerance of African Americans. *Review of Education, Pedagogy, and Cultural Studies, 16,* 411-425.

Power, F., Higgins, A., & Kohlberg, L. (1989). *Lawrence Kohlberg's approach to moral education.* New York: Columbia University Press.

Powers, D. A., & Ellison, C. G. (1995). Interracial contact and Black racial attitudes: The contact hypothesis and selectivity bias. *Social Forces, 74,* 205-226.

Pratte, R. (1985). Tolerance, permissiveness, and education. *Teachers College Record, 87,* 103-117.

Price, V., & Hsu, M.-L. (1992). The role of misinformation and attitudes toward homosexuals. *Public Opinion Quarterly, 56,* 29-52.

Prothro, J. W., & Grigg, C. M. (1960). Fundamental principles of democracy: Bases of agreement and disagreement. *Journal of Politics, 22,* 276-294.

Quillian, L. (1995). Prejudice as a response to perceived group threat. *American Sociological Review, 60,* 586-611.

Quinley, H. E., & Glock, C. Y. (1979). *Anti-Semitism in America.* New York: Free Press.

Rahe, P. A. (1994). *Republics ancient and modern* (3 vols.). Chapel Hill: University of North Carolina Press.

Rawls, J. (1993). *Political liberalism.* New York: Columbia University Press.

Ray, J. J. (1983). Reviving the problem of acquiescent response bias. *Journal of Social Psychology, 121,* 81-96.

Reed, J. S. (1980). Getting to know you: The contact hypothesis applied to sectional beliefs and attitudes of White southerners. *Social Forces, 59,* 123-135.

Remmers, H. H. (1963). *Anti-democratic attitudes in the American schools.* Evanston, IL: Northwestern University Press.

Rich, H. E. (1980). Tolerance for civil liberties among college students: A multivariate analysis. *Youth & Society, 12,* 17-32.

Ringer, F. K. (1969). *Decline of the German mandarins.* Cambridge, MA: Harvard University Press.

Ringer, F. K. (1979). *Education and society in modern Europe.* Bloomington: Indiana University Press.

Rivkin, S. G. (1994). Residential segregation and school integration. *Sociology of Education, 67,* 279-292.

Rokeach, M. (1960). *The open and closed mind.* New York: Basic Books.

Rose, E. J. B., in association with Deakin, N., Abrams, M., Jackson, V., Peston, M., Vanags, A. H., Cohen, B., Gaitskell, J., & Ward, P. (1969). *Colour and citizenship: A report of British race relations.* London: Oxford University Press.

Rossi, P. H., & Berk, R. A. (1985). Varieties of normative consensus. *American Sociological Review, 50,* 333-347.

Rothbart, M., & John, O. P. (1985). Social categorization and behavioral episodes: A cognitive analysis of the effects of intergroup contact. *Journal of Social Issues, 41*(3), 81-104.

Rothbart, M., & John, O. P. (1993). Intergroup relations and stereotype change: A social-cognitive analysis and some longitudinal findings. In P. M. Sniderman, P. E. Tetlock, & E. G. Carmines (Eds.), *Prejudice, politics, and the American dilemma* (pp. 32-59). Stanford, CA: Stanford University Press.

Royce, R. J. (1982). Pluralism, tolerance, and moral education. *Journal of Moral Education, 11,* 173-180.

Ruggiero, G. de. (1942). Religious freedom. In E. R. A. Seligman & A. S. Johnson (Eds.), *Encyclopedia of the social sciences* (Vol. 13, pp. 239-246). New York: Macmillan.

Sack, R. (1973). The impact of education on individual modernity in Tunisia. *International Journal of Comparative Sociology, 14,* 245-272.

Sampson, W. (1986). Desegregation and racial tolerance in academia. *Journal of Negro Education, 55,* 171-184.

Sanders, C., Lubinski, D., & Benbow, C. (1995). Does the defining issues test measure psychological phenomena distinct from verbal ability? *Journal of Personality and Social Psychology, 69,* 498-504.

Sanford, N. (1973). Authoritarian personality in contemporary perspective. In J. N. Knutson (Ed.), *Handbook of political psychology* (pp. 139-170). San Francisco: Jossey-Bass.

Schauer, F. (1982). *Free speech: A philosophical inquiry.* Cambridge: Cambridge University Press.

Schelling, T. C. (1971). Dynamic models of segregation. *Journal of Mathematical Sociology, 1,* 143-186.

Schelling, T. C. (1978). *Micromotives and macrobehavior.* New York: W. W. Norton.

Schofield, J. W. (1982). *Black and White in school: Trust, tension, or tolerance?* New York: Praeger.

Schofield, J. W. (1986). Black-White contact in desegregated schools. In M. Hewstone & R. Brown (Eds.), *Contact and conflict in intergroup encounters* (pp. 79-92). London: Basil Blackwell.

Schofield, J. W. (1993). Promoting positive peer relations in desegregated schools. *Educational Policy, 7,* 297-317.

Schommer, M. (1993). Comparisons of beliefs about the nature of knowledge and learning among postsecondary students. *Research in Higher Education, 34,* 355-370.

Schuman, H., & Bobo, L. (1988a). An experimental approach to surveys of racial attitudes. In H. J. O'Gorman (Ed.), *Surveying social life* (pp. 60-71). Middletown, CT: Wesleyan University Press.

Schuman, H., & Bobo, L. (1988b). Survey-based experiments on White racial attitudes toward residential integration. *American Journal of Sociology, 94,* 273-299.

Schuman, H., Bobo, L., & Krysan, M. (1992). Authoritarianism in the general population: The education interaction hypothesis. *Social Psychology Quarterly, 55,* 379-387.

Schuman, H., & Johnson, M. P. (1976). Attitudes and behavior. *Annual Review of Sociology, 2,* 161-207.

Schuman, H., & Presser, S. (1981). *Questions and answers in attitude surveys: Experiments in question form, wording, and context.* New York: Academic Press.

Schuman, H., Steeh, C., & Bobo, L. (1985). *Racial attitudes in America: Trends and interpretations.* Cambridge, MA: Harvard University Press.

Scott, J., & Schuman, H. (1988). Attitude strength and the abortion dispute. *American Sociological Review, 53,* 785-793.

Scott, R. R., & McPartland, J. M. (1982). Desegregation as a national policy: Correlates of racial attitudes. *American Educational Research Journal, 19,* 397-414.

Searle, J. R. (1994). Rationality and realism: What is at stake? In J. Cole, E. Barber, & S. Graubard (Eds.), *The research university in a time of discontent* (pp. 55-83). Baltimore: Johns Hopkins University Press.

Sears, D. O., & Allen, H. M. (1984). The trajectory of local desegregation controversies and Whites' opposition to busing. In N. Miller & M. B. Brewer (Eds.), *Groups in contact: The psychology of desegregation* (pp. 123-151). New York: Academic Press.

Selznick, G., & Steinberg, S. (1969). *The tenacity of prejudice.* New York: Harper & Row.

Sen, A. (1995). *Inequality reexamined.* Cambridge, MA: Harvard University Press.

Serow, R. C. (1983). *Schooling for social diversity: An analysis of policy and practice.* New York: Teachers College Press.

Shea, C. (1995, January 13). Disengaged freshmen. *Chronicle of Higher Education, 41,* A29-A31.

Shea, C. (1996, January 12). New students uncertain about racial preferences. *Chronicle of Higher Education, 42,* A33-A35.

Sidanius, J., & Pratto, F. (1993). The inevitability of oppression and the dynamics of social dominance. In P. M. Sniderman, P. E. Tetlock, & E. G. Carmines (Eds.), *Prejudice, politics, and the American dilemma* (pp. 173-211). Stanford, CA: Stanford University Press.

Sidanius, J., Pratto, F., & Bobo, L. (1996). Racism, conservatism, affirmative action, and intellectual sophistication: A matter of principled conservatism or group dominance? *Journal of Personality and Social Psychology, 70,* 476-490.

Sigel, R. S. (Ed.). (1989). *Political learning in adulthood: A sourcebook of theory and research.* Chicago: University of Chicago Press.

Sigelman, L., Shockey, J. W., & Sigelman, C. K. (1993). Ethnic stereotyping: A Black-White comparison. In P. M. Sniderman, P. E. Tetlock, & E. G. Carmines (Eds.), *Prejudice, politics, and the American dilemma* (pp. 104-126). Stanford, CA: Stanford University Press.

Simmel, G. (1955). *Conflict and the web of group-affiliations* (K. H. Wolff & R. Bendix, Trans.). Glencoe, IL: Free Press.

Simon, H. A. (1983). *Reason in human affairs.* Stanford, CA: Stanford University Press.

Simon, H. A. (1993). Decision making: Rational, nonrational, and irrational. *Educational Administration Quarterly, 29,* 392-411.

Slavin, R. E. (1985). Cooperative learning: Applying contact theory in desegregated schools. *Journal of Social Issues, 41*(3), 45-62.

Slavin, R. E. (1990). Achievement effects of ability grouping in secondary schools: A best-evidence synthesis. *Review of Educational Research, 60,* 471-499.

Slomczynski, K. M. (1989). Effects of status-inconsistency on intellective process. In M. L. Kohn (Ed.), *Cross-national research in sociology* (pp. 148-166). Newbury Park, CA: Sage.

Smith, A. W. (1981a). Racial tolerance as a function of group position. *American Sociological Review, 46,* 558-573.

Smith, A. W. (1981b). Tolerance of school desegregation, 1954-1977. *Social Forces, 59,* 1256-1274.

Smith, T. W. (1984a). Nonattitudes: A review and evaluation. In C. F. Turner & E. Martin (Eds.), *Surveying subjective phenomena* (Vol. 2, pp. 215-255). New York: Russell Sage Foundation.

Smith, T. W. (1984b). The subjectivity of ethnicity. In C. F. Turner & E. Martin (Eds.), *Surveying subjective phenomena* (Vol. 2, pp. 117-128). New York: Russell Sage Foundation.

Smith, T. W. (1990). The sexual revolution? *Public Opinion Quarterly, 54,* 415-435.

Smith, T. W. (1991). *What do Americans think about Jews?* New York: American Jewish Committee.

Sniderman, P. M., Brody, R. A., & Kuklinski, J. H. (1984). Policy reasoning and political values: The problem of racial equality. *American Journal of Political Science, 28,* 75-94.

Sniderman, P. M., & Piazza, T. (1993). *The scar of race.* Cambridge, MA: Harvard University Press.

Sniderman, P. M., Tetlock, P. E., & Carmines, E. G. (Eds.). (1993a). *Prejudice, politics, and the American dilemma.* Stanford, CA: Stanford University Press.

Sniderman, P. M., Tetlock, P. E., & Carmines, E. G. (1993b). Prejudice and politics: An introduction. In P. M. Sniderman, P. E. Tetlock, & E. G. Carmines (Eds.), *Prejudice, politics, and the American dilemma* (pp. 1-31). Stanford, CA: Stanford University Press.

Sniderman, P. M., Tetlock, P. E., Carmines, E. G., & Peterson, R. S. (1993). The politics of the American dilemma: Issue pluralism. In P. M. Sniderman, P. E. Tetlock, & E. G. Carmines (Eds.), *Prejudice, politics, and the American dilemma* (pp. 212-236). Stanford, CA: Stanford University Press.

Sniderman, P. M., Tetlock, P. E., Glaser, J. M., Green, D. P., & Hout, M. (1989). Principled tolerance and the American mass public. *British Journal of Political Science, 19,* 25-45.

Spicer, D. N. (1994). World view and abortion beliefs: A replication of Luker's implicit hypothesis. *Sociological Inquiry, 64,* 114-126.

Staub, E. (1989). *The roots of evil: The origins of genocide and other group violence.* Cambridge: Cambridge University Press.

Steeh, C., & Schuman, H. (1992). Young White adults: Did racial attitudes change in the 1980s? *American Journal of Sociology, 98,* 340-367.

Stehr, N. (1994). *Knowledge societies.* Thousand Oaks, CA: Sage.

Stembler, C. H. (1961). *Education and attitude change: The effect of schooling on prejudice against minority groups.* New York: Institute of Human Relations Press.

Stephan, W. G., & Brigham, J. C. (1985). Intergroup contact: Introduction. *Journal of Social Issues, 41*(3), 1-8.

Stephan, W. G., & Stephan, C. W. (1984). The role of ignorance in intergroup relations. In N. Miller & M. B. Brewer (Eds.), *Groups in contact: The psychology of desegregation* (pp. 229-255). New York: Academic Press.

Stipp, H., & Kerr, D. (1989). Determinants of public opinion about AIDS. *Public Opinion Quarterly, 53,* 98-106.

Stouffer, S. A. (1955). *Communism, conformity and civil liberties: A cross-section of the nation speaks its mind.* Garden City, NY: Doubleday.

Sullivan, J. L., Avery, P., Thalhammer, K., Wood, S. L., & Bird, K. (1994). Education and political tolerance in the United States: The mediating role of cognitive sophistication, personality and democratic norms. *Review of Education, Pedagogy, and Cultural Studies, 16,* 315-324.

Sullivan, J. L., & Marcus, G. E. (1988). A note on "Trends in political tolerance." *Public Opinion Quarterly, 52,* 26-32.

Sullivan, J. L., Marcus, G. E., Piereson, J., & Feldman, S. (1979). The development of political tolerance: The impact of social class, personality, and cognition. *International Journal of Political Education, 2,* 115-139.

Sullivan, J. L., Piereson, J., & Marcus, G. E. (1982). *Political tolerance and American democracy.* Chicago: University of Chicago Press.

Sullivan, J. L., Shamir, M., Walsh, P., & Roberts, N. S. (1985). *Political tolerance in context: Support for unpopular minorities in Israel, New Zealand, and the United States.* Boulder, CO: Westview.

Suzman, R. M. (1973). Psychological modernity. *International Journal of Comparative Sociology, 14,* 273-287.

Tajfel, H. (1978). *Differentiation between social groups.* London: Academic Press.

Tapp, J. L., & Kohlberg, L. (1971). Developing senses of law and legal justice. *Journal of Social Issues, 27*(2), 1-16.

Taylor, D. G., Sheatsley, P. B., & Greeley, A. M. (1978). Attitudes toward racial integration. *Scientific American, 238*(6), 42-49.

Tedin, K. L. (1994). Self-interest, symbolic values, and the financial equalization of the public schools. *Journal of Politics, 56,* 628-649.

Thalhammer, K., Wood, S. L., Bird, K., Avery, P., & Sullivan, J. L. (1994). Adolescents and political tolerance: Lip-synching to the tune of democracy. *Review of Education, Pedagogy, and Cultural Studies, 16,* 325-347.

Thomas, R. M. (1992). *Comparing theories of child development* (3rd ed.). Belmont, CA: Wadsworth.

Torney, J. V., Oppenheim, A. N., & Farnen, R. F. (1975). *Civic education in ten countries.* New York: John Wiley.

Torney-Purta, J. (1990). From attitudes and knowledge to schemata: Expanding the outcomes of political socialization research. In O. Ichilov (Ed.), *Political socialization, citizenship education, and democracy* (pp. 98-115). New York: Teachers College Press.

Tsukashima, R. T., & Montero, D. (1976). The contact hypothesis: Social and economic contact and generational changes in the study of Black anti-Semitism. *Social Forces, 55,* 149-165.

Turner, C. F., & Martin, E. (Eds.). (1984). *Surveying subjective phenomena* (2 vols.). New York: Russell Sage Foundation.

Ullman, W. (1975). *Law and politics in the Middle Ages.* Ithaca, NY: Cornell University Press.

Umberson, D., Chen, M., House, J., Hopkins, K., & Slaten, E. (1996). The effect of social relationships on psychological well-being: Are men and women really so different? *American Sociological Review, 61,* 837-857.

U.S. Department of Commerce, Bureau of the Census. (1992). *Statistical abstract of the United States: 1992.* Washington, DC: Government Printing Office.

Useem, E. L. (1992). Middle schools and math groups: Parents' involvement in children's placement. *Sociology of Education, 65,* 263-279.

Vogt, W. P. (1990, August). *Social origins of toleration.* Paper presented at the annual meeting of the American Sociological Association, Washington, DC.

Vogt, W. P. (1993). Durkheim's sociology of law: Morality and the cult of the individual. In S. P. Turner (Ed.), *Emile Durkheim: Sociologist and moralist* (pp. 71-94). London: Routledge.

Voltaire, F.-M. A. (1980). *Letters on England* (L. Tancock, Trans.). London: Penguin. (Original work published 1734)

Voltaire, F.-M. A. (1985). *Philosophical dictionary* (T. Besterman, Trans.). London: Penguin. (Original work published 1764)

Wagner, U., & Machleit, U. (1986). "Gastarbeiter" in the Federal Republic of Germany: Contact between Germans and migrant populations. In M. Hewstone & R. Brown (Eds.), *Contact and conflict in intergroup encounters* (pp. 59-78). London: Basil Blackwell.

Wagner, U., & Schonbach, P. (1984). Links between educational status and prejudice: Ethnic attitudes in West Germany. In N. Miller & M. B. Brewer (Eds.), *Groups in contact: The psychology of desegregation* (pp. 29-54). New York: Academic Press.

Walker, L. J. (1984). Sex differences in the development of moral reasoning: A critical review. *Child Development, 55,* 677-691.

Walsh, M. (1996). But words will never hurt me. *Education Week, 15*(26), 28-31.

Walzer, S. (1994). The role of gender in determining abortion attitudes. *Social Science Quarterly, 75,* 687-693.

Weil, F. D. (1984). Review of Sullivan et al. 1982. *American Journal of Sociology, 89,* 963-966.

Weil, F. D. (1985). The variable effects of education on liberal attitudes: A comparative-historical analysis of anti-Semitism using public opinion survey data. *American Sociological Review, 50,* 458-474.

Westie, F. R. (1965). The American dilemma: An empirical test. *American Sociological Review, 30,* 527-538.

Whitt, H. P., & Nelson, H. M. (1975). Residence, moral traditionalism, and tolerance of atheists. *Social Forces, 54,* 328-340.

Wilcox, C. (1990). Race differences in abortion attitudes: Some additional evidence. *Public Opinion Quarterly, 54,* 248-255.

Wilcox, C. (1992). Race, religion, and abortion attitudes. *Sociological Analysis, 53,* 97-105.

Williams, J. A., Nunn, C. Z., & St. Peter, L. (1976a). Origins of tolerance: Findings from a replication of Stouffer's *Communism, conformity, and civil liberties. Social Forces, 55,* 394-408.

Williams, J. A., Nunn, C. Z., & St. Peter, L. (1976b). "Origins of Tolerance": Reply to Crockett. *Social Forces, 55,* 413-418.

Williams, R. M. (1947). *The reduction of intergroup tensions.* New York: Social Science Research Council.

Williams, R. M. (1988). Racial attitudes and behavior. In H. J. O'Gorman (Ed.), *Surveying social life* (pp. 331-352). Middletown, CT: Wesleyan University Press.

Wirt, F. M., & Kirst, M. W. (1992). *Schools in conflict: The politics of education.* Berkeley, CA: McCutchan.

Wolff, R. P. (1968). *The poverty of liberalism.* Boston: Beacon.

Wolff, R. P. (1969). Beyond tolerance. In R. P. Wolff, B. Moore, Jr., & H. Marcuse, *A critique of pure tolerance* (pp. 3-52). Boston: Beacon.

Wolff, R. P., Moore, B., Jr., & Marcuse, H. (1969). *A critique of pure tolerance.* Boston: Beacon.

Wood, S. L., Thalhammer, K., Sullivan, J. L., Bird, K., Avery, P., & Klein, K. (1994). Tolerance for diversity of beliefs: Learning about tolerance and liking it too. *Review of Education, Pedagogy, and Cultural Studies, 16,* 349-372.

Wuthnow, R. (1988). *The restructuring of American religion.* Princeton, NJ: Princeton University Press.

Wynne, E. A. (1985). The great tradition in education: Transmitting moral values. *Educational Leadership, 43,* 4-9.

Yee, A. H., Fairchild, H. H., Weizmann, F., & Wyatt, G. E. (1993). Addressing psychology's problems with race. *American Psychologist, 48,* 1132-1140.

Young-Bruehl, E. (1996). *The anatomy of prejudices.* Cambridge, MA: Harvard University Press.

Zalkind, S. S., Gaugler, E. A., & Schwartz, R. M. (1975). Civil liberties attitudes and personality measures: Some exploratory research. *Journal of Social Issues, 31*(2), 77-91.

Zellman, G. L. (1975). Antidemocratic beliefs: A survey and some explanations. *Journal of Social Issues, 31*(2), 31-53.

Zellman, G. L., & Sears, D. O. (1971). Childhood origins of tolerance for dissent. *Journal of Social Issues, 27*(2), 109-135.

Index

About the Author

W. Paul Vogt teaches sociology of education and research methods in the Department of Educational Administration and Policy Studies and is Interim Associate Dean in the School of Education at the State University of New York at Albany. He is the author of the *Dictionary of Statistics and Methodology* (Sage Publications, 1993) and numerous articles and reviews appearing in such journals as the *Journal of Higher Education, History and Theory, Journal of the History of the Behavioral Sciences, Review of Education, Pedagogy and Cultural Studies, Contemporary Sociology, Comparative Education Review, History of Education Quarterly,* and *Revue française de sociologie.*